C708 019 030 065 4X

THE DOOG

The Incredible Story of Derek Dougan:
Football's Most Controversial Figure

KNOW THE SCORE BOOKS PUBLICATIONS

CULT HEROES	Author	ISBN
CARLISLE UNITED	Mark Harrison	978-1-905449-09-7
CELTIC	David Potter	978-1-905449-08-8
CHELSEA	Leo Moynihan	1-905449-00-3
MANCHESTER CITY	David Clayton	978-1-905449-05-7
NEWCASTLE	Dylan Younger	1-905449-03-8
NOTTINGHAM FOREST	David McVay	978-1-905449-06-4
RANGERS	Paul Smith	978-1-905449-07-1
SOUTHAMPTON	Jeremy Wilson	1-905449-01-1
WEST BROM	Simon Wright	1-905449-02-X

MATCH OF MY LIFE	Editor	ISBN
DERBY COUNTY	Nick Johnson	978-1-905449-68-2
ENGLAND WORLD CUP	Massarella & Moynihan	1-905449-52-6
EUROPEAN CUP FINALS	Ben Lyttleton	1-905449-57-7
FA CUP FINALS 1953-1969	David Saffer	978-1-905449-53-8
FULHAM	Michael Heatley	1-905449-51-8
LEEDS	David Saffer	1-905449-54-2
LIVERPOOL	Leo Moynihan	1-905449-50-X
MANCHESTER UNITED	Ivan Ponting	978-1-905449-59-0
SHEFFIELD UNITED	Nick Johnson	1-905449-62-3
STOKE CITY	Simon Lowe	978-1-905449-55-2
SUNDERLAND	Rob Mason	1-905449-60-7
SPURS	Allen & Massarella	978-1-905449-58-3
WOLVES	Simon Lowe	1-905449-56-9

GENERAL FOOTBALL	Author	ISBN
2006 WORLD CUP DIARY	Harry Harris	1-905449-90-9
2008 CHAMPIONS LEAGUE YEARBOOK		978-1-905449-93-4
BOOK OF FOOTBALL OBITUARIES	Ivan Ponting	978-1-905449-82-2
BURKSEY	Peter Morfoot	1-905449-49-6
The Autobiography of a Football God		
HOLD THE BACK PAGE	Harry Harris	1-905449-91-7
MY PREMIERSHIP DIARY	Marcus Hahnemann	978-1-905449-33-0
Reading's Season in the Premiership		
OUTCASTS	Steve Menary	978-1-905449-31-6
The Lands That FIFA Forgot		

PARISH TO PLANET A History of Football	Dr Eric Midwinter	978-1-905449-30-9
TACKLES LIKE A FERRET (England Cover)	Paul Parker	1-905449-47-X
TACKLES LIKE A FERRET (Manchester United Cover)	Paul Parker	1-905449-46-1

CRICKET	Author	ISBN
ASHES TO DUST	Graham Cookson	978-1-905449-19-4
GROVEL! The 1976 West Indies Tour of England	David Tossell	978-1-905449-43-9
MOML: THE ASHES	Pilger & Wightman	1-905449-63-1
MY TURN TO SPIN	Shaun Udal	978-1-905449-42-2
WASTED?	Paul Smith	978-1-905449-45-3

RUGBY LEAGUE	Author	ISBN
MOML WIGAN WARRIORS	David Kuzio	978-1-905449-66-8

FORTHCOMING PUBLICATIONS IN 2007

MATCH OF MY LIFE	Editor	ISBN
BRIGHTON	Paul Camillin	978-1-84818-000-0
IPSWICH TOWN	Mel Henderson	978-1-84818-001-7

GENERAL FOOTBALL	Author	ISBN
EUROPEAN FOOTBALL YEARBOOK 2008	Mike Hammond	978-1-84818-400-8
BEHIND THE BACK PAGE	Christopher Davies	978-1-84818-506-7
FORGIVE US OUR PRESS PASSES	Football Writers' Association	978-1-84818-507-4
JUST ONE OF SEVEN	Denis Smith	978-1-84818-504-3
MAN & BABE	Wilf McGuinness	978-1-84818-503-6
PALLY	Gary Pallister	978-1-84818-500-5
PLEASE MAY I HAVE MY FOOTBALL BACK? 	Eric Alexander	978-1-84818-508-1

RUGBY LEAGUE	Author	ISBN
MOML LEEDS RHINOS	Caplan & Saffer	978-1-905449-69-9

THE DOOG

The Incredible Story of Derek Dougan:
Football's Most Controversial Figure

David Harrison & Steve Gordos

www.knowthescorebooks.com

First published in the United Kingdom
by Know The Score Books Ltd, 2008

The right of Steve Gordos & David Harrison to be identified as the authors of this work has been asserted by them in accordance with sections 77 and 78 of the Copyright, Designs and Patents Act, 1988.

Know The Score Books Limited
118 Alcester Road
Studley
Warwickshire
B80 7NT
01527 454482
info@knowthescorebooks.com
www.knowthescorebooks.com

A CIP catalogue record is available for this book from the British Library
ISBN: 978-1-848185-02-9

Jacket design by Graham Hales

Printed and bound in Great Britain
By Cromwell Press, Trowbridge, Wiltshire

Mixed Sources
Product group from well-managed
forests and other controlled sources
www.fsc.org Cert no. TT-COC-2082
© 1996 Forest Stewardship Council
FSC

Photographs in this book are reproduced by kind permission of:
Jutta Dougan, Belfast Evening Telegraph and Birmingham Mail.

Disclaimer:
Despite every effort, the authors have been unable to trace the copyright holders of several photographs included in this book. Any photographer involved is cordially invited to contact the publisher in writing providing proof of copyright.

Front cover:
Burning passion in the eyes of a legend.

Rear cover:
Left: Dougan gives thanks for Wolves' League Cup victory over Manchester City in 1974.

Right: Striding out as captain of Northern Ireland alongside England's Bobby Moore.

Heartfelt thanks to all the interviewees who kindly gave their time and thoughts about Derek Dougan. Also to David Instone, Richard Roper, Tony Lyons and Simon Lowe, without whom this book would not have been possible.

CONTENTS

FOREWORD BY MARTIN O'NEILL   I

INTRODUCTION   V

1.   THE FAMILY MAN   1

2.   FROM BELFAST TO HALMSTAD   13

3.   AN IRISH ROVER   27

4.   A FATAL NIGHT   35

5.   DIVERSION VIA LONDON ROAD   51

6.   INSTANT FOLK HERO   65

7.   YOU'RE BANNED   81

8.   CHAIRMAN AT LAST   99

9.   EUROPEAN GOAL KING   109

10. WEMBLEY GLORY DAY   125

11. WOLVES AT THE DOOR   137

12. HOW NOT TO RUN FOOTBALL   145

13. THE TAINTED HERO   157

14.   TWO OF US   165

15.   UNWANTED HEADLINES   175

16.   AND IN THE END   191

       STATISTICAL RECORD   196

       BIBLIOGRAPHY   202

FOREWORD

BY MARTIN O'NEILL

I WAS SADDENED TO HEAR about the death of Derek Dougan. But I wasn't the only one because 'The Doog', provocative, disputatious, iconoclastic, but with a big heart, touched the lives of all of those who had come to know him, however briefly. Like that other Belfast Colossus, George Best, I thought he would never die. Heroes never do. And Derek Dougan was a hero to me.

Northern Ireland's colourful exploits in 1958 came a little too early in my life to truly appreciate. I remember seeing the World Cup Final between the host nation and Brazil on TV in a neighbour's house, his being the only living room for miles that contained a set.

However by 1960, our family possessed our own television, which took the place of the large wireless in the corner. Here I watched the FA Cup final between Wolverhampton Wanderers and Blackburn Rovers unfold. Rovers had a young Irish lad playing at centre-forward that fateful afternoon. I found out later that he had asked for a transfer the very morning of the game. Yes, the flamboyant Dougan's career was cranking into full swing. And he would spend the rest of his football days being just what he was, charmingly controversial.

I loved him from a distance. He, Best and that fantastic goalkeeper Pat Jennings became everything to us kids growing up in Northern Ireland with a dream and an ambition. They were living the dream. They had made the big time. Derek was in the spotlight and revelling in his infamy. He seemed to be handling things pretty OK as well.

I met him in 1972. The English League season had just ended, but the Home Internationals were just about to get under way – three matches against the Home Countries in the space of a week. The Northern Ireland squad had gathered in a hotel in Troon, Ayrshire, overlooking the famous golf course. We were preparing for our first game against Scotland at Hampden Park in a few days time, anxiously awaiting the arrival of George Best. He didn't turn up. As a group we were distraught.

However, Dougan became our talisman. He took control, assuming natural leadership of the team. Little gatherings in the hotel foyer with The Doog holding court became the order of the week. Espousing all kinds of theories and viewpoints from the offside law to Martin Luther King's 'I Have A Dream' speech in Washington, Dougan had us spellbound.

I was very young and consequently spoke only when spoken to. Derek was fascinating. I felt particularly encouraged by his warmth and generosty towards a relative newcomer. Anyway, he roused us all to such an extent we managed to beat England at Wembley for the first time in many a long year, with The Doog in a starring role.

The ten days spent in his company seemed like ten minutes. I left the group a more enlightened young man. Dougan, by the sheer weight of his personality, had lifted our spirits to heights we didn't think possible.

A year later I played alongside Derek at Lansdowne Road, Dublin for an All-Ireland Select Team against the reigning world champions, Brazil. It was a momentous occasion. The game was played against the backdrop of immense political upheaval, Northern Ireland especially being in a state of turmoil. Derek played a major role in the organising of the match. Not everyone was in favour of an All-Ireland team. However, Derek cared little about religious background. He felt that the match might help unite communities on either side of the political (and religious) divide.

Unfortunately for Derek, the match spelled the end of his international career and that was the saddest part of all. I think he may well have guessed the outcome, but he felt so strongly about this particular game that he was prepared to accept the consequences. And so, my days and hours with him grew less frequent. I missed him a lot on those Northern Ireland get-togethers.

We met again at George Best's funeral. Perhaps heroes were mortal after all. Still when I saw Derek, all the memories of a generation past came flooding back to me. We talked awhile. I'm not sure exactly of all the subjects covered, but he still retained that zest, that enthusiasm and that warm personality.

I pretended to argue with some long-standing Dougan viewpoint, but in truth, I was deferring to my hero. I told him that my younger brother had supported Wolves for years and that he had idolized The Doog. "You have already told me that," said Derek. I looked surprised. "Back in Troon in 1972," he said!!

His death had a profound effect on me. His funeral was indeed very moving. The people of Wolverhampton lined the streets to pay their respects to one they loved dearly. He had performed many a heroic deed at that wonderful Molineux stadium just a stone's throw from the church where he now reposed.

Derek Dougan's life had ended, but his legend burned as brightly as ever.

Martin O'Neill
March 2008

INTRODUCTION

To QUOTE THE WORDS of one of his favourite songs by Nat King Cole, Derek Dougan was 'unforgettable in every way.' It summed up his life, his playing career, his work as a crusader for footballers past and present, his marriage to wife Jutta and relationships with women and ordinary people whose lives he touched in an extraordinary way.

However, there were other times when the things Derek Dougan did were unforgivable. He could hold a room full of people spellbound with the magnetism of his personality. Then he could destroy a perfectly pleasant occasion with a crass remark or outrageous act. Only Dougan knew whether this was deliberate. You often felt he craved attention so badly he did not care how he got it.

Nor did this garrulous contradiction of a man care whom he upset as long as he regarded them as more pompous than himself. He loved to thumb his nose at the establishment and authority. He prided himself on being a true man of the people.

And the people gave him back what he loved most – adulation, respect and affection. He was never happier than when he was surrounded by a gathering of supporters, entertaining, cajoling and bringing joy to their lives. To see him work such an audience was to witness a master communicator. It came as a natural gift to someone who had no highbrow or formal kind of education He learned his lessons on the streets, in the bars and in the dressing rooms of everyday life.

In the final interview before his death, given to Clive Corbett author of the lovingly-produced book, *Those Were The Days*, Dougan said: "Quite simply I have always wanted to play with the best players, but unfortunately I have been described as the rebel which is nonsense. I had 30 managers in my career and when the man who is the manager of the football club has got less intelligence than you, it's sometimes very difficult to take."

To some that sounds like arrogance, to others the words of a man with supreme self-belief. His followers would hang on his every word. His detractors would dismiss them as conceited nonsense. Few divided opinion as widely as the Doog.

When he was in his pomp at Wolves during the halcyon days of his playing career, the chant would go up from his worshippers on the North Bank: "What's his name?" The spontaneous and deafening retort rang around Molineux: "DOUGAN!"

For Wolves fans he was unforgettable … in every way.

Steve Gordos & David Harrison
March 2008

Chapter One

THE FAMILY MAN

IT WAS LOVE AT FIRST SIGHT for Derek Dougan when he first set eyes on the beautiful German teenager. She was Jutta Fichtl, a 19-year-old au pair girl working for the Moyle family in the upmarket Edgbaston district of Birmingham. He was the Aston Villa centre-forward, an instantly recognisable character who had already made his name for his outrageous behaviour as much as his football skills.

Dougan decided within days of meeting the unsuspecting Jutta that he wanted to marry her. His romantic feelings, though not rejected, had to overcome some major obstacles before they were fulfilled, however. They would marry and the partnership survived, in name at least, for over 40 years, taking the couple on a memorable journey. Theirs was a tempestuous adventure from its early financial hardships, through to the glamorous world that opened up as footballers gradually began to obtain celebrity status and brought the attention of television cameras, glossy mags and gossip columnists.

Jutta could justifiably claim to be football's first WAG – the acronym given to the wives and girlfriends of modern day players whose main objective in life is to flash their gold credit cards and acres of flesh, gripping tightly on to the arms of their partners. In the early days of their marriage, the Dougans never enjoyed such luxury. However, through Jutta's housekeeping and motherly instincts and her husband's growing reputation as a sporting and media star, they built a life that gained its share of fame and fortune. The arrival of their two sons Alexander and Nicholas completed the perfect family picture.

Underneath it did not always follow such a smooth course. Dougan was always too much of a maverick character to accept the blissful married life, but Jutta was always there waiting for the happy wanderer to return home. In an exclusive interview for this book Jutta talks revealingly and lovingly for the first time of her life and times with Derek. It is a story which sums up the endearing complexities, qualities and failings of this unique individual, one of football's true superheroes. It ends with his death in a final chapter of heart-breaking poignancy.

"It was 1961. I was just 19 years old and had not long arrived in England to work for the Moyle family in Augustus Road, Edgbaston," Jutta recalls. "I met up with some of the other au pairs working in the area and we used to congregate in a café somewhere off New Street in Birmingham city centre. That's where Derek and some of the Aston Villa players sometimes went. I think the players used to come in because they had heard these young foreign girls would be there. The first time I saw him he had a woollen hat on. I soon discovered that he had completely shaved off his hair.

"Eventually we got talking and I found out he was a footballer, but that meant nothing to me. In Germany we did not have professional players then. I could not believe that someone could actually get paid for playing football. We got on well and then he got around to asking me out on a date. But it wasn't easy for me. The family I worked for were very strict. Back home in Munich I would always be out at carnivals and dances and not be home until seven in the morning. With the Moyle family in England I was not even allowed to have a key. I only had two afternoons and two evenings off – Tuesdays and Thursdays – and had to be in by 11pm. Mrs Moyle would always be up waiting for me 'til I got back. The other au pair girls I knew were being taken out to the theatre and made to feel part of their families. I wasn't allowed to do anything. I became an au pair because I was going to be a stewardess with Lufthansa and needed to learn English. But I ended up spending my time doing slave labour. I had to be up at seven to clear up the mess made by the family's two dogs in the breakfast room, break up coal, light fires and clean the shoes of the master and his son. I had to clean the downstairs of the house during the week and upstairs at the weekend.

"On my days off I wasn't allowed to leave the house 'til four in the afternoon. I went to school between seven and nine for my English lessons and had to be back by 11. It didn't leave much time for socialising. In seven months I was only allowed two Saturdays off. Otherwise I stayed in my little box room. I wasn't even allowed to go back home at Christmas even though my family had sent me return tickets. They needed me at Edgbaston because Mrs Moyle had planned a few parties."

Then along came The Doog to sweep her off her feet. He was living in digs in the Handsworth area with the Truman family who ran a pub called the Stork Hotel. He arranged to meet Jutta for occasional dates which were very brief. He always had to leave her at 10.30pm so she could obey her curfew. However, within months he had asked the new love of his life to marry him. She agreed, but knew there were problems ahead before they could tie the knot. The first one to overcome was the dreaded Moyle family of Edgbaston.

Jutta says: "When I told her who I had met, Mrs Moyle was not very pleased and said Derek had a bad reputation. I tried to get an au pair job with another family, but she stopped that by offering me more time off. I then decided to go back to Germany and never return to that house. When I told her I was leaving, she went to the police and tried to stop me ever coming back to England.

"I intended to eventually come back to Birmingham to be with Derek at the Stork Hotel. The Truman family were to become our adopted parents. Derek had been away from Belfast for so long they were his English family. We even called them mum and dad. We stayed in touch with them all their lives.

"After I left for Germany in January, Mrs Moyle was very angry with me for leaving her. She wrote a letter to my parents warning them about the man their daughter was associating with. She wrote that Derek had a very bad reputation and that he lived in a second rate hotel. I got hold of that letter and sent it back to Handsworth to Derek's 'mum and dad'. They took it to a solicitor because it amounted to defamation of character. Mrs Moyle also had to take a solicitor and apologise.

"Derek and I parted company and I just thought he would go off with other women after I returned to Germany. But he gave me a little gold ring and that was special. When I told my parents I had met him and he wanted to marry me they were most upset. They couldn't believe it. I had only met him in the November and by January, I was being asked to get married. At home the whole of my family got involved. There were many meetings and many tears. In the end they took my passport off me. Under German law you had to be 21 to get married without your parents' permission, so I had to get a job and stay in Germany."

That was not good enough for Dougan. He was totally smitten by his fraulein. She immersed herself in a new social life in Munich and got a job with a film company called Bavaria Films, but he bombarded her with letters and phone calls. Jutta was living life to the full and admits she had more or less forgotten about Derek until he announced he was going to visit her in Germany. "My father said, 'I'll throw him out. I don't want to see him,'" recalls Jutta. "But my mother said: 'Bring him home for coffee so I can have a look at him.' He couldn't speak German, so I did all the translating and he turned on the charm for my mother and I think it worked. Then a few months later he came back and said he was taking me to England to marry him.

"I was just turned 20 and I still needed my parents' signature. I just ground them down. And then they just gave up. Eventually my parents came to love England, especially my father who kept coming to visit Derek and me. He would cycle around, went shopping for me, loved meeting people and really enjoyed being with us. Later on my parents would come to babysit for us, so that Derek and I could have a holiday alone. Sometimes they would come with us to Spain or Croatia.

"Derek had such charisma. He had a lovely voice and would sing songs to me, mostly Nat King Cole or Tony Bennett and also Dean Martin and Frank Sinatra. That was very romantic. He was so good looking – especially when he grew his hair back. He shaved it because he thought it was going thin and by having it all cut off, it would grow back stronger. He was far ahead of his time. Many years later someone sent me a cutting from the *Liverpool Echo* newspaper, showing pictures of Derek and David Beckham side by side. Derek had his head shaved, so did Beckham. Derek had a Mohican cut, so did Beckham. Derek grew his hair long, so did Beckham. But Derek had done it all years before."

The couple were married and soon had to uproot and move to Peterborough after Dougan completed a £21,000 move in the summer of 1963. Although that brought a wage rise they had no savings to invest in such luxuries even as a dining table! They moved into a small semi-detached house provided by the club and it was a very Spartan existence to begin with.

"My parents gave us a bit of money," recalls Jutta. "But we didn't have much. The boxer Johnny Prescott was our best man and he gave us a television set as a wedding present. I had to put a few suitcases on top of each other and cover them with a cloth to use as a makeshift dining table. We had two knives, two forks and two spoons. Once when a friend called Arthur Hall came to visit us from Birmingham, I had to go to the hardware store to buy an extra knife, fork and spoon. The man in the shop said: 'Having a visitor, are we?' He didn't know how true that was.

"Derek was one of the top wage earners at Peterborough – I think it was about £20 to £30 a week – but it was still a bit of a struggle. But I was so happy. Eventually we bought our first home for less than £3,000. We didn't know whether we could afford the mortgage. I wasn't working. I was already pregnant with Alexander. At first we had no carpets. I had to sand down the upstairs floorboards to stop us getting splinters in our feet. I threaded some wool through a coal sack to use as a rug in front of the fire-place in the lounge. I didn't have a washing machine. When Alexander was born I had to boil the nappies in a bucket on the gas stove.

"It wasn't an extravagant lifestyle by any means. If we wanted anything we saved for it because we didn't want to go into debt, apart from the mort-gage. I did all the financial things and the practical ones. If something needed to be mended I did it. Derek wasn't practical at all. If you asked him to paint something he would do three brush strokes and complain that the fumes were bad for his chest. Once he decided to cut the lawn in his silk suit. He pushed himself away from the wire fence, got caught up in it and ended up with a triangular rip in his trousers. That was the end of his lawn cutting."

Dougan moved up the football and social ladder when he joined First Division Leicester City for £12,000 in May 1965, but the two years at the East Midlands club were unremarkable for Jutta. The last and best spell of their lives together would have to wait until he moved to Wolves for £45,000 in March 1967. Then the good times would roll.

"My main memory of Leicester was that our son Nicholas was born there," says Jutta. "He was born on December 6, St Niklaus Day in Germany. But I don't remember too much about the football. I know that Gordon Banks was their goalkeeper and Peter Shilton was an apprentice. Derek told me that Peter used to clean the pros' boots. I don't remember going into the town or mixing too much socially at Leicester. But I was pregnant with Nick and also had to look after little Alexander, so there was not much time to socialise. It was the move to Wolves which moved us into a new world and lifestyle.

"We were into the Swinging Sixties by then and I was wearing skirts just a few centimetres above the knee. When I went back to Germany wearing one my mother went mad at me saying: 'Jutta, you are a mother. You shouldn't be dressed like that.' Later the skirts went even shorter.

"Derek was earning good money when he signed for Wolves. You could say that Wolves made Derek, but in many ways Derek made Wolves. He was very generous with his money. We didn't have the fortunes that the modern players have, but it was much more than we'd had before. Once I saw a beautiful coat with a black fox collar. It cost £50, which was a lot for a coat in those days. I told Derek, 'I will never ask for anything else at Christmas or birthdays, if you buy me that.' He got it for me – and many more birthday and Christmas presents afterwards.

"We made some lifelong friends in Wolverhampton – men like the former Wolves chairman John Ireland, a wonderful man, and the former goalkeeper Malcolm Finlayson, who would drive me to away games. He had so many cars, a Jaguar, Aston Martin and Rolls-Royce, to name a few. I liked football, but I didn't watch much of it. I could never remember the players' names. Derek once took me to Gordon Banks's testimonial match at Stoke City. I noticed Bobby Charlton was playing in a red shirt and thought it was Manchester United until it was pointed out to me he was a guest for Stoke. Eusebio was also playing in red, so I asked Derek, 'When did Eusebio sign for Stoke?' He said, 'I am not bringing you again.'

"At Wolves' home games the players' wives would sit on the first row. It was a fashion show and one could not go to matches in the same outfit twice. Sometimes the season ticket holders behind us would give out abuse to the team. If one of the wives said, 'How dare you call my husband that?' they would reply, 'Shut up. At least we paid for our tickets, unlike you.' Once I was alone at an away game at Anfield and I sat next to a beer-bottle-swigging Liverpudlian who kept calling Derek an 'Irish git'. I kept very quiet and did not want him to know I was Dougan's wife.

"I occasionally socialised with the other wives at coffee afternoons, but not much. We had loads of friends, but they tended to be outside football. Derek was recognised whenever we went out, but he was always pleasant to the fans and never refused an autograph request. He was becoming a celebrity with his own column for the *TV Times* magazine and later as a panellist on football programmes. When Derek was a panellist during the World Cup finals I accompanied him for weeks at a time to London. We had a nanny then for the children. I had a lovely time roaming around London and meeting people like the wonderful Brian Moore, film and television stars, playwrights and, of course, lots of footballers. Once we were flown to Cherbourg to board the QE2 when Derek was a judge for the Miss TV Times competition along with the racing driver James Hunt and footballer Johan Cruyff. We had a first class cabin with butler service.

"There were invitations to 10 Downing Street and one of these led to a big row between Derek and me. He was always blaming me for being late. This time I was drying my hair on the landing at our home and forgot I had left the bath tap running because of the noise of the hairdryer. The water came through the kitchen ceiling. The house was flooded and I had to try to mop up all the water with towels.

"It meant we were late leaving for London. He was doing his nut. My hair was still in rollers under a scarf and all the way to London we were arguing and bickering. First he had to go and visit a book editor in Soho. Derek parked the car on yellow lines in a narrow street and it was pouring with rain. Derek went in to see the editor and, while he was away, I started turning on the blowers and wipers so I could see out of the windows. When I saw there was a space on a meter over the street I tried to start the car and the battery was flat. I had to go into the office in my rollers to tell him what had happened. He was so embarrassed – and angry.

"We had to wait an hour for the AA man to arrive and when he did the battery had recuperated and the car started with the first turn of the key. We had arranged to go to our friends' flat to change before going to Downing Street and after we had changed the car wouldn't start again. We ended up having to push it off the road. I was wearing an evening dress and high heels and Derek an evening suit.

"We ended up going to Downing Street in a taxi. Derek was steaming because we were going to be late, but when we arrived it was all smiles and he was the perfect gentleman. At No. 10 we met people like the Canadian Prime Minister Pierre Trudeau and the ballet dancer Rudolph Nureyev, who asked me what my husband did. I told him he was a professional footballer and when Derek joined us a few minutes later Rudolph squeezed his thighs to test his muscles!"

Apart from playing the role of society wife, Jutta also had to be mother and housekeeper. Their second son Nicholas had been born and, with Derek often travelling away with the team, it was her job to keep the family home in order. They had a nanny to look after the children, but otherwise Jutta took on the full range of financial and household duties and still had time to take a hairdressing course at college in Wolverhampton.

"Derek would be away at training camps or travelling to games, so I would be left with the kids," she said. "One summer they played in America for six weeks as the Los Angeles Wolves and I was left at home with all the responsibility. I was effectively father and mother to the boys for long periods of time. Sometimes Derek would moan that I was too strict with Alexander and Nick. He would let them get away with anything. He idolised them. But sometimes I had to put my foot down. Normally he wasn't there, so they had to listen to somebody – and it was me."

The marriage was not always on an even keel, however. There were tears and tantrums, but the Dougans stayed together. Rumours of Derek's womanising began to surface, but his wife turned a deaf ear to most of them even though she suspected at least a few of them were true. She tolerated it until their relationship reached breaking point in 1985 because of his infidelity. Jutta recalls, "I left him. That says it all. Maybe I had enough. There were other women. There were days on end when he never came home. It was hard to be left there waiting alone for him. There were rows and tears. I was getting all the rumours. And there would be lipstick or make-up on his clothes. He would just laugh it off and say it was just some woman he had met who had given him a hug. What could I do? Once he went missing for three days and he came home with blood on his shirt. He said he had been mugged and been in hospital. We had not a clue where he had been.

"Once he rang up and was drunk and said, 'Jutta, if anyone rings, you don't know where I am.' As if I did anyway! I just ran the house and got on with my own life as best I could. Then I found out about one particular affair and that was it. I'd had enough. I went back to Germany. I still loved him, but I couldn't stay with him."

Sons Alexander, who went to Warwick University to take a law degree, and Nick, who was taking his A levels before starting out on a career with NatWest Bank, lived in England, but divided their lives by regularly visiting Jutta in Munich. It was tough to see their mother and father living apart, but they enjoyed the love of both of their parents and remained loyal to each of them. They even spent plenty of time back together in Wolverhampton as a family unit.

Nick worked with his dad for a while on business projects in Belfast and then moved to work in Germany near his mum. He speaks with great affection for Derek, even though he appreciates how much hurt he caused. "Dad was one of life's characters," he said: "He liked to have fun. He was my dad and I loved him for being my dad. He probably wasn't the best dad around, but that didn't make me love him any less. Just because my parents were living apart, they were both there for us just the same.

"My brother and I tended to live in this cocooned world. It was nice. Mum would protect us from some of the things that were going on. The hardest part was having to watch mum going out of that front door and pretending everything was OK. But all we needed to know was that both our mum and dad loved us. We grew up bilingual with a family in England and one in Germany and that was a great upbringing.

"It was great when dad went back to Wolves in the 1980s as chairman and chief executive. That was a real exciting time for me. I would go to all the home games. He knew everyone. I could go to places like The Rock and Eves Nightclub and get in for free. He never encouraged me to play football. I played a bit of rugby, but he just left me to my own devices. To me he was the loveable Irishman. He was street-wise, but some of his decisions were a bit ill-judged."

Back in Germany, Jutta started a new life, but did not cut herself off completely from Dougan. Her sons were still in Wolverhampton with their dad and that was a natural point of contact. Eventually she would revisit the family home and still regarded Derek as a special friend. Deep down she suspected she still loved him, even though there were now even more women in his life and he was free to operate as a single man. Remarkably, divorce was only mentioned once.

Jutta said, "Either I upset him or he upset me on one occasion and we talked about divorce, but that soon passed. We always kept in touch. Of course, there were the kids and I always needed to know how they were getting on. At first Derek couldn't believe I had left him. Maybe he forgot the reasons why. He didn't tell the neighbours for about a year. If they asked about me, he would just say, 'She's fine. She's just back in Germany for a holiday.' Derek's sister told me he did not let her know for over a year that I had left him.

"Eventually I started coming back twice a year for three weeks at a time. I would spring clean the house, shop and cook meals to put in the deep freeze. Derek would have about 30 shirts under his bed waiting for me to iron. There was still a close bond. I would never have wished him anything bad. I sometimes helped him financially and sent money over to him. Once someone broke into the family house at Keeper's Lane and smashed up the porch. He needed 4,500 marks (about £1,500) for the repairs, so I sent it to him. I never saw it again, of course, even when the insurance money came though."

Jutta's visits stopped when her husband developed a serious relationship with a woman called Virginia Taylor-Potts, who moved into Keeper's Lane along with her ageing parents. "Typical of dad's generosity he took Virginia's parents in," recalls Nick. "The father had had a stroke, but dad was great with him, always helping him with his exercises and keeping him clean. I had moved to Germany by then. I liked Virginia and once told mum, 'Mum, I would like you to meet her. Virginia is the salt of the earth.'"

However, Jutta went on the warpath when she discovered that Dougan planned to swap the Keeper's Lane property for a bungalow in the Stockwell End area of Wolverhampton, owned by his pal, Doug Hope. The bungalow was close to an old people's home which would have been an ideal residence for Virginia's elderly parents. Jutta was furious because she rightly claimed the house in Keeper's Lane was half hers.

"I wasn't jealous of Virginia," says Jutta. "It didn't matter to me that she was living with him. I was mad with Derek. I was upset because half that house belonged to me. He just sent me a card saying he had met someone and she was moving into Keeper's Lane.

"A few days before Derek's funeral Virginia asked me via my best friend if she could come to the service. Not only did I say yes, I rang Virginia and invited her to come to sit with us in church in the family pew and to the wake at Molineux afterwards. This was where Virginia and I met for the first time in our lives and we got on great together. I discovered what a warm-hearted, lovely person she is.

"When I heard Derek was swapping the house I rang him and asked him what was going on. He said, 'I can't talk now. I have to fly to Belfast. My heart is not too good. I will ring you.' I waited and he didn't ring. So I thought, 'Right I'll stop you selling the house. It is half mine.' I was put in touch with a solicitor in Bristol who said she would put something called an 'F charge' on the house. It meant my name would go to the land registry and no-one could buy the house without my approval.

"Derek was informed by my solicitor about the F charge. He rang me. He was furious. He said, 'You bastard. I'll have you for everything you have got. See you in court.' I couldn't sleep all night. Fortunately for Derek, my solicitor in Bristol made two mistakes. She registered the F charge in the name of Derek Dougan. His full name is Alexander Derek Dougan. And she registered our house in Codsall in the West Midlands. It should have been Staffordshire. Derek and the buyer's solicitors could therefore ignore the F charge. So he got the house deal through on these technicalities. I had lost half of the house because of these mistakes and Derek registered the new house in his name. I was so annoyed. Not only that but I had lots of things in Keeper's Lane – handbags, shoes, a sheepskin coat, books, lots of things I valued. Either they were left rotting in the garage or they were dumped in the tip. But I got over the shock of him stitching me up and we still exchanged Christmas and birthday cards."

By now Dougan's health was deteriorating. He had suffered a heart attack, but still maintained his hectic pace of life, pursuing the cases of retired footballers who had fallen on hard times as well as enjoying an active social life. When Virginia Taylor-Potts left his house in Stockwell End, it gave Jutta the chance to revisit him.

She says, "I knew he had suffered a heart attack and wasn't in good health. When Virginia moved out, I came over for Alexander's 40th birth-day for a few days. We had a great time. When I arrived in England two days before the party, Alexander asked me if I could do the catering. He told me he had invited 120 people. With the help of some friends I just got stuck in."

Derek's death in the summer of 2007 came as a hammer blow to Jutta. She was devastated by the loss of the man who was still her husband and who had figured large in her life for better or worse for over 40 years. The news came to her suddenly and sadly when she was at a family celebration in Germany.

"My mother's cousin had a birthday and there was a party in this place which wasn't even a village," she recalls. "There were just three farm houses and a pub. My mobile phone didn't work there. There was no reception. When I left that place I went back to the cousin's house and checked my mobile. There were many messages, all of them from Nick. I still have them on my phone now. One said, 'Mum. Ring please. It's bad.' He had heard from his brother his dad had died and could not get hold of me. I couldn't believe it. I flew to England next day for the funeral preparations."

Jutta had a secret which until now she has only shared with those closest to her. It has given her a final memory of her husband which brought her peace and happiness at a time of great sorrow. Three months before he died, Derek asked her to go back to him.

"When he asked me I said, 'Yes. I would love to come back,'" she says. "It was the nicest thing I had heard for years. All those things he had done wrong were suddenly wiped away. I am so happy now that even though he has died, I have the memory that we were getting back together. All my hurt had gone when he asked me that question.

"All the trouble over the house and the different women, they didn't matter any more. The fact that we never divorced always suggested, even in a subconscious way, that there was still something there for us to cling on to. I realised when Derek asked me to go back, he needed me. He realised he was poorly and that his life wasn't in good order. I could help look after him, cleaning and cooking and organising his home and his finances for him. He knew that when I was with him everything was well. He could still have his freedom.

"I gave in my notice to leave my job in Germany and had to apply for my old age pension. That was going to take a few months, so I had to wait for that before I returned to Derek. I am an only child and my mother is 87. I decided what I would do was to spend a week in Germany with her and a week in England with Derek. Nick would look after my mother when I was away. I couldn't believe it. I was coming back home to be with Derek.

"My dearest and closest friends are in England. I have missed England all these years back in Germany and always dreamt of coming back one day. But then Derek died . . . and now I only remember the good things. I did enjoy it. I had a great life, an exciting life. I am old now and it's nice to look back and have those lovely memories."

Chapter Two

FROM BELFAST TO HALMSTAD

THOUGH ALEXANDER DEREK DOUGAN established himself over 18 seasons as one of English football's finest goalscorers, he always thought of himself as a lapsed centre-half. He believed a position at the centre of defence was what suited him best. Others thought differently and were proved right. His lean frame and speed off the mark made him far better suited to poaching goals rather than preventing them. Not that either role at first occurred to Dougan as a youngster growing up in east Belfast.

In the playground at Mersey Street School young Dougan used to love to run, but not with a ball at his feet. He just loved running. He was good at it and rarely got out of breath. Fortunately one of his teachers, a Mr Mawhinney, noted the fleet-footed schoolboy and suggested that he join the school football team. "The way you can shift, you'll do all right," he told him. The teacher was spot on in his analysis, but in his first match the nine-year-old Dougan started out up front before being switched to centre-half and soon found in subsequent games that it was the position he preferred. If not centre-half he thought of himself as a left-half.

Dougan's schooling had started when he was little more than three. Born on 20 January 1938, Dougan was evacuated during the War to Bangor and it was there he first went to school. Returning to Belfast he would attend Belvoir School before moving on to Mersey Street where his football potential was first spotted. Once bitten by the football bug, there was just no stopping him. He would play with his pals after school and would hone his heading talent by nodding a ball up against the side of any available house. Sundays would see him and many other local lads playing on a piece of land at the bottom of Avon Street, known as the Meadow. He would break off to nip home to 31 Avon Street, change into his best clothes to attend Sunday school for a couple of hours before dashing home to change back into his ordinary clobber to return to the on-going match on the waste land. It was a scenario re-enacted all over Britain in those years immediately after the war. Young boys on coming home from school had no TV to watch and no

PCs to play upon, so they would be out in the street or on the nearest open space to have an impromptu game of football.

While Dougan saw himself as a half-back, others still saw his potential as a striker and he was often played there. A few years later the national schools selectors took note of him and Dougan set his sights on winning a schoolboy cap. However, he was due to leave school and would thus have missed his chance. So he managed to pass an exam to go to Belfast Technical High School. That enabled him to continue his schooling long enough to win three schoolboy caps – against Wales in Cardiff, England at York and Scotland in Belfast. In the game at York, the England side, who won 5–0 were skippered by Manchester lad Wilf McGuinness, later to play for England and both to play for and manage Manchester United.

Jim Dobbin was goalkeeper in the schools side with Dougan and in a Northern Ireland youth side who played in the 1955 international tournament in Italy. "We played in Pisa and Florence and we had some great times," said Dobbin. "We would meet up in the town centre with players from other countries. Derek was always full of fun. He was a joker, nothing malicious, just liked to enjoy himself. He used to love to sing that Dean Martin song, Amore. You know the one . . . 'When the moon hits your eye like a big-a pizza pie.' He loved that. He was always singing it. There were some good players in that youth squad, like John Crossan and Bobby Braithwaite."

Dobbin became firm friends with Dougan after they got to know each other in the Irish schools side and would often pal around in the mid-1950s. "He would come to see us down in Larne and we were at an age when the Teddy Boy cult was the big thing. We'd wear the flamboyant suits, but they did not always fit Derek as his arms were so long. We'd go to dances at the King's Arms in Larne and the Belfast Plaza."

Like Dougan, Dobbin had trials in England – with Wolves and Birmingham. "Derek went over to turn professional with Portsmouth, but I was an unattached amateur. Wolves wanted to take me on, but I was learning my trade as a sign-writer. The signing-on fee was only about £10 or £15 and I was doing better than that at home – and I was homesick. I met Billy Wright and Harry Hooper at Wolves when I went over there. Harry was also at Birmingham when I had my trial there. They were all nice to me at Wolves and Stan Cullis said that if I signed he would expect me to behave myself. He wanted no nonsense. When I turned down Blues there was a story in the Birmingham paper from the manager Arthur Turner and the headline was 'Sign writer sticks to paints'.

"After Derek had signed for Portsmouth we had been out in Belfast one night and he said to me, 'I've got a surprise for you' and he took me round by the side of City Hall and showed me where he'd parked a green Ford Prefect that he'd bought. He ran me home in it. He always kept in touch after he moved to England. Whenever he was over he would come and visit us. In later years he'd bring over people like Ian St John and Denis Law for speaking engagements and he used to do a lot of promotional work, like officially opening car showrooms. He always kept in touch with his old friends."

His schoolboy caps duly won, Dougan left school to work first at the Tri-ang toy factory and then as an apprentice electrician at the Harland and Wolff shipyard where his father was also employed. As a member of Cregagh Boys' Club, the same one attended a few years later by George Best, Dougan was able to continue his football. He also signed amateur forms for Linfield but they took little interest in him. As a lad from the east side of Belfast his natural loyalty was to Glentoran, but a scout who looked at him reported, 'He's not too bad on the ball but would not get in our fourth team regularly.' With Linfield and Glentoran not too bothered about him, Dougan left to join Distillery and soon made his first team debut. "I shall never forget my 16th birthday," he wrote many years later, "playing my first game for Distillery against Glenavon in the Irish Cup. I was at centre-forward. I didn't like playing in this position, but when you make your debut you are happy to play anywhere in the side." Dougan emphasised, "My favourite position was centre-half or left-half. To this day I still regard myself as a makeshift centre-forward!"

Dougan had the last laugh over Glentoran as he helped Distillery beat them in the 1956 Irish Cup final after two replays. The sides drew 2–2 and 0–0 before Distillery won 1–0, all the games being at Windsor Park, Belfast's principal ground. The evening before the third game, Dougan still found time for a street kick-around, according to his cousin Jimmy Kitchen, and it could have spoiled his cup final chances. Said Kitchen, "We were playing in the street which was being dug up. I sold him a dummy and he fell into the building works. He got out and he was going to kill me because he could be hot-tempered. He was not hurt though – but that was Derek playing in a kick-about before a big game."

As young lads, Kitchen and Dougan had knocked around together and loved to wind each other up. "Just after the Blackpool-Bolton Cup Final we were going to the pictures and talking about the match," remembered Kitchen. "He said that fella Mortensen was some player and I said I liked

Matthews. All Mortensen could do was score goals. Big Dougie's eyes were out like organ stops. 'That's the whole object of the game, you cretin,' Big Dougie said," Kitchen added, "We never called him Doog back home. It was always Big Dougie."

It was not long after his Distillery debut that Dougan's mother, Josie, died of cancer. That strengthened his determination to leave the city to pursue a football career in England. He said, "She had been the centre of my life there and now she was gone I felt no pull from the grass roots. I wanted to get away." Dougan, one of six children, described his mother, in his book *The Sash He never Wore . . . Twenty Five Years On*, as 'the author of my commandments for life and living, the lady who knew nothing of hate and everything of love.' No doubt her death influenced his willingness in later life to help charities connected with cancer research and treatment.

Someone who did cross the water before Dougan was Distillery inside forward Brian Moore. He joined West Ham and that led indirectly to Dougan getting a game against the London club. Part of the Moore deal was that a friendly would be played and Dougan was in the Distillery party who flew to London for the match at Upton Park. Though he did not remember the score, the match stuck in his memory because of the speed of the Hammers outside-right – Harry Hooper. "He was the fastest thing I had seen in football boots," was Dougan's verdict on a player who would soon join Wolves as the successor to Molineux legend Johnny Hancocks. Hooper had a memorable first season with Wolves, but then fell out of favour with manager Stan Cullis and missed out on the greatest three seasons in the club's history, which brought successive First Division titles and then the FA Cup. Brian Moore did not have much luck in London and made only nine first team appearances.

One Belfast boy who did make a successful career in England was Sammy Chapman, a close pal of Dougan's who crossed the water before him. Chapman, who first went to England for a spell in Manchester United's youth squad, said, "We were born in the same street and there was only about a month between us, Derek being slightly the older. His family moved to Avon Street, so he went to Mersey Street school. I was at Templemore Avenue, so we were rivals, but we were also friends. I knew his family, his dad was a good man and his sister Pearlie used to look after the family after Derek's mother died. I played in schoolboy matches with him and I could see he had what it took to be a great player."

Chapman warms to the recollection of the young Dougan. "You could see he had it all. He had an unbelievable talent, everything you could wish for in a player. It was a God-given talent. It was all so easy for him. He was tall, slim and never had a weight problem later on and, of course, he was left-sided which was a big asset and he was so fast – you were never going to catch him."

An important factor in Dougan's development was the arrival at Distillery in July 1955 of experienced former Charlton and Plymouth player Maurice Tadman to take over from Jimmy Macintosh. Tadman helped Dougan on two fronts. Firstly he was sympathetic to Dougan's wishes to play centre-half or left-half and, secondly, he was a centre-forward himself and so eased the pressure on Dougan to play there. In two seasons with Distillery Tadman scored 55 goals in only 62 games. He also had enough faith in Dougan to make him one of the youngest players ever to captain the club. Because Tadman allowed Dougan to play mostly in defence or midfield, there was less opposition on the occasions when the boss said, "We're in a spot, I want you to play up front." Thus Dougan would on occasions play centre-forward or inside-left and it was during one of his spells up front that he attracted the attention of scouts from English clubs.

Another trip to England came in September 1956 when Dougan played in the Northern Ireland side beaten 5–2 by England in an amateur international at Bromley. Fate took a hand to enable Dougan to add that amateur cap to those gained at schoolboy and youth level. Ray Gough, a Crusaders wing-half just a few days younger than Dougan, was first choice but had to cry off through injury. Dougan stepped in at left-half and did well despite the scoreline. Though Gough was fit for the next amateur international, against Wales at Ebbw Vale, and took Dougan's place, Dougan had obviously impressed the selectors and was retained in the team though switched to inside-left. The Welsh won the game 3–1 with Phil Woosnam, a future team-mate of Dougan's at Villa, scoring twice. The match was in January 1957 and Dougan could hardly have realised that in six months he would be making headlines in the First Division of the Football League. As for Gough, who was talked of as a star in the making, there would be no fame and fortune. He did not move to England until 1964 when he spent a year with Exeter without making an impact before going to Millwall where he made only 13 appearances.

Dougan rated Ebbw Vale one of the bleakest places he had ever visited. No doubt it looked even bleaker on a cold Saturday in January. In stark contrast, before the year was out, Dougan's talents would be seen at such hotbeds of English football as Highbury, Old Trafford and Roker Park.

Before the game at Ebbw Vale he had agreed to sign professional for Distillery, but the club held back his resignation so that he still qualified to play one last time as an amateur.

Dougan went to England for trials at Preston and Bury which came to nothing but as his displays for Distillery improved he began to attract interest from Football League clubs, Wolves, Blackpool and Leeds being among them while Scottish giants Celtic also took a look at him. However, it was Portsmouth whose eye the rangy youngster really caught. Dougan played well at inside-left against Linfield in front of a huge crowd attracted by the presence in the visitors' side of former Newcastle and England legend Jackie Milburn. Among the spectators was Portsmouth scout Jack Tinn (manager of their successful 1939 FA Cup-winning team), who sent back a favourable report to Eddie Lever, the Pompey boss. Lever came to see for himself and saw Dougan have an average game against Bangor in a 1–1 draw, but he stayed in Ireland to watch him again the following Saturday when Dougan crowned a much better display with a goal from 25 yards in a 3–0 defeat of Ards. That was enough for Lever and after the game he asked him to sign for Pompey. Dougan jumped at the chance. He moved to Portsmouth in the summer of 1957, little realising how quickly he would get a chance to play in top-flight English football. According to the pen picture in the 1960 FA Cup final programme, 'The day Pompey signed him, in the stand also watching were managers Stan Cullis (Wolves), Raich Carter (Leeds) and Johnny Carey (Blackburn).'

Dougan had enjoyed his time at Distillery, a club with no particular religious affiliation, which was something Dougan liked. Reflecting in 2006 on his time at Grosvenor Park he said, "It was probably the happiest time of my entire footballing life. That was brought about by the camaraderie of the players. If you believe people who should know better, they say there's a terrible conflict between Protestants and Catholics. I'll tell you I don't think there is. I played in a team that was six Protestants and five Catholics – or it could have been the other way round!"

Ray Crawford, later to achieve fame with Ipswich where his goals helped make the East Anglians unlikely First Division champions in 1961/62, was given the Pompey number-nine shirt for the opening of the 1957/58 season. That allowed Jackie Henderson, another future Wolves man, to revert to outside-left, having played centre-forward for two or three seasons. Crawford did well as Pompey managed three wins and a draw in their opening five games, but he chipped a bone in his ankle in the home match with Sheffield United.

This injury eventually let Dougan into the side, but he was not manager Lever's first choice as deputy. In fact, Lever would try four others at centre-forward before giving the raw recruit his chance. Sid McClellan, Derek Weddle, Ron Newman and Henderson were all used up front in the seven games which followed Crawford's injury. Then Dougan was finally given his opportunity – against Charlton in the Southern Floodlit Challenge Cup.

Football under lights was still a novelty in those days and Portsmouth had had the honour of staging the first ever floodlit Football League match – against Newcastle in February 1956. While Wolves had staged friendlies against top-class foreign opposition attracting huge gates and huge interest, other clubs had pioneered floodlighting with domestic competitions such as the one which gave Dougan his first chance to shine in the Portsmouth first team. Full-back Jack Mansell, given a chance at inside-left, scored two goals as did inside-right Johnny Gordon in a 4–1 win at The Valley on Monday 14 October 1957. Though Dougan did not score he must have done enough to impress Lever as he retained his place in the side to visit Old Trafford the following Saturday. It was as tough a league debut as you could get. United had been champions for the previous two seasons and were hoping to make it a hat-trick despite the fact that Wolves had set the early-season pace. Dougan was up against his fellow countryman Jackie Blanchflower and though he did not score had another useful game as Pompey gained a shock 3–0 win, all the goals coming before half-time.

Teams that day, Saturday 19 October:
Manchester United: Wood; Foulkes, Peter Jones; Colman, Blanchflower, McGuinness, Berry, Whelan, Dawson, Viollet, Pegg.
Portsmouth: Uprichard; Gunter, Wilson; Albury, Rutter, Dickinson; Harris, Gordon, Dougan, Henderson, Newman.
Scorers: Harris, Henderson, Newman.
Attendance: 38,253.

Missing from the United side were three Old Trafford legends, Roger Byrne, Duncan Edwards and Tommy Taylor. They were on duty for England helping their country beat Wales 4–0 in Cardiff. League games were played on the same day as internationals in those days and if a club had lost men to their national sides then they just had to get on with it and field reserves. Dougan would never get the chance to play against those three greats. By the time the return game took place at Fratton Park, they were dead, victims of the Munich Air Disaster which also claimed the lives of five other United men, David Pegg, Liam Whelan, Eddie Colman, Geoff Bent and Mark Jones.

Dougan may have been awaiting his first goals for Pompey, but he quickly showed his scoring prowess four days after the United match when he was selected for Northern Ireland's B team against Rumania B at Belfast. He hit a hat-trick in a 6–0 win. Also on the scoresheet with a penalty was Sammy Chapman, who was then still with Mansfield, but would later join Dougan at Portsmouth.

Dougan's home League debut was in the 2–0 win over Leicester and, though he did not score in this match nor in the 2–1 defeat at Villa which followed, he would open his account the next time he turned out at Fratton Park. More of that in due course, because the Villa game alerted a fellow Irishman to his potential. Winger Peter McParland, one of Northern Ireland's true greats, could hardly believe what he saw.

"Our centre-half Jimmy Dugdale was one of the best in the country at the time, probably only kept out of the England side by Billy Wright," recalls McParland, "but Derek gave him a real going over, really tore him apart, ran him all over the pitch. Jim had played against the best centre- forwards of the day, Tommy Taylor, Nat Lofthouse and the rest and had taken care of them but he could not handle Derek that day."

It did not end there. "I had heard about Derek from people in Ireland, but I had never met him before," says McParland. "Well after the game that day I had come out of the bath and was sitting down in the dressing room getting dressed. Next thing I know, standing in front of me is Derek. He said he had just come to say hello to me. I can't remember all he said, but I just remember this chap in front of me. He was full of confidence and he made a big impression on me."

McParland was among the top names in English football at the time, having scored the two goals earlier that year which won Villa the FA Cup at Wembley thus preventing Manchester United's ill-fated Busby Babes from doing the Double. Yet Dougan was not in awe of him and, as McParland put it, came in 'bold as brass' to make himself known to an established star player from his own part of the world. McParland adds tellingly, "I'm not sure what I said to him had any effect. I told him that Jimmy Dugdale was one of the best centre-halves in the country and said how well he'd done against him, but I felt it all went over Derek's head. That's the sort of person he was, he was never bothered about praise." Having shown his prowess in that game at Villa Park it was no surprise when Dougan kept up the good work just a week later.

There was something almost pre-ordained about Dougan's football career in England in that his first goal in this country should be hit against Wolves, the club to whom he would eventually give his best years. It came at Fratton Park on Saturday 9 November 1957 when Portsmouth faced Wanderers, then top of the First Division and boasting an array of England internationals. Foremost among them was Billy Wright and it would make national headlines when the youngster from Belfast not only gave England's captain and centre-half a busy afternoon, but climaxed it with the equalising goal in a 1–1 draw. Then, as now, it seemed fashionable to try to undermine national sporting icons. Wright was such at that time and a 19-year-old rookie from Belfast giving the run-around – or alleged run-around – to England's main man meant Dougan was the name in most of the headlines in the Sunday papers.

Dougan believed he would do well against Wright. Height and speed were on his side, but vast experience was on Wright's. However, Dougan's trump card was the fact he was an unknown quantity and he admitted that had he played against Wolves a week later he would not have enjoyed as much success. They would have then known what he was all about.

The moment of that first English goal was something he would always remember as it was not a tap-in or a lucky touch – it was a real gem. This is how he described it in his book *The Sash He Never Wore . . . Twenty Five Years On*: 'I drifted to the right side of the pitch in the six-yard box. I spun round Billy Wright and another Wolves defender, worked the ball on to my left foot – my "natural" one – and hit it with everything I had. It seemed to fly past Noel Dwyer, the Wolves goalkeeper, and then into the net.'

Not that it was all praise for Dougan for, on scoring, he had without thinking raised his arms above his head to acknowledge the cheers of the fans. As celebrations go it would be mild by 21st Century standards, but in the 1950s such a gesture was thought of as over-demonstrative and not the done thing. One or two sportswriters picked up on this and manager Eddie Lever was forced to answer the criticism. He defended Dougan, saying, "It was the natural elation of a youngster scoring his first goal for his club. He's a bit of a showman, I'll admit, but there is nothing wrong with that."

The gesture did not surprise his cousin Jimmy Kitchen, who reckoned Dougan had told him beforehand he would do something spectacular. "He used to write to me just about every week when he first went to England and he told me that if nothing else he was going to nutmeg Billy Wright during the game." The way Kitchen recalls it is probably with a little exaggeration as he adds, "After he scored he ran up to Billy Wright, shoved the ball up Wright's shirt and patted him on the head." One suspects distance may have lent enchantment to whatever the extent of Dougan's celebration was, but there is no doubt that it was an early example of the exhibitionism that would become his trademark and would endear him to his fans, though probably not the opposition's. "I'm sure there was an open letter in one newspaper," Kitchen adds, "about the audacity of this young fella in doing that to the England captain but the thing was that it was not spontaneous. It was planned. That was Derek."

Some might have thought that Dougan's gestures were part of a stereo-typical mad Irishman character. They were nothing of the sort. He realised very early on that the paying public were as much a part of the football drama as were the players. He made them feel they were special and he would always have them on his side virtually throughout his playing career. Back to cousin Jim Kitchen, "Derek was not the character the general public thought he was. Some of them thought he was an idiot. In fact he was anything but an idiot. When he first went over the water to Portsmouth he told me, 'I'll have about 15 years at this and I'm going to make a name for myself. I want to be in television or films or make a record.' He couldn't sing to save his life, but he was determined he would be somebody. We were best mates and he always kept in touch after he went to England. He kept writing to me and even sent me a couple of suits."

Crawford, the man whose injury had eventually led to Dougan getting his chance, remembers well that game against Wolves. "I was in the stand watching and he was unbelievable that day. He was doing his tricks and trying flicks, using his speed and his quickness of thought. All this against the great Billy Wright." Crawford felt he could have hit it off with the young Irishman in the same forward line. He recalled, "I would have loved to have played with Derek for a long spell, but it was not to be."

Sammy Chapman, Dougan's old Belfast pal, had moved to England in October 1956 and would leave Mansfield Town to team up with Dougan at Fratton Park, but not until February 1958. However, he remembers seeing Dougan play against Wright, particularly one incident. "The ball came to Derek and he let it go through his legs. Billy Wright did not expect that and Derek was round him and gone. It was a special moment."

Chapman adds that it was because of Dougan that he moved to Portsmouth. "We shared the same digs for a time. And you could say I slept with Derek Dougan because we had to share a bed at first! We had some good times together because Pompey was a wonderful city, a lovely place and we were only 20 years of age. Derek was a good-looking lad and he always dressed immaculately and there was plenty of entertainment around. Not that Derek was a big drinker, certainly not in those days. We used a club which was non-alcoholic. We would drink coffee there and it would stay open late. Sometimes there was live music, jazz, just easy-going stuff and dancing though nothing too heavy, just mild dancing. It was basically just a nice place. We had some lovely times there."

Ray Crawford also remembers Dougan arriving at Portsmouth and was quickly taken with him. "He was very likeable, like so many Irishman. He was not shy and he settled in immediately. I think he had been given a bit of money when he signed. It would not have come from Portsmouth because clubs did not do anything like that in England. It was illegal in those days, but I think Distillery gave him a bit, maybe £350 or so. I know he soon bought a great big car, a Ford Consul, I think, with an open top. He used to ride around with some of the other young lads, Sammy Chapman, Brian Carter and Alec Stenhouse."

The word back in Belfast was that Dougan had received £600 for signing on. If so, it was a sizeable sum for those days.

It may have been that 1957 match that many years later led Dougan to say of Wright, "I never thought Billy was that outstanding a player", something of a sacriligious statement in Wolverhampton. Yet before that 1957/58 season was out Dougan would twice more face Wolves. In the FA Cup fourth-round clash at Molineux, Pompey were beaten 5–1 and in the return league fixture lost 1–0, the *Express & Star's* Phil Morgan writing that Wright 'reduced the lanky Dougan to ordinary proportions.'

When Crawford was fit again he took over at centre-forward with Dougan moved to inside-left. However, when Crawford came back after another injury spell he had to play on the left wing as Dougan had by then established himself in the number-nine shirt, a spell of five goals in as many games meaning he finished his inaugural season in England with eight from 26 league appearances, not a bad return for a youngster in a struggling side who escaped relegation only on goal average. They, Newcastle and Sunderland finished on 32 points, just one above bottom-placed Sheffield Wednesday.

What proved a vital point in their relegation escape came against Manchester United before Fratton Park's biggest gate of the season, 39,975 turning up in midweek for the game against a side urgently re-built after the horrors of Munich. The young United side, who had against all the odds reached the FA Cup final, led Pompey 2–0 at half-time, but an exciting second half saw the game end 3–3, Dougan hitting one of the goals. There were two matches left in the league season and Portsmouth did their best to give the fans palpitations. They lost at Leeds and then at home to fellow strugglers Sunderland, whose win was still not enough to save them. Dougan missed that game through injury and also the final of the Southern Floodlit Cup, which Pompey won by beating Reading 2–0 at Elm Park. Dougan's goal in the 1–0 semi-final victory at Watford had got them to the final.

Dougan's displays, plus that B international hat-trick, had done enough to thrust him into the Northern Ireland selectors' deliberations. The Irish, along with Wales, Scotland and England, had qualified for the summer's World Cup finals in Sweden, still the only occasion all four Home nations have made it to the last stage. Northern Ireland were a fine side at the time. Indeed, three days before Dougan had scored his first league goal, in the game against Wolves, his countrymen had gained a famous victory at Wembley, beating a very good England side 3–2. However, if Northern Ireland did have a problem position it was centre-forward, though Billy Simpson of Rangers seemed to have made the spot his that season. Dougan was named in the squad for Sweden, as was his pal Sammy Chapman, though a non-travelling reserve.

It got better than that for Dougan. An injury to Simpson during training meant that Dougan, allocated the number-16 shirt, was selected for Northern Ireland's opening group game which brought a 1–0 win over Czechoslovakia in Halmstad. The Irish would memorably go on to reach the quarter-finals under the managership of former international Peter Doherty, but Dougan played no further part in their heroics. The group game after the Czech match saw Northern Ireland beaten 3–1 by Argentina and Dougan posed the question in his book, Attack, many years later, 'Why change a winning team? I am not saying that we would have won had the team been unchanged, neither am I saying that we would still have lost. It is one of those imponderables.'

Rather than stick with a centre-forward who had made a considerable impression in his inaugural First Division season, the selectors (Doherty, in keeping with the other three Home nations' managers, did not have a say in the eleven men he had to mould into a team) turned to Nottingham Forest's Fay Coyle for the Argentina match. He had played three times for his country while with Coleraine, but in 1957/58 had just three games in the Forest first team and those would prove to be his only league games in English football. Coyle did not impress against Argentina and was dropped in favour of Tommy Casey, a Newcastle half-back. John Scott of Grimsby, who, like Dougan, had not been capped before the finals was then asked to lead the line in the group play-off game and the quarter-final, which the Irish lost 4–0 to France. For the record, unlike Dougan, neither Coyle nor Scott played for Northern Ireland again.

Peter McParland was Northern Ireland's goalscoring hero in that tournament, with five of the six his country scored in Sweden, and he felt the selectors may have been a bit hasty in dropping Dougan after just one match. "He was a bit miffed about that," recalled McParland. "He did not have a good game but, being the type of player he was, I feel if they had kept him in he would have got going. He was probably the best centre-forward we had in our squad. I suppose because we were lacking a bit there I tended to come in from the left wing and that's why I scored all those World Cup goals. I think the only British player to score more in the finals than me is Gary Lineker. Derek should've stayed in the side, but if he had, maybe I would not have got my goals."

Talking in 2006 Dougan offered what he believed was behind his lone appearance in Sweden. He maintained, "The real reason that Fay Coyle made his international debut (sic) was that in those days committees helped pick the team and Coleraine got another two or three thousand pounds if he became an Irish international. That was the reason they left me out. They weren't bothered about winning the World Cup or reaching the next round. Peter Doherty pulled me to one side and said, 'You had a wonderful game against the Czechs, but I don't think I'm going to play you again because you're just here for the experience.' I said, 'Well I thought I came here to play football.' I seriously regret I did not play more in that (tournament) because we went on to the quarter-final. The Derek Dougan of ten years later would have challenged Doherty, confronted him and said, 'I'm going to strip and go out and play and you can do what you want.'"

Dougan's theory about Coyle could be right, except that the Argentina game was not his debut. Coyle was already an Irish international when he joined Forest. Extra payment would have been far more likely once he had played a certain total of League games. Dougan's recollection that Doherty had told him he had played well is also open to doubt. Most reports of the Czech match, as well as McParland's recollection, suggest Dougan had hardly sparkled. For a final word, step up Albert Sewell, a journalist who followed Northern Ireland during the finals and made this contribution about the Czech game to John Camkin's book *World Cup 1958*, "One goal was decisive – a header by Cush from a centre by McParland after 21 minutes – but the Irish passage could have been so much smoother if

Dougan had been quicker in thought and movement." So, despite what Dougan may have said, it seems the reason he was dropped after just one outing is simple – he did not play very well.

Chapter Three

AN IRISH ROVER

IF IT HAD NOT BEEN a bad club campaign for Dougan it had been a poor one for Portsmouth and manager Eddie Lever inevitably got the sack. Dougan liked Lever and not merely because he had been the man who brought him to England. He later said he reckoned him to be one of the most genuine and considerate managers he had known in his career. 'It was his straight thinking, his fair dealing and integrity that I admired,' Dougan wrote of Lever. 'He respected other people's views and did not try to subvert them to his own.'

Lever's replacement was Bournemouth boss Freddie Cox, the one-time Arsenal winger. In 1957 he had steered Bournemouth to FA Cup giantkilling wins over Tottenham and Wolves before losing to Manchester United in the quarter-final. Cox's arrival was bad news for Dougan and not too good for the club either. They were relegated at the end of the 1958/59 season. Dougan played in the opening match then lost his place to Crawford for a couple of games before Cox signed Ron Saunders from Gillingham to be first-choice centre-forward. Crawford was soon trans-ferred to Ipswich and Dougan would leave Fratton Park before the end of the season, though not before he had worn shirt numbers seven and eleven which meant in his brief spell at the club he had played in all the five forward positions that were then the norm.

Crawford was a little surprised to be shown the door. He remembers, "Freddie Cox just called me in and said I had no future at Fratton Park. I had scored nine goals in 19 league games, which I did not think was a bad return, but he just said I had no future and sold me to Alf Ramsey. In fair-ness he bought a useful replacement in Ron Saunders. Ron was a good player, but I was still surprised to be sold."

Crawford has a high opinion of Dougan. "He was up there with the best, but he did have that thing about wanting to be a centre-half. I came upon him once walking purposefully up the players' tunnel and I said 'What are you up to?' and he said 'I'm going to see the manager. I want to revert to centre-half.' I had just scored a couple of goals and was doing quite well and he said he did not think he would get into the team at centre-forward. So the manager agreed to play him at centre-half in the reserves. Anyway he played about 15 minutes at centre-half and I think he must have given away about 15 free-kicks. He might even have given away a penalty as well. The result was they switched him up front as quickly as they could for the rest of the game." Thus chastened, Dougan shelved for the moment any desires to be a central defender once more. As Crawford drily recalls: "At that stage I don't think Portsmouth were ready for a ball-playing centre-half."

Portsmouth had been champions of England in successive seasons, 1948/49 and 1949/50, but those heady days were just a memory by the time Dougan joined the club, as Sammy Chapman confirms. "I suppose we arrived at the wrong time. The great side had broken up and there were only three of them left – Norman Uprichard, Peter Harris and Jimmy Dickinson. We had other good players like Jack Mansell, Jackie Henderson and Phil Gunter, but it was a transitional period and things just did not work out. It changed when Freddie Cox arrived. Derek left, but I hung on because I did not want to go. He wanted rid of me but I liked Pompey. It was only when George Smith took over that I finally left and went back to Mansfield."

Dougan admitted there was a personality clash between him and Cox – "the Irish terrier and the English sheepdog did not see eye to eye" was how he, typically, put it. Dougan took offence when Cox wanted to know why he had moved digs. Unlike today, clubs wanted to know where their players were living and if it met with their approval. It would be none of the club's business today, but times were different then. Dougan regarded it as an intrusion into his private life. Where he chose to live was his business. It was such niggling things that would irk him and almost always throughout his career, provoke a response.

Portsmouth also had a rule that players should walk to the ground as the exercise would be good for them. Dougan thought this was nonsense and he and one or two others would drive most of the way to Fratton Park before parking their cars just around the corner and then walking the last few yards.

In that second season at Fratton Park, Dougan, after being dropped, spent much of the time sidelined. His injury was at first diagnosed as a sprained ankle. After eight weeks he managed to get through a third-team game and was given an outing in the reserves. That lasted just ten minutes before he hobbled off the pitch. An X-ray this time revealed the ankle was broken. While the training staff had been treating him for a sprain for two months or more he had in fact been nursing a break.

Training for the start of the 1958/59 season, Dougan had sustained an ankle injury, though not as serious as the later one, but it brought a further decrease in his respect for the club. As a member of the Irish squad which had captured the imagination of their fans by reaching the World Cup quarter-finals, he was invited to a special celebration in Belfast where each player would receive a commemorative medal. The club said he should stay at home and concentrate on getting fit. Dougan did not see it that way, "I felt that if I had gone home to Ireland for a while I would have been in better mental shape to deal with the injury. The medal came by post. It was a bitter disappointment to miss the celebration. I needed the break to renew an emotional link with home at a time when my ankle was holding back my progress." Many years later Dougan would say the award from the Irish FA was not a medal, but a gold watch.

Pompey's wretched season saw them amass only 21 points and their relegation was virtually sealed as early as March when they lost 5–1 at home to Newcastle. The day after that match Freddie Cox sent a message to Dougan's digs saying he wanted to see him. Dougan was surprised to find the boss in an untypically friendly mood which was quickly explained when he said, "Blackburn want to sign you." Though Dougan was happy to get away and to stay in the First Division, there was a certain irony. His recall to the first team after his injury had been against Blackburn at Ewood Park and he had remembered thinking how fortunate he was to be living on the South Coast rather than in that grimy northern town. He snatched the opportunity, however, and before the season closed there was time for Dougan to make four appearances for Rovers and score one goal – on his debut in a 1–1 draw at Arsenal.

While the heavy defeat by Newcastle was Dougan's final game for Pompey it was also the first for Ron Howells, a Welsh wing-half signed from Wolves. There was, Dougan maintained many years later, a move by Wolves director Jim Marshall to set up a swap deal rather than cash, with the Irishman moving to Molineux at a point when Wolves were seeking to maintain the supremacy of their all-conquering team of the 1950s which was in the process of winning back-to-back titles in 1957/58 and 1958/59. Whether this was a serious approach or just a casual inquiry is not known. Dougan reckoned it was very much a serious possibility and that his eventual move to Wolverhampton and ultimate cult status could have happened nine years earlier than it eventually did. It was probably a good thing the swap deal did not go through as it is open to question whether he would at that time have been ready to put down permanent roots, the next few years bringing instability and no little infamy to the reputation of The Doog.

In a 2006 interview on Isle of Wight radio, Dougan said how happy he had been in his first year at Portsmouth, living at Southsea. "It was idyllic and you could go up town to the market and to little cafes to have a cup of tea. There was a store that was a lovely place to walk around. I loved Southsea." Dougan also confirmed his views on his second Pompey manager, "Freddie Cox was a man that absolutely ruined the morale of not only the football club but the town."

Dougan's initial view of Blackburn did not alter once he moved there. Though he came to like the people he could not adapt to the change of scenery, missing the sea breezes and lively atmosphere of Portsmouth. After just a few months there he decided he wanted to leave only to be told by manager Dally Duncan, "Don't be silly, lad, you're with a good club."

Rovers may have been a good club though their League form in Dougan's first full season was disappointing, despite fielding what Dougan regarded as the best forward line he had played in – Douglas, Dobing, Dougan, Vernon, McLeod. On occasions it all clicked into place as on the day in December 1959 when Blackburn beat erstwhile First Division pace-setters West Ham 6–2. Hammers centre-half Ken Brown had made his international debut a few weeks before, in the latest attempt to find a successor to the recently retired Billy Wright, and had seen a Dougan-less Northern Ireland beaten 2–1 at Wembley. Brown must have wondered why the Irish selectors chose to ignore the centre-forward when he saw his display at Ewood Park. Dougan scored four times in 31 first-half minutes, the last goal a solo effort which saw him run half the length of the field.

The fans soon took to Dougan and he was dubbed 'Cheyenne' because they reckoned he looked like hunky American actor Clint Walker who played the eponymous hero in the TV series Cheyenne which ran from 1955 to 1963. The nickname could not have been more apt. Dougan may not have been quite so strapping as the 6ft 6in actor, but there was a certain resemblance and, more to the point, the TV character was a drifter, never really settling down. That was Dougan, all right.

Before the season ended. Roy Vernon would be sold to Everton, much to Dougan's disgust, and England winger Bryan Douglas was switched to inside-left, thus giving Rovers a Three-D inside trio of Dobing, Dougan and Douglas. This combination, fired by England skipper Ronnie Clayton at half-back, would make up for the poor league performances by helping

Rovers reach the FA Cup final, then the glorious climax of the English season, Dougan clinching their place with both goals in a 2–1 semi-final win over Sheffield Wednesday at Maine Road, Manchester. Dougan was up against Peter Swan that day. A player who would be capped by England that summer, Swan was a more than useful defender, but Dougan had one of his special days. Legend among Rovers fans was that after leaving Swan sprawling to score the second goal he shouted in the defender's ear on the way back to the centre circle, "How many tickets do you want for Wembley?" It may or may not be true – but it would certainly be typical and merely added more grist to the mill of the growing Dougan legend. Typically he never sought to scotch that rumour.

However, Dougan was still not happy at Blackburn. He felt the dourness of the club matched that of the town and, though he did make a few friends there he recalled, "I could not shake off a depression that caused me to wake each day regretting that I had to go to the ground." He said there was virtually no contact between the club's officials and the players. 'This was before players in the '60s earned the right to be treated as equals,' wrote Dougan some years later. 'One small incident illustrates the social unease that I had never known in Ireland. A director, trying to be matey, came to us on the coach as we were about to leave for an away game and handed to us boiled sweets. He meant well, but we felt like schoolboys.'

Dougan's unhappiness did not ease despite the looming Wembley date with Wolves. As is well-documented, he put in an official transfer request on the morning of the big game. He answered suggestions that he had done this because he was a sensation seeker by saying that he did not choose the moment, it chose him. "I had intended to ask for a transfer when Blackburn were knocked out of the Cup," he explained. "It never occurred to me, or anyone else, that we would get to Wembley. Six times previously I had made verbal requests, but had not been taken seriously. Not wanting to embarrass the club I had decided to wait for an opportune occasion."

A pulled muscle made Dougan a doubt for the final in any case. He bluffed his way through a fitness test a few days before the game by making sure no-one noticed the pain he was in as he did a few sprints. In hindsight he felt he was wrong to play. He was not fully fit. He also regretted making that transfer request on the day of the final.

"In posting my transfer request on the morning of the Cup Final, my mind ruled my heart. I had made two decisions. Both were wrong, Looking back with a more temperate mind I acknowledge that I did Blackburn Rovers a double disservice. I should not have asked for a transfer when I did and I should not have played in the Cup Final." The young Dougan, however, could not bring himself to pass up the opportunity to play in the greatest showpiece of the season, perhaps understandably. He would never again have the chance to play in an FA Cup final.

Within minutes of the game beginning he knew he was not fully fit and that contributed to his below-par display. After Wolves had taken the lead, Rovers' hopes were given a body blow when full-back Dave Whelan, the man who would many years later guide Wigan Athletic to Premier League status as multi-millionaire owner of retailer JJB Sports, broke his leg in an innocent-looking challenge with Norman Deeley. There were no substitutes in those days and ten-man Rovers were beaten 3–0. Confirmation that Dougan did not do himself justice came in the Playfair Football Annual for 1960/61. The magazine's Cup Final report said Rovers had 'tried hard with some players shining stars, but the losers had players who disappointed – including centre-forward Dougan.'

When news of Dougan's transfer request leaked out, he came in for plenty of criticism, not least from the Press. Reporters wanted to know the inside story and offered him large sums of money for an exclusive interview. Dougan declined, saying there was no "inside story". He could only explain that he had made many verbal requests and that it seemed as good a time as any to make it official. It was a depressing period and, listless and unhappy, he went to discuss terms with a Belgian club, though nothing came of it. He even thought of quitting football altogether and returning to Portsmouth to set himself up in a business of some sort. But surely what he sought was a happy home for his considerable talent? For all his misery at Rovers he had still scored 17 goals in 42 league and cup appearances that season.

Dougan had begun the 1959/60 season in good form and it earned him his second international cap, though he hardly set the game alight as Scotland won 4–0 at Windsor Park, Belfast, before 56,000. The Irish had the bulk of the play, but failed to take their chances and were three goals down at the break. Dougan had not impressed and to add insult to injury he was replaced at centre-forward for the next game, against England, by Wilbur Cush of Leeds – a 5ft 5in tall half-back. Dougan's international career was not put entirely on hold and he was included in the Northern Ireland B squad to meet France at Windsor Park in November 1959. Despite having scored five goals at that stage of the season and looking good at centre-forward in a useful Rovers forward line, Dougan was played in his old schoolboy position of centre-half. Maybe there was a late injury crisis or perhaps Dougan nagged the selectors into letting him play in the role he still felt was his natural one. No-one seems to know, but his cousin Jim Kitchen well remembers the match if not the exact reason for his selection.

"His real preferred position was centre-half," says Kitchen. "It was only when he went over to England that they thought of him only as a centre-forward. I was at the B international and he did not last the game. He was hurt when he came over. I seem to remember he had his thigh strapped up. He told me he still wanted to play at centre-half and he must have persuaded them to let him."

William Rainey, was a young Belfast boy who watched the game and recalls, "I know Derek did not last the game out. Albert Campbell of Crusaders came on for him." Many years later Rainey would meet Dougan in very different circumstances. "I worked in the Royal Victoria Hospital where Derek spent time recovering from his heart attack. I spoke to him about the games I saw him play and he was a lovely guy."

That B international match on 11 November ended 1–1 and Dougan had some good defenders around him in full-backs Bill McCullough (Arsenal) and Alex Elder (Burnley), plus half-backs Martin Harvey (Sunderland) and Jimmy Nicholson of Manchester United. Even allowing for the injury, Dougan had obviously not done enough to convince anyone that his best position was anything other than centre-forward. It would be many more years before he was again allowed to wear the number-five shirt in a first-class game.

In the summer after Blackburn's disappointing Wembley visit manager Dally Duncan and Rovers parted company. Dougan spoke to the club chairman and said he was still unhappy and it was in the club's interests to let him go. The chairman would not hear of it. When Dougan scored a hat-trick in a 3–1 win over Manchester United on the opening day of the 1960/61 season people may have got the impression that he had changed his mind and was now happy to stay at Blackburn. That was not the case. "Had I scored three hat-tricks it would have made no difference," was how Dougan summed it up. However, he was always proud to boast in later years that he was still the only Blackburn player to hit a hat-trick at Old Trafford.

Jack Marshall took over as manager. He was christened 'Jolly Jack' as he was always telling jokes, though not always appreciated by his audience. Dougan thought he might get on with him and dropped his transfer talk for a while. Soon his discontent returned as he found Marshall's regime a petty one, such as when he tried to deny players £1 spending money on away trips. Then Dougan found he had been offered terms which were lower than those offered to some of the reserve team players. He tore up the offer letter in the secretary's office and knew once and for all that he had to get out of Ewood Park. Dougan recalled, "A few days after scattering waste paper in the secretary's office I was offered a rise. It was too late."

There was at last an extended run in Northern Ireland's team during 1960/61, although it came to an end when he fell foul of the referee in Athens. Dougan collected four caps in a struggling team who were beaten 5–2 by England and 5–1 by Wales, both games at Windsor Park. In the latter game Dougan at last scored a goal at international level and he struck again in the next match, a 3–2 defeat by Italy in a friendly in Bologna. The Athens match was a World Cup qualifier against Greece which the Irish lost 2–1. All four caps were at inside-forward, with the centre-forward berth firmly in the grip of Bolton striker Billy McAdams.

It seems Dougan was harshly treated in Athens. He recalled, "I was not only shadowed by, but plagued by, a Greek defender. If I went up for the ball, there he was on my back. If I was running with it, there he was elbowing me in the ribs. If I was waiting for a move to begin, there he was leaning on me. There was bound to be a bust-up. I raised my arm and clenched my fist as a gesture to warn him off. The referee did not see it as a gesture. He thought I had struck the player in the face. There was the player falling back as if I had delivered a sharp upper-cut, so the referee assumed the worst. I had not even touched him. The crowd yelled abuse and threw cushions at me. The referee gave me a stern lecture. He had not seen the constant provocation."

Dougan escaped dismissal, but the Irish selectors left him out for the World Cup clash with West Germany a week later. Said Dougan, "I was not sent off, but being dropped for the match at the Olympic Stadium in Berlin was just as bad."

Apart from the international appearances, it had been a good season domestically. Having hit 16 goals in 30 league and cup games in 1960/61, Dougan had proved his worth and Villa boss Joe Mercer was on the lookout for a centre-forward having just sold England star Gerry Hitchens to Inter Milan. Mercer needed a replacement and Dougan fitted the bill. He finally ended his Ewood Park nightmare and signed for £15,000 in August 1961.

Chapter Four

A FATAL NIGHT

JOE MERCER WAS ONE OF football's great characters. As a player he had won a championship medal before the war with Everton as well as five England caps. It seemed his best footballing years had been lost because of the hostilities, only for Arsenal to buy the veteran wing-half in 1946 for £9,000 and allow him to enjoy even more success. The Gunners twice won the First Division title under his captaincy as well as the FA Cup in a playing career that lasted past the age of 40. He was voted as Footballer of the Year in 1950, the same year as he lifted the Cup. As a manager he would go on to achieve great things with Manchester City in the late sixties and 1970s with Malcolm Allison as his lieutenant. At Villa Mercer did not have a character like Allison to work with his players and, though he'd had a spell in charge of Sheffield United, he was still comparatively new to management. He was one of the old school, whereas Dougan was among the new breed ready to question authority if he did not agree with their ideas.

Yet it all began well at Villa Park. Dougan actually lodged at Mercer's home for a month before moving to the house of Scottish inside-forward Bobby Thomson. Dougan got off to a great start. After losing their opening game of the 1961/62 season at Everton, Villa won two and drew one of their next three games. The draw was at Molineux where Wolves took a two-goal lead despite being reduced to ten men when young full-back Johnny Harris was carried off with a broken leg. It was in the days before substitutes and Wolves could not hang on as two goals from Dougan ensured a share of the points. Many years later Dougan would say of Wolves, "I always tended to do well against them for all my other clubs." This was just not so. He faced Wolves on ten occasions in all and in fact was never on the winning side. His very first league goal, upsetting Billy Wright when at Portsmouth, and those two at Molineux for Villa were the only ones he scored against Wolves.

After that Molineux match, Dougan scored again the following Saturday as Villa won 2–0 at Sheffield United. Despite continuing to maintain that he was a lapsed centre-half, Dougan looked the embodiment of a modern centre-forward. He was not the burly up-and-at-em type like Nat Lofthouse of Bolton or Spurs Double team star Bobby Smith. Dougan had pace and skill on the ball and the sort of panache that would fleetingly make Stan Collymore look so good many years later. Manager Mercer even spoke of Dougan in the same breath as Real Madrid legend Alfredo di Stefano. There could be no higher compliment. The football world seemed to be at Dougan's talented feet. However, fate was about to take a hand.

The first League Cup competition, launched the previous season, had dragged on, so much so that by the time Villa and Rotherham had reached the two-legged final it was May and so it was decreed that they would meet at the start of the next season to settle who would be the inaugural winners of the trophy. Villa lost the first game of a two-legged final 2–0 at Millmoor, but won the return leg 3–0 at Villa Park on Tuesday 5 September 1961, thanks to an extra-time winner from Peter McParland, deputising for the cup-tied Dougan.

This was a rare cause for celebration for Villa and it was a few hours after the final whistle when Dougan, his housemate Thomson and sports writer Malcolm Williams, of the Wolverhampton-based Express & Star, finally made their way home. It was a journey that ended in tragedy in the early hours. Thomson's black Vauxhall Velox car crashed in Willenhall town centre and Williams, who was travelling in the back, was killed. Thomson injured his leg, while Dougan sustained a broken arm and head injuries that needed over 50 stitches.

A headline in the *Express & Star* the next evening screamed, 'Villa footballers in fatal car crash'. The report began, 'A few hours after their team won the Football League Cup last night two Aston Villa players were injured and a passenger killed when the car in which they were travelling crashed in Willenhall. The injured Villa players are Irish international Derek Dougan (23) and the car owner inside-forward Bobby Thomson (24). Killed in the crash was a member of the *Express & Star* sports editorial staff 26-year-old Malcolm Williams of Chaucer Avenue, Straits Estate, Sedgley. The accident occurred at about 2.30 this morning when the car crashed into a tree on the edge of the Round House Cafe car park in Walsall Street, Willenhall. All three men were rushed to the Royal Hospital, Wolverhampton, but Malcolm Williams was found to be dead on arrival.'

It went on, 'Malcolm Williams joined the *Express & Star* and *Sporting Star* in April 1958. Previously he had been on the editorial staff of the

Walsall Observer. Well liked by Villa and other club players and managements, he had covered Villa and other club matches for the past three seasons and was also a speedway reporter for the two Wolverhampton papers. Son of Mr and Mrs J R Williams of Cope Street, Leamore, Walsall, he leaves a widow and two children, Stephen (five) and Stuart (four).'

The tragedy meant the newspaper was without a report of the previous night's match. That may have been insignificant in comparison with the loss of young life yet a report was still needed. Rodney Foster, an *Express & Star* news reporter, who had been at the game, supplied the piece for the sports pages. Foster later become a respected broadcaster with the BBC.

Thomson was allowed home later in the day before then being admitted to the Queen Victoria Nursing Institution and had time to give some quotes to the paper. "I don't know exactly how long we stayed in the dressing room," he said. "I should say it was about 11 o'clock when we left and went to a small cafe and club about 300 yards from the ground. We had some sandwiches and then we had a sing-song. I remember Malcolm saying 'What a wonderful evening' or 'What a marvellous evening' or something like that. It was about half past one when we set out for Wolverhampton. We stopped by the Gaumont cinema at Walsall and Malcolm got out to get some cigarettes from a machine there. We were about ten minutes then we carried on. In Walsall Street there was a crash. I don't remember exactly what happened. It all happened so quickly. Malcolm had been sitting in the back and Derek had been sitting next to me. I think Derek and I were both thrown out of the car. I remember walking around dazed and somebody had come up to us by that time."

Aston Villa manager Joe Mercer was generous in his praise of Williams. In the same newspaper report he said, "Malcolm Williams was the most wonderful fellow in the reporting world that I have ever met. He had a wonderful sense of humour and we all loved him very much indeed. He was a great bloke. He was definitely the nicest reporter I have ever met. He was keen on his job and did it right and straight. It's a sad loss to us all."

Mercer and the Villa players attended Williams's funeral where the family mourners were led by his wife Hazel and his parents Mr and Mrs James Williams. *Express & Star* colleagues acted as bearers, among them sports editor George Gillott and Tony Cox, whose sports gossip column was a regular feature in the paper for many years. There were representatives from other local newspapers, football clubs and local football leagues

Among the wreaths was one from Gerry Hitchens, whose signing for Inter Milan had led to Dougan's arrival at Villa Park. The message on the flowers was, 'With fondest remembrances Malcolm'.

There was inevitable speculation that the three in the car had been drinking heavily. This Dougan always hotly denied, as in his book *Doog*, published in 1980.

'I did not play in the match against Rotherham because I was cup-tied,' he wrote. 'The match went into extra-time and did not finish until 9.45pm. After the presentation on the pitch it was after 10.30 before the players had come out of the showers and changed, which proved we could not have been drinking. Naturally there was a lot of jubilation, which does not necessarily mean drinking. We did not leave Villa Park until just after midnight and then went to private premises for an hour. I had a couple of lagers there. Although it was getting late, Malcolm had to return to his office to write his report. It was a dreadful accident, but it had nothing to do with post-match celebrations. Malcolm had barely two pints of beer, as was later revealed at the autopsy.'

Some 26 years later, in an interview with John Hannam on Isle of Wight Radio, Dougan put the accident down to a 'blow out' – a burst tyre – and stressed again that they had not been drinking alcohol at the after-match celebrations. "It was tea or coffee in those days." He referred to the ill-fated journalist as 'Malcolm Johnson', maybe confusing him with Tom Johnson, the man who took over the task of reporting Villa games for the *Express & Star*. Dougan also said the number of stitches he needed was not 50 but 150. These may be small inaccuracies, but are nothing compared with Thomson's recollection of that traumatic night.

"I talked Malcolm into going to a little cafe with us after the match," said Thomson, speaking in 2007. "It was near Villa Park, called Ernie's, or something like that, and had a backroom bar. I said I'd drive him home. There was no way I was drunk, I would not do that when I was driving. I knew the road through Willenhall like the back of my hand. I knew there was a bad S bend there, but Derek was up to his antics. He put his leg across mine and that's how it happened. He was always doing silly things when I was driving. He had a deerstalker-type hat which he'd put on my head and pull over my eyes or he'd just put his hand over my eyes. The trouble with Derek was he used to get drunk very quickly. I don't remember much more about the accident. I think I must have come out of the windscreen. I know I went over to Derek and said something like 'All right, son? I'm not going to move you' and then I must have passed out. Somebody said to me later it was a good job I passed out and did not look in the back of the car. When I woke up in hospital they told me what had happened to Malcolm. He was a lovely man. I still think about him. I eventually went home in a wheel chair and they took Derek to the QVNI in Wolverhampton."

It was at the QVNI (Queen Victoria Nursing Institution) in Bath Road, Wolverhampton, that Ron Warrilow, a young reporter with a freelance agency in the town, had his first meeting with Dougan. He still remembers it well. "I was detailed to try to get an interview with him. I went along to the QVNI and as luck would have it, Derek was leaning out of an open window. I just noticed the shaved head and knew it was him. I shouted up to ask how he was, but he just said he could not talk to me and closed the window."

Dougan said little to Thomson about the accident or how it had happened. "It was never ever mentioned," maintains Thomson. "He never broached the subject. Maybe he blamed me, or fate, I don't know. All he said to me was 'It was a bit of luck I had my head shaved, so they could put the stitches in more easily.' He knew what he had done."

Journalist John Dee also has cause to think fate took a hand in Williams's death. Gloucester-born Dee joined the Express & Star about that time, having worked for the *Wednesbury Borough News*. It was when with that paper that Dee met Williams. Dee had ambitions to be a sports writer and used to cover Villa matches. "I was a big mate of Malcolm's and because he did not drive I used to give him lifts," explained Dee. "If I had been there that night he would have come home with me, but I had a few days off and went back home to Gloucester with my wife. Malcolm and I always went to the Villa matches together. We went all over the country. I knew nothing about it until my mother rang me and said an *Express & Star* reporter had been killed in a crash. I went to the funeral at Gornal crematorium and it was packed."

Without having mentioned to Dee what Thomson had told us about the accident we asked Dee if he had any memories of Dougan because Dee eventually took over the coverage of Wolves for the *Express & Star* when Phil Morgan retired. Dee told us of an incident when he stayed with the team, by then managed by Bill McGarry, during their build-up to the 1974 League Cup final. The players had been to Wembley on the Friday before the game to take a look at the pitch and were being bused back to their hotel driven as usual by coach driver Sid Kipping. "McGarry wasn't with the team, so I found myself sitting at the front of the coach next to Doog," said Dee. "I think we were on the North Circular Road at the time. Doog picked up one of the blankets that were in the coach for putting over the directors' knees to keep them warm. He gave me a nudge as if to say 'Watch this' and he put the blanket over Sid's head and then slowly pulled it back and put it down. He laughed his socks off at this, but I thought 'Christ, Sid could crash here.' It's a good job Sid was not driving fast. He was only doing about 25 or 30, Sid always drove sedately."

In the light of Thomson's explanation of what had happened in that crash 13 years before it is an eerie tale.

An attempt to apportion blame for the fatal crash proved a shambles as the prosecution failed to establish in court who had been the driver. It does not appear that Dougan was called as a witness yet he surely would have been able to confirm that Thomson was at the wheel. This is how the *Express & Star* reported the case on 3 November 1961:

'Aston Villa footballer Bobby Thomson was found not guilty at Willenhall yesterday afternoon of driving carelessly the car in which he and another player were injured and *Express & Star* sports writer Malcolm Williams was killed on September 6. The South Staffordshire stipendiary magistrate Mr H W Maitland Coley said that from the evidence it could not be said that Thomson – Robert Gillies McKenzie Thomson (24) of 73 Canterbury Road, Penn, Wolverhampton – or anyone else was driving. It could be assumed that one of the three men was driving, but it could not be said that a case had been made out against Thomson.

The decision followed a submission by Mr J G B Thorne (defending). Mr Thorne said that Thomson had taken the course of leaving it to the police to prove the case, on his advice. "The man who died was a charming and talented young man and a personal friend of the defendant. The whole thing is a public matter and I trust I have done right in leaving the police to prove the case," he declared.

Mr E Hiscox (prosecuting) had said that it was alleged that the car involved in the crash at 2.30am on September 6 was being driven by Thomson. With him were Alexander Derek Dougan and Malcolm Williams. Dougan, Mr Hiscox said, was travelling in the front nearside passenger seat. Williams was in the nearside back seat. As the car being driven from Walsall towards Willenhall town centre came to the right-hand bend near the Round House Cafe it seemed that – from marks found later on the road – the vehicle mounted the pavement and first collided with a tree and then with a trolley wire standard. From there the car appeared to have travelled across to the other side of the road, slewing round to face the opposite direction. Its rear end collided with a trolley wire standard at the corner of King Street. Then it came into contact with an advertisement hoarding.

No-one saw the accident. A nearby resident heard the sound of the crash and went to the scene. All three occupants were injured, but Williams was found to be dead on arrival at the Royal Hospital. "It is alleged that the defendant was driving this car and was not exercising sufficient care in his driving at a double bend where the road narrowed," Mr Hiscox said. At this point Mr Thorne said he was not challenging the fact that the car had been driven carelessly. The question was: Who was the driver?

Herbert Edward Bailey of Flat 1, 34 Walsall Road, Willenhall, said he saw three people at the scene shortly after the crash. One was hanging from the back nearside door. Another – who he thought was Thomson – was lying on the ground at the front nearside of the car. A third man was walking around in front of the car.

Police Constable Kennett said that when he arrived at the scene he noticed that the car's speedometer was stuck at 50mph. Seen later at the Queen Victoria Nursing Institution, Thomson declined to make a statement but said, "I put everything in the hands of my solicitor." Nothing was said at the scene of the accident about who was driving the car.'

After the dismissal of the careless driving charge, Thomson admitted an offence of having no excise licence for the car. Mr Thorne said the crash had happened during the 14 days' grace allowed for renewing the licence and it was purely a technical matter. Thomson was given an absolute discharge on payment of 4s (20p) costs. So the matter was closed, but the crash has remained the subject of speculation ever since.

At the time of the Willenhall car crash, Dougan was living with Thomson at his home in Canterbury Road, Penn, Wolverhampton. "Our neighbours were the Kings and they had a young son called Mervyn. I think he's done quite well for himself," recalls Thomson with a laugh.

"Derek was just going to stay with us a few weeks, but I could not get rid of him," Thomson went on. "He had a girlfriend from his Blackburn days who used to come down and stay from time to time. She was a right one. My missus did everything for us and I used to say to him, 'It's about time you went, if not you'd better start paying rent.' In the end it was nine months before he left."

He and Dougan were two fiery characters and Thomson said that Dougan once punched him on the nose during a five-a-side game which led to a scuffle between them before they were separated. They still used to pal around together, however.

"We'd often go out with Nigel Sims (Villa's goalkeeper) to places like Himley House or the Kingfisher Club at Wall Heath. I was once going to meet up with Johnny Prescott, the boxer, at Sutton. I said I'd make my own way there, but Doog said, no, he'd pick me up. But he never turned up and we fell out over that."

In the end they probably had one fall-out too many and did not make their peace, something Thomson regrets. "I was a bit sad that we never did make it up. About three weeks before he died I was sitting at home and thinking I'd get in touch and say, 'We're a pair of prats, I'm over 70 and you're nearly 70, isn't it time we made it up?' I never did get chance to do it. It was one of those things."

Thomson recalls a touch of Dougan humour when they were first intro-duced at Villa Park. "Joe Mercer brought him over and said 'This is Bobby Thomson. He can play forward, he can play in midfield, he can shoot, he can dribble, he can do the lot,' and Derek just said, 'What did you say his name was? Pelé?'

"He went on to make quite a few goals for me, but I always thought he was a better player at home than away – and I've seen a few of those in my time. He once said to our winger Jimmy MacEwan, 'You don't like, me do you?' and Jimmy said, 'It's not that I don't like you, it's that when you lose the ball you stand there laughing.' You see we were a team and if we lost the ball to an opponent we chased after them. Derek would stand there with his arms by his side. He fell out with one or two at Villa Park. To be fair, I don't think he was used properly. Being a big fella they thought he had to be played up front. At Wolves they played him deeper and he used to get the flick-ons for John Richards. That was when you saw the best of him."

That young neighbour of Thomson's, Mervyn King, the future governor of the Bank of England, confirmed that it was indeed the presence of the players on his doorstep that made him a Villa fan. In fact when Dougan came to lodge next door with Thomson it meant there were three Villa men in the same street, as goalkeeper Nigel Sims lived opposite. Sims, like Thomson, was an ex-Wolves man.

"They were very friendly," King remembers, "and would kick the ball if they walked by when we were playing in the street. I was about 11 when we moved to Wolverhampton and followed Villa first during the 1959/60 promotion season. They got to the FA Cup semi-final that year. I was not old enough to go and listened to it on the radio." Although the first match he saw was Wolves against Manchester United, the presence of Thomson and Sims in the neighbourhood was the deciding factor in King's football affections. The first match he attended at Villa Park was in October 1960 when Villa beat Newcastle 2–0. "We had some friends of my father's who came from Newcastle and they came down to see the match. I started going from then and it has not stopped since, really.

"Once, Bobby Thomson's car broke down and my father drove him to Villa Park. We got there about ten to three having been given a police escort. I don't think Bobby Thomson played very well that day and scored an own goal. My favourite player was Gerry Hitchens. I also liked Harry Burrows, who used to play left wing and had one of the hardest shots in football."

It was indeed Hitchens's transfer to Inter Milan that had led to Villa signing Dougan, and King, as well as admiring him as a player came to admire him as a man. "I met Derek several times in the last few years in his work with Xpro. He was a very intelligent man and we need more people like that in the game."

Dougan, however, was nothing if not controversial. In 1961 he hit the headlines once again by virtue of his haircut – an almost unimaginable occurrence in that day and age.

Veteran radio broadcaster Tony Butler recalls Dougan's days living in Canterbury Road. "My mother lived nearby and when Derek shaved his head he went round to show her. He knocked on the door and said, 'What do you think of this?' She said, 'You look absolutely ridiculous.' He went off in quite a huff. One thing I do remember about him while he was living there was that he used to go down to the playing fields in Windsor Avenue and take the young kids in football practice. He did not run a club or anything like that, but he would just go down there, organise them into two teams and would play with them for ages. He would do things like that and fair play to him. The youngsters thought he was wonderful."

Apart from the trauma of seeing a good friend killed, Dougan had to face many weeks without football as he slowly recovered from his injuries. He missed 14 league games before making a scoring comeback in a 2–0 win at

Leicester on 2 December. He ended the season with 10 goals from 23 league outings and also scored twice as Villa reached the sixth round of the FA Cup before losing to Tottenham, who were on their way to winning the trophy for a second year running.

Villa had some useful players, many of them with youth on their side like centre-half John Sleeuwenhoek, wing-half Alan Deakin, winger Harry Burrows and full-back Charlie Aitken. During Dougan's absence after the car crash, veteran left-winger Peter McParland often deputised at centre-forward, but Dougan's return paved the way for the departure of his fellow Northern Ireland international. McParland was sold to Wolves as Molineux supremo Stan Cullis tried to bolster the fortunes of a club who found themselves in the unlikely position, after so many years of dominance, of fighting a relegation battle.

Dougan had clearly made an early impact with his new club, who finished a respectable seventh in the First Division. The Irish Rover felt he was at last at somewhere special in terms of football tradition and football potential.

"I woke each morning full of enthusiasm, eager to get to the ground," he recalled. However, there was still a feeling that the potentially electric Dougan was not doing his talents justice on a regular basis. That inconsistency would dog Doog in his early days. In the *Sports Argus* annual, veteran football writer Tom Duckworth said of Dougan that he 'was brilliant one game and the reverse the next. He remains unpredictable.'

There was hardly any sign of unpredictability when the 1962/63 season began. Dougan was on target on the opening day when West Ham were beaten 3–1 at Villa Park and scored both goals as the mighty Tottenham were beaten 2–1, also at Villa Park, in front of nearly 65,000 fans. He did not score when Villa made it three wins a row by beating Manchester City 2–0 at Maine Road, but was on target as they lost the return with Spurs 4–2 at White Hart Lane.

Four goals in four games seemed too good to last – and it was – but the team were still playing well and near the top of the table. Looking back, Dougan said, "There were tears of happiness in Joe Mercer's eyes when we beat Tottenham. Villa were riding high. Our confidence soared. There was nothing we could not do. This was where Villa belonged, reaching for the top of the First Division."

Villa's good start had Dougan revelling in the team's form but controversy was always lurking just around the corner and it came in September 1962 at the City ground, Nottingham – he was sent off. Dougan may have established a reputation for being fiery and outspoken but most of the time he kept his temper under control on the field. He earned his share of bookings but had not been dismissed until the bizarre incident against Nottingham Forest. After about half an hour of the game Villa inside forward Ron Wylie collided with home goalkeeper Peter Grummitt and the ball bounced between the two of them. Dougan tried to deflect it round the keeper towards goal but Grummitt managed to recover and boot the ball clear, falling backwards as he did so. The referee's verdict was that Dougan had kicked Grummitt and off he had to go.

In his book, *Attack!*, Dougan summed up his feelings. "I felt like a schoolboy who has been singled out for a misdemeanour he had not committed and sent to the headmaster's study. In the melée, the referee imagined I had kicked Peter Grummitt. On circumstantial evidence I was being condemned to the long, long walk off the pitch."

On Joe Mercer's advice, Dougan did not attend the FA disciplinary committee's meeting and hoped the officials would see sense as Grummitt had admitted after the game that the Villa man had not touched him and there had been letters to Dougan from Forest fans confirming that the ref had got it wrong. Despite all this, Dougan was suspended for two weeks.

The season began to go wrong for Villa when the awful winter set in and brought football to a virtual halt. Dougan recalled that in the street he slipped on some ice and twisted his knee and when matches got going again Villa slumped badly and a run of 11 successive defeats took them to within two points of the relegation places before they pulled themselves together. They were beaten by Manchester United in the FA Cup, but again reached the League Cup final. Dougan was sidelined and missed the two-legged clash with arch rivals Birmingham City which Villa lost. Dougan recalled, "Through most of this I had been hobbling on the sidelines." His memory may have played him tricks, though, as he never missed more than two games in a row and made 28 league appearances. His nine goals was a disappointing total after his sparkling start to the campaign.

That early form had brought Dougan a recall to the Northern Ireland side and he played in both games against Poland in the European Nations Cup, scoring in the 2–0 win in Katowice, but not in Belfast when the Irish won by the same score. In between those two he played in the Home International Championship clash with Scotland at Hampden Park. The Scots won 5–1 and Dougan was given little chance to impress by Dundee centre-half Ian Ure.

Dougan gradually became disillusioned at Villa Park. It was a familiar story after his experiences at Fratton Park and Ewood Park. "I tried to adapt myself to Mr Mercer's tactics," he said, "but something had changed, something radical that gave me an uneasy feeling that I had become an outsider."

As ever, Dougan had firm views on what needed to be done to make a promising team into a very good one. He felt they should sign West Bromwich Albion's former England striker Derek Kevan. He wanted a move and could have been bought for £30,000. That would have enabled Bobby Thomson to play in midfield where he was happier and would have complemented the robust Vic Crowe at right-half. That was the Dougan view, but Mercer instead signed West Ham's skilful scheming inside forward Phil Woosnam. Dougan was deflated. "When he (Woosnam) came Vic Crowe's style appeared to alter. He became more cultured and academic. Our aggressiveness declined. Bobby Thomson was never really happy as a striker. He was best suited to midfield."

This may well have been the cause of the end of Dougan's love affair with Villa. He reckoned the management did not know what to do once results went against them and consequently his relationship with Mercer deteriorated until the manager circulated clubs that Dougan was 'open to offers'. They talked things over one morning during training as Dougan recalled:

"Mr Mercer came to me and said, 'Let's go for a walk.' He appeared to be in a contrite mood. The father and son kind of relationship that had begun to develop when I stayed at his home reasserted itself. 'You know I sometimes say things I don't mean,' he confided. 'I didn't mean to put you on the transfer list. You can forget it.' I could not forget it and told him, 'You can't just crumble my world and then say forget it. It's not as simple as that.'"

Later that week it was announced in the Press that Dougan was on the transfer list. His days at Villa Park were numbered.

Dougan had pointed out to Mercer that for many of Villa's games he had been injured, but the manager replied, "That's why I'm blaming you, because you did not play." That, thought Dougan, was a strange left-handed compliment.

The relationship had also been soured by rumours that Dougan was spending too much time in Birmingham's night spots and there was even a story that that he had been in a night club brawl and had been thrown down the stairs. He went to see Mercer at his home and told him that stories of him being a lothario, a late night hell-raiser and a social buffoon were not true. Mercer assured him he did not believe all the tittle-tattle. He knew that players had only to be seen somewhere near a night club and people would put two and two together and make five.

Despite the fall-out and the decision to list him, Dougan was chosen for the last but one league game of the season – against Liverpool. His name was on the team sheet, but the list was then amended to give young George Graham his first-team debut. The club told the Press that Dougan was unfit, but he knew that if he had done well against Liverpool at Villa Park it would have brought the wrath of the fans upon Mercer. Dougan had become a huge terrace favourite at Villa just as he was with the fans at all his other clubs. Villa duly beat Liverpool with Graham, eight years later a Double hero with Arsenal, scoring on his debut.

That did not quell the unrest, however. Villa received many letters from supporters saying Dougan should not be allowed to leave. Dougan had a couple of meetings with Villa chairman Chris Buckley, who said he wanted him to stay but could not interfere with the manager's decision. Dougan fully understood that and realised that the time had come to move on. It was a reluctant parting as he loved the club – "Looking over the ground, even when there was no-one in the stands and on the terraces, I felt a deep affinity with the club. There is a mystique about Villa Park. Tradition rises from the ground like a vapour."

Dougan reckoned Villa needed to shake off the cobwebs and a few years later, by which time the club were in the Second Division, he believed that new manager Tommy Docherty was the man to do it. 'Docherty's forthright, uncompromising and resolute approach to the game and the enthusiasm of Doug Ellis, Villa's new chairman, should bring Villa back to its rightful place in the soccer hierarchy,' wrote Dougan. Not for the first time his judgment was wrong. Docherty succeeded only in taking Villa into the Third Division and was duly sacked.

Dougan's stay at Villa was never short of incident, never more so than when he decided to shave his head. Some reckoned that making himself look like film star Yul Brynner, of *The King and I* fame, was just another example of his attention-seeking. Dougan was cagey about it all and there were even theories that his streamlined head would make him quicker or possibly would make him a better header of the ball. It was nothing of the sort, of course, as Dougan readily admitted a few years later. "My hair had showed signs of thinning and I had heard that if it was completely shaved it would grow again more strongly." He reckoned it did the trick, too, though he was always concerned about his hair loss and would even have a hair weave during his Wolves days.

Many years later when Manchester United star David Beckham attracted considerable coverage in the tabloid newspapers after he adopted a Mohican hairstyle, Dougan maintained that he had done it 40 years earlier. Yet Dougan did not initially adopt it, he shaved his head completely. Later he did develop it into a Mohican which involves leaving a strip of hair down the middle of the head with only the sides shaved.

Peter McParland recalls the shaven head incident. "I was getting changed ready for training and Nigel Sims, our goalkeeper, came in and said, 'Wait till you see what's coming in' and then Derek came through the door with a hat on, took it off and showed us the bald head. We played Everton at Goodison Park next day and of course the Scousers gave him a right chorus. They kept making Red Indian calls, but it did not bother him."

The inconsistency of Dougan's time at Villa Park is confirmed by McParland. "When he came to Villa I got the impression that life was not serious to him. He would have a good game and really turn it on, then there would be others where he didn't. He certainly did not seem to take the game seriously, but something must have happened when he went to Wolves because he proved himself there. I saw enough at Villa Park, though, to know he could have been a world beater if he put his mind to it.

"He was the fastest thing I had seen. I think only Stan Matthews was quicker over a 15 or 20-yard burst. There was vapour coming from behind him the pace he used to go at. He could run all day and in training if you set a task for him, like a sprinting exercise, he would leave everybody standing. If we did a cross-country run no-one could keep up with him. I'm sure he could have been a top class cross-country runner if he hadn't been a footballer."

It was not only for his playing exploits that McParland recalls Dougan with affection. "I have very fond memories of Derek. Over the years he always kept in touch. He would come on the phone sometimes yelling and bawling about something that had annoyed him yet my wife would sometimes answer the phone first before putting him on and she'd say afterwards, 'What a real gentleman that Derek is' because he'd been charm itself to her. Then he'd get me on and he'd start ranting. I think I spoke to him just three or four days before he died. He always kept in touch with people. If ever I was in Birmingham we would always meet up. He loved to talk and he was great company."

Sammy Chapman, his childhood friend from Belfast and team-mate at Portsmouth, has his views on why Dougan did not make the impact at Villa that he should have done. "He was a natural and a terrific athlete and Villa should have been the platform for him, but I think he got caught up in the glamour of the thing instead of showing what he could do. Let's face it he had a thoroughbred type of build and that helped him survive for so long. Perhaps if he had really turned it on when he was younger he would not have lasted as long. In later years he was a terrific example to younger players, the way he looked after himself and the way he trained."

The bald facts for the hair-restored Dougan at the end of 1962/63 were that once again he was unhappy and needed a change of scenery, but his next move would take the football world by surprise – he joined Peterborough United of the Third Division. He must have impressed them in Villa's League Cup run to that final date with Blues. He scored a hat-trick as Villa beat Posh 6–1 in the first round at Villa Park.

Chapter Five

DIVERSION VIA LONDON ROAD

DOUGAN'S MOVE TO LONDON ROAD caused a minor sensation at the time. Peterborough United had been a Football League club for only three seasons. Having been a prominent non-league side for many years they made the most of their chance when finally voted into the Fourth Division for the 1960/61 season. They won immediate promotion to the Third Division with a goals total of 134 that still stands as the most scored by any team in an English league season. Their centre-forward Terry Bly scored a remarkable 52 goals in that inaugural campaign and another 29 when Posh finished fifth in the Third Division the following season. However, former Fulham forward Jimmy Hill, having played his part in getting the maximum wage abolished, was then cutting his teeth as an innovative manager of an ambitious Coventry City side and so bought Bly for the Sky Blues. Though Peterborough finished sixth in 1962/63 they still needed someone to take Bly's place and manager Jack Fairbrother boldly set his sights on Villa's unsettled enigma. As a player Fairbrother's job had been to stop goals and he was Newcastle's goalkeeper when they won the FA Cup in 1951, only for injury the following season to allow Ronnie Simpson to make the Geordies' keeper spot his. Fairbrother became player-manager at Peterborough in 1952, moving on to manage Coventry and coach the Israeli national side before eventually returning to Peterborough in 1962 following in the footsteps of another former keeper, George Swindin of Arsenal fame. As a manager, Fairbrother put the emphasis on scoring goals and wanted Dougan to continue the trend.

Rumour was that a couple of First Division clubs were interested in signing the seemingly permanently unsettled centre-forward, but if there were, Dougan never learned of any firm offers. One of the factors which led him to join Peterborough, apart from their obvious ambition, was their persistence. They tracked him down while on holiday. Without consulting him, Villa had agreed a fee with the Cambridgeshire club and said if they could find him they could talk to him. After a number of telegrams were dispatched, he was finally tracked down in Munich visiting Jutta's family and asked to return to England. Fairbrother impressed him and Dougan duly agreed to the £21,000 move, though many of his friends inside and outside the game counselled against it. He was by then 25 and should have been at the peak of his career in the top flight not dropping down two divisions. He was said to be the highest-paid player in the Third Division at the time, in this first season following the abolition of the maximum wage, and initially liked the look of the town where he moved into the house once occupied by former Posh manager Jimmy Hagan.

Peterborough did not figure in the promotion race in 1963/64 as Jimmy Hill's Coventry ran away with the Third Division title on their way to the top flight for a stay which would last into the new century, but Posh did finish a comfortable 10th. There were some experienced men in the side, in addition to Dougan, notably former Charlton goalkeeper Willie Duff, ex-Cardiff central defender Frank Rankmore and former West Brom striker Keith Smith. Dougan finished top league scorer for the club with 20 goals from 38 games in a season which saw an unexpected change of manager. Fairbrother decided to quit football in February 1964 and Gordon Clark was drafted in.

A full-back who reached no greats heights, but was good enough to play 55 games for Manchester City before the Second World War, Clark had managed Dougan's old club Distillery and later became boss of West Bromwich Albion. Perhaps because of the Irish connection, he and Dougan hit it off straight away. Clark made it clear who was boss, but at the same time he was willing to listen to Dougan's problems and his point of view. "I always felt that I could go to his office to discuss a problem," said Dougan, "and know that he would give his time and understanding, not to mention endless cups of tea. I knew that he was boss and he knew that I knew. I never tried to take any liberties with him and played as well for him as I possibly could."

Dougan had found Peterborough United something of a culture shock after enjoying the facilities befitting a club with the traditions of Aston Villa. Posh's training ground was a public park, where players had to fight for space with children and dogs while their version of a gym was a room under the stands. The players were expected to know their place and when Dougan was first shown around the London Road ground and spotted a ladies' tea room it was quickly made clear to him that it was for use by the wives of directors and not for players' wives. The players' partners were expected to wait outside the ground to meet their men after games. On one particularly cold day they forced their way past the doorman despite his protests that it was against club rules for them to come inside. Dougan found this intolerable.

Clark undertook to change things and having a storeroom converted into a tea room for players' wives and installing card tables in the team coach were little things which made the players think they were valued. The manager had ambitions to take the club to greater heights and shipped out many players. Among those he brought in were Dougan's old Villa team-mate Vic Crowe. He also signed former Wolves, Arsenal, Stoke and England half-back Eddie Clamp. Crowe would prove a hit, but Clamp played only a few games. However, the signings showed that Clark was determined to shake things up and for a while Dougan thought he could be a part of the push to reach the Second Division.

It was not only manager Clark who impressed Dougan at London Road. The physio Albert Preston earned his lasting gratitude for helping ease the ankle trouble which had been with him since he had broken it when at Portsmouth. Preston was head of a special injuries unit at a local hospital and recommended a surgeon to Dougan. Recalled Dougan some 40 years later, "They corrected this injury that I'd had for five years and I never missed another match through this particular defective ankle. Only problem I've got is that it's now riddled with arthritis." He added, "I'm so grateful to Albert Preston. He was ahead of his time."

A promotion challenge did not materialise in 1964/65 and Peterborough finished eighth, though only eight points off a promotion place. However, there was a glorious diversion in the shape of an FA Cup run which saw Dougan get the better of Billy Wright, just as he had done over seven years earlier. The run began in the first round with a 5–1 home win over Western League side Salisbury Town, with Dougan hitting a hat-trick. After a 2–1 extra-time win over fellow Third Division outfit QPR in a second-round replay following a 3–3 draw at Loftus Road, Dougan struck another hat-trick as Posh won 3–0 at Chesterfield. That set up the dream fourth-round tie – Arsenal at home.

With Wright their manager, the Gunners, may not at that time have been the force they once were or would become again, but they were still a magical name in English football. Wright had brought some big names to the club in a bid to recapture their former glory, notably former England full-back Don Howe, Scotland centre-half Ian Ure and star forwards Joe Baker and George Eastham. John Radford, a future star of the 1971 Double team, but then a mere 17-year-old, put the visitors ahead just before half-time and the north London side must have thought the hard work had been done. Peterborough kept battling and with 17 minutes to go it was Dougan who silenced the singing Arsenal fans and set the home crowd roaring.

This is how Dougan described his goal. "Vic Crowe started a move down the line. Ron Barnes, the right-winger, took the ball on. I dummied to go to the right of Ian Ure, dummied back again and Ron read the move perfectly. He laid the ball clear of Ure and after a precision pass from Oliver Conmy I steered the ball past Tony Burns for the equaliser. Crowds surged over the pitch, delirious with excitement and relief."

A draw and a replay at Highbury would have been a great result, but Posh were not finished. Barnes did the groundwork and Peter McNamee was able to tap in the winner to complete a bad day in Arsenal history. It may not quite have been on a par with their sensational defeat at Walsall in 1933, but it was close. Wright took defeat with the sort of dignity he had shown as a player and when the Peterborough doctor popped his head around the away dressing room door to ask if there were any injuries, he was told by the Highbury boss, "No, only 11 broken hearts." There was extra satisfaction for Dougan in the way he had played against Ian Ure, the man who had made life so difficult for him at Hampden Park.

Teams that day:
Peterborough: Duff; Cooper, Singleton, Crowe, Rankmore, Orr, Barnes, Conmy, Dougan, Deakin, McNamee.
Arsenal: Burns: Howe, Clark, McLintock, Ure, Court, Skirton, Radford, Baker, Eastham, Armstrong.
Attendance: 30,056.

Peterborough was buzzing after the win, but Clark, the realist, told the Press it would be three to five years before he had the club running the way he wanted. More immediately there was a fifth round game against Second Division Swansea, who themselves had conquered Newcastle United. The attendance at London Road for the Arsenal match was a club record and that figure was increased by another 40 for the visit of the Welsh side. It proved an anti-climax as Posh were held 0–0. However, they bounced back and promptly won the replay at Vetch Field 2–0 with a goal in each half from Peter Deakin.

The reward was a quarter-final trip to face high-riding First Division Chelsea. Dougan and the rest of the squad were taken away to Blackpool to tune up for the big game and found their opponents had got the same idea. Team-mate Peter McNamee recalled in an interview with the *Peterborough Telegraph*, 'We went up to Blackpool to train and get away from all the media attention, but the first people we saw up there were the Chelsea squad, so we got to know them before we played. They were really friendly and chatty but on the day they clearly meant business, whereas everything that could have gone wrong did go wrong from our point of view. It should have been a great day. We had 25,000 Posh fans travel to London and the atmosphere was stunning.' The things that went wrong were an injury to Vic Crowe and a rare off day for goalkeeper Duff who had been one of the stalwarts of the Cup run.

For Dougan, though, this meant he was back on the big stage and, in the atmosphere of a packed Stamford Bridge, realised what he was missing. Alas, he had little chance to sparkle. Crowe was injured in the first few minutes and, with no substitutes in those days, it was 10 fit men against 11 for the rest of the game. Crowe did return to limp along in attack and even scored a goal. By that time a Chelsea side featuring Ron Harris and Peter Osgood on the cusp of a glorious decade, had scored four without reply and eventually hit another to end the Cup fairytale 5–1. That quarter-final remains Peterborough's best performance in the FA Cup.

By now Dougan had realised he wanted to get back into the top flight. He had enjoyed his full season with Clark and rated it the best he had had in England as far as a manager-player relationship was concerned. Although he was relishing every game and performing consistently, Dougan had itchy feet once more. Apart from needing to play against the best players, Dougan also wanted to be playing on the international scene. He had not won a cap during his two seasons at London Road. Once when driving through Peterborough town centre he spotted a newspaper placard proclaiming 'Irish selectors to watch Posh player.' When he raced into the newsagent's to buy a paper he found that it was teammate Oliver Conmy who was the target of the selectors – and it was not even Northern Ireland's, it was the Republic's. Dougan reckoned that not once did his country's selectors watch him during his Third Division exile, even though his 25 league and cup goals in 1964/65 was the best seasonal total of his career up to then. Clark had told him he was sure a First Division side would soon come in for him, even though it was almost unheard of for a player to return to the top flight after being sold to a Third Division club. Yet, Dougan's life was one of constantly being an exception to rules and so it proved once again.

Dougan's move back to the First Division took him to Leicester in May 1965 for a reported fee of £12,000. City were on a spree as boss Matt Gillies was said to have spent double that on bringing Dunfermline winger Jackie Sinclair to Filbert Street. Both players would impress in their first season in the East Midlands, the diminutive Sinclair even outscoring Doog.

Dougan likened his return to the First Division to heavyweight boxer Floyd Patterson winning back his world title after losing it to Ingemar Johansson. It was not about money. He had been well paid at Peterborough and took a drop in wages to join Leicester.

In his book, *The Sash He Never Wore . . . Twenty Five Years On*, Dougan described the day he learned of his impending move. 'One morning I was up rather early and shaving when the phone rang. It was Gordon and I was to be down at the ground in an hour's time. I was out of this world. I could not get down to the ground quickly enough, even though I still did not know who wanted me. I parked my car, almost ran to the club and dashed into Gordon's office. He was sitting there as calm as anything and when I asked him who it was he told me Leicester City.'

Team-mate Ollie Hopkins was also at the ground and told him, "Well, Doog, you're back where you belong." That was the consensus of opinion, but he had enjoyed his two years in the game's lower reaches. The fans took to him and so did the players.

Peter McNamee says: "Derek was great fun. He was outspoken in his days with us, so much so that he used to take over the team talks from the manager before matches. We were all surprised when he signed for us, but he soon became one of the lads. He was a great player for us, though, brilliant in the air and always talking and telling us what to do. He used to love a game of cards, but as he was on more money than the rest of us he used to raise the stakes too high."

The question also has to be asked, at this point in his career, was this an indication of the true level of his abilities? And could he bring that level of goalscoring form into the First Division? His potential was undoubted, but Dougan had now reached a crucial point in his career, the beginning of the years in which any player should be in their prime, performing to their utmost potential. As yet he had only truly achieved this in the Third Division.

City, who had finished runners-up to Chelsea in the League Cup in 1964/65, were a useful side and Dougan assumed they had ambition. The season before, 1963/64, they had gone one better and won the League Cup thanks to a two-leg victory over Stoke City. Ironically at least one source credited that win as one of Dougan's honours. There was indeed a Dougan in that City line-up in the final games, but it was Max Dougan, a Scottish wing-half, not Derek.

The Foxes' spending was not finished and during the season they paid Cardiff what was then a club record £40,000 for Peter Rodrigues, a Welsh international full-back. They finished a respectable seventh in 1965/66 as Dougan hit 20 league and cup goals, three fewer than top scorer Sinclair. He had made his point in the top echelon of the game. However, City were an unpredictable side. One Saturday in November 1964 they lost 5–0 at home to Manchester United, only to win 5–1 at Newcastle a week later. They boasted future England World Cup hero Gordon Banks in goal and at the end of Dougan's first season with them, Leicester blooded a 16-year-old keeper named Peter Shilton,

Banks's view of Dougan makes interesting reading. In his autobiography, *Banksy*, the goalkeeping legend wrote, "Derek had no qualms about voicing his opinions on football and its establishment figures. He was a radical and original thinker whose caustic wit and sharp brain made many a manager think twice about taking him on. The fact that he was playing his football in the Third Division was in all probability due to his reputation as a troublemaker. Why on earth Matt Gillies signed him, I don't know. What I do know is that Derek was a stylish and formidable player who, in his time at Leicester, channelled his undoubted intelligence on to the field of play to the great benefits of the team and the constant delight of the supporters."

High praise from Banks and he went further. "We often hear today about players having cult status. Derek Dougan was one of the originals. Many people thought his best days were behind him when he came to Filbert Street, but in his two years at Leicester and subsequent eight years at Wolverhampton Wanderers he was to play the best football of his career, maturing into an intelligent and unselfish striker of the highest calibre. He was a windmill of a striker whose talent and swirling personality were to leave their mark not only at Leicester City but on football in general."

Dougan took time to settle at Filbert Street, not scoring his first goal for Leicester until the fifth match of the season, a 4–1 home win over Sunderland. He hit two in a 5–2 win at West Ham and two more as Leeds were held 3–3 at Filbert Street. In all, he had scored five goals in a five-game sequence and it was enough to persuade Northern Ireland's selectors to end his spell of nearly three years in the international wilderness. Since his last game for his country, there had emerged an Irish talent, which Dougan would readily admit was even greater than his – George Best. During

Dougan's two-season spell at Peterborough, Best had broken into the Manchester United side and become a permanent fixture in the Irish team. Now Dougan would be inside-left with Best at outside-left against Scotland at Windsor Park. It proved a triumphant return for The Doog.

With Burnley's Willie Irvine in the number-nine shirt, Dougan formed a twin strike partnership and it worked well. Spurs' Alan Gilzean headed home a Willie Henderson centre to put the Scots ahead, but Dougan marked his return at a packed Windsor Park with the equaliser at the end of the first half. This is how he described it in an article under his name in the Boys Book of Soccer 1966: 'George Best appeared to be fouled in the area by a Scottish defender and I half stopped, expecting the whistle to be blown for a penalty. Nothing happened, but the ball ran loose to me about 18 yards out. I thumped it as hard as I could and saw it crash against the underside of the bar and enter the net. What a moment!'

In the second half Gilzean cancelled out a goal from Johnny Crossan, but Dougan would play his part in the winner. Jimmy McIlroy's free-kick was headed back by Dougan at the near post for Irvine to score spectacularly, hooking the ball in with an overhead kick while in mid air. It was a day to savour for Dougan with his friends and family watching. He was pleased not only because of the result, but because he had scored with his 'weaker' right foot. Dougan confessed he had been apprehensive before the game, feeling he had yet to prove himself at this level. He need not have worried. His goal was his fourth in ten games for his country. Somewhat surprisingly, Dougan would score only four more times in a further 33 appearances for Northern Ireland. He was often playing in a struggling side and in an era when football was becoming more and more defensive, yet even taking that into consideration, his scoring record at international level did not do his undoubted talents justice.

Teams that day in Belfast, Saturday 2 October 1965:

Northern Ireland: Jennings (Tottenham); Magill (Arsenal), Elder (Burnley), Harvey (Sunderland), Neill (Arsenal, captain), Nicholson (Huddersfield), McIlroy (Stoke), Crossan (Manchester City), Irvine (Burnley), Dougan (Leicester), Best (Manchester United).

Scotland: Brown (Tottenham); Hamilton (Dundee), McCreadie (Chelsea), Mackay (Tottenham), McNeill (Celtic, captain), Greig (Rangers), Henderson (Rangers), Law (Manchester United), Gilzean (Tottenham), Baxter (Sunderland), Hughes (Celtic).

Referee: Jack Taylor (England). Attendance: 50,000.

It was a heartening return to international football for Dougan, but this initial success would be followed by anti-climax for him and his Irish team-mates. They all desperately wanted to reach the World Cup finals being staged that summer for the first time in England. They were in a qualifying group that gave them every chance. Only one could qualify from the Irish, Switzerland, Holland and Albania. Holland were not then the great world football power they would later become, so it was a contest between three well-matched teams and the Albanian minnows. As so often happens in World Cup qualifying groups it is results against the minnows which often prove crucial. So it was this time for Northern Ireland.

The side who had beaten Scotland were named for the game against England at Wembley and did not do too badly in losing 2–1 and so got a vote of confidence for the vital trip to Tirana to face an Albanian side who had lost all five of their previous games in the group, scoring only one goal – perhaps significantly, against Ireland in Belfast – and conceding 11. A win for the Irish would have put them level on points with Switzerland at the top of the final group table and that would have meant a play-off. However, Albania held the Irish 1–1 and Dougan's chance of playing in the finals for a second time was gone. He would proudly boast later in life that he had taken part in five World Cup campaigns yet his first cap for his country remained his only game in the finals. George Best would not even get one appearance in the finals and he and Dougan would have dearly loved to figure in the 1966 tournament on what to them was home territory. If the Irish had made it to England they may well have caused an upset or two, but, as someone once said, 'if' is the biggest word in football.

All that was left for Dougan and Co, after beating Wales 4–1 in Cardiff in the final match of the Home International championship, was to provide warm-up opposition in Belfast for two of the World Cup finalists. Though they lost 2–0 to the Germans, they beat Mexico 4–1 to show what they might have done had they qualified.

If his return to the international stage had ultimately ended in frustration, Dougan could be satisfied with his return to top-flight League football. Yet he had still not found his spiritual home or, more to the point, a manager whom he could respect and who would value his advice. Dougan always felt strongly that managers should listen to players rather than treat them like subordinates. Matt Gillies was not a manager who shared that view and not someone to whom Dougan warmed. Typical of Gillies' personality was his reaction to Dougan after that win over the Scots. As a Scot, Gillies had brought several of his fellow countrymen to Filbert Street. After the win in Belfast Dougan enjoyed some good-natured banter with Leicester's Scottish contingent but Dougan wrote in his book, Doog, 'Matt Gillies could not find it in his heart to congratulate me. He made some banal remark which left me with the feeling that in being associated with Northern Ireland's victory over Scotland I had let him down.' It was early evidence that the two would not hit it off, Dougan adding, 'I felt that my days at Leicester were numbered – though I was to remain another 18 months – and that in the meantime only virtuoso performances by me would keep me in the first team.'

The bluff striker once again proved he was easy to wound. But a wounded animal often bites back and evidence that Dougan would not treat Gillies with the deference he expected from his players came when the team were setting off to meet Manchester City in a fifth-round FA Cup tie. The club chairman's bag was on the ground waiting to be loaded into the coach and Gillies told Dougan to carry it. "I asked him if the chairman was ill or something and could not carry it for himself," Dougan recalled. "He repeated the instruction, which I refused to carry out. One of my team-mates was then told to carry it and he complied. This must have confirmed for Matt Gillies that I was a threat to him."

It was just a petty incident, but there would soon be another clash with the manager when Dougan was asked by Professional Footballers' Association secretary Cliff Lloyd to join the PFA committee. Dougan regarded it as one of the biggest compliments ever paid to him at that stage of his career and out of respect told Gillies so that he would know about it before it appeared in the newspapers. Rather than congratulate him Gillies riled Dougan further saying, "I don't want any dressing room lawyers here." Yet during his playing days at Bolton, Gillies had himself been a PFA delegate, so his reaction just added to Dougan's disdain for him.

Dougan made the point that he had always been a conscientious PFA member, always paid his subs and thought the manager would, like him, regard it as an honour for the club that he had been appointed to the PFA executive. "Not so Matt Gillies," Dougan recalled, "or was his terse uncongratulatory reaction due to MY involvement? Would he have taken this attitude if another player had been invited? If I had been a Scot, I have no doubt I would have been accepted by him."

The manager-player relationship was not helped when Dougan asked for more money. He had a mortgage to pay and Jutta was expecting their second child. He could point to evidence of his value to Leicester. When he was unfit for a match against Blackpool, he was told not to mention it to anyone as his absence might affect the gate. Gillies' attitude to Dougan's pay request was that he ought to be grateful the club had brought him out of the obscurity of the Third Division. Dougan pointed out he had taken a £750 drop in annual pay by leaving Peterborough and that failure to give him a rise would leave Gillies with an unhappy player on his hands. The manager's reaction? "Then I will have to put up with an unhappy player."

To Gillies's credit, he did not let the lack of rapport with Dougan stop him selecting him week in week out. Dougan repaid that faith by showing some of the most consistent form of his career to that date. It won him a special place in the affection of the fans, something he achieved at all his clubs, with graffiti hailing 'The Doog' being scrawled on walls and even school blackboards on a regular basis across the city. The Irish firebrand's flair, dynamism and goals consistently won a very special place in the hearts of supporters to the point that even now, in many cases 40 or even 50 years on, his name brings a smile to the face and a torrent of Doog-related stories from any fan lucky enough to have witnessed Dougan wearing his club's colours, no matter how long that may have lasted.

For all his disillusion with the Leicester manager, Dougan still had the future of the club at heart and felt they had the basis of a good side which could be improved with a few more astute signings. One such could have been Terry Cooper, a few years later to become a regular member of the England side. At that stage he had not established himself as a permanent member of the Leeds team and Dougan and team-mate Davie Gibson got talking to him after a match at Elland Road and found that Cooper would certainly be keen on a move to Leicester. The pair relayed the information to Gillies and were surprised when the manager showed no enthusiasm for the deal, even though the fee would probably have been about £25,000.

Dougan felt the addition of Cooper could have been another step towards transforming Leicester from a useful team into a very good one. Cooper remained at Leeds and eventually won a place at full-back at the expense of Willie Bell as Don Revie's team changed the football landscape of the country, challenging for honours consistently for the next decade and winning both the FA Cup and league title, and reaching the 1975 European Cup final, during that period. Ironically, it would be Bell that would join Leicester just over a year later. Dougan's view that the club lacked ambition was borne out by the fact they eventually sold both himself and England goalkeeper Gordon Banks, although Banks's replacement, Peter Shilton, was no slouch in anyone's book. Gillies went, too, and in 1969 Leicester, despite reaching the FA Cup final, were relegated. Dougan was not surprised.

If he was unhappy off the pitch, Dougan certainly did not let it affect his performances on it. He began 1966/67 in scintillating form. By the end of October he had collected 17 goals, 12 in the League and five in the League Cup. His League haul included a hat-trick in a 5–0 hammering of one of his former clubs Aston Villa, who were destined to be relegated that season. At one stage a 12-match spell brought him 14 goals. As happens to all strikers, no matter how prolific they may be, a lean patch followed. He ended the drought with a goal in a 2–1 home win over Arsenal on 11 February, but just over a month later he would be on his way out of Filbert Street.

The inevitable move from Leicester still came out of the blue. When told by the reserve team trainer to report to the manager's office Dougan wondered if it might just be news of a new contract. So it was a shock when Gillies told him Wolves wanted to sign him and that terms had been agreed. Such was the way players were dealt with in those days that Gillies told him he needed an answer by noon. That gave Dougan about ten minutes and he was visibly shaken. "Thanks for giving me so much time." he snorted.

Having checked with his wife, who said she would back him whatever he decided, Dougan agreed to meet Wolves manager Ronnie Allen, who suggested a venue in Birmingham. However, Dougan was in such a state by then that he did not trust himself to drive any great distance and Allen agreed a rendezvous at a motel near Leicester. The discussions on the proposed move took place in Allen's car in the car park where one of the first questions Dougan asked was how long Wolves had been interested in signing him. Allen told him six weeks. Yet Dougan had been given ten minutes to make up his mind!

There was no time to think as the transfer deadline was that day, but Dougan did not need any when he heard Wolves' terms and, more important, Allen's ambitions for the club. Those ambitions seemed to contrast starkly with those at Leicester where their willingness to let Dougan go surprised Gordon Banks. The England goalkeeper recalled in *Banksy*, 'The Doog was a cult figure at Filbert Street, as he would become at Molineux. His contribution to the team had been significant and he was enjoying playing First Division football again. Derek wasn't keen to go, but when your club values your transfer fee above your contribution to the team, you might as well move on.'

Leicester fans were sorry to see the big centre-forward leave. Long-time supporter Derek Allen explains, "We only tended to sell players when they were finished. I think Gillies sold him too early. The fans really warmed to him because he was a flamboyant character. There was one game where he was really taking the mickey out of the opposition, beat one of their defenders who then tried to kick him, but missed and ended up kicking the linesmen. I can't remember who it was against as it was a long time ago, but it was a big talking point at the time. The defender probably got booked. The away fans were also a bit confused when they came to Filbert Street because they thought we were booing a lot but it was the chant of 'Doog', which we used to stretch out and it sounded like boos."

Bill Chettle says, "I first saw Dougan at Villa Park and he led their line when we lost 8–3 there in 1962. He scored two goals and I thought what a good player he was. When he came to us there was never a dull moment. He was a real crowd pleaser, everybody loved Doog. I wish we had somebody like him at number-nine now. He was brilliant." John Chapman agrees, "He gave us another dimension. He may have been mostly left-footed, but that didn't matter and he was excellent in the air, scored some great goals with his head. He was just what we needed at the time, a good centre-forward, and he really hit it off straight away. There was a lot of disappointment when he left Leicester and we started to get a reputation as a selling club after that."

Chapter Six

INSTANT FOLK HERO

AT THEIR PEAK IN THE 1950s, when three times under manager Stan Cullis they had been champions of England, Wolverhampton Wanderers had been relegated to the Second Division in 1965. Under Ronnie Allen, a young go-ahead coach, they were back on track and looking good for a return to the top flight. The missing piece in the jigsaw was a centre-forward of stature. Allen believed that Dougan, though by then 29, could provide the ingredient which would see Wolves safely over the final hurdles to promotion. Allen, himself an England centre-forward who had starred for West Bromwich Albion throughout the 1950s and scored a dramatic penalty equaliser in the 1954 FA Cup final when the Baggies beat Preston 3-2, was proved spectacularly right. News of Dougan's departure did not go down well with the Filbert Street fans. Just as those at Villa had done, they bombarded their club with letters of protest.

Signed for £45,000 on 16 March 1967, Dougan made his Wanderers debut against Plymouth at Home Park two days later in conditions not best suited to good football. Apart from a sandy pitch which made control difficult there was a gusty wind that helped neither side. Phil Morgan in his *Express & Star* report noted, 'Shots into the wind by Dave Wagstaffe in the first half and Mike Everitt in the second described fantastic arcs. Many a ball kicked from defence soared suddenly upwards or dropped as quickly.'

Morgan added, 'This was no setting against which to judge the ability of new signing Derek Dougan to settle in with his new Molineux comrades or, for that matter, their aptitude for accepting his long-striding high-leaping style. And Dougan? He was closely shadowed by Andy Nelson, who did not hesitate to give away many of the free-kicks with which the game was far too liberally laced. Not that Dougan was completely subdued for there were moments when he showed the know-how, although never allowed a scoring chance.' The game was decided by its only goal when Peter Knowles struck for Wolves on 55 minutes, heading the ball in when goalkeeper Pat Dunne could only palm into the air one of winger Terry Wharton's trademark hot shots.

If Dougan's first game for Wolves was low key his second was the stuff of which legends are made. Indeed, his home bow has gone into Wolverhampton folklore, not merely for the fact he scored a hat-trick in a 4–0 defeat of Hull City, but for the manner in which he completed it – with a goal still talked about today by those fans who witnessed it. Phil Morgan summed up Dougan's Molineux arrival superbly in the *Express & Star*, writing, 'They came, they saw, he conquered.'

The first goal came when Hull keeper Ian McKechnie could only palm into the air a shot from full-back Bobby Thomson and Dougan was on the spot to put the ball home. That was eight minutes before half-time and 15 minutes after the restart he glided home a shot to finish off a move begun by Mike Bailey and Wharton.

The third goal was special indeed. The move began when left-winger Dave Wagstaffe turned up on the right wing. He beat one defender before centring to the far side of the six-yard area where Wharton headed back across goal. The ball was dropping behind Dougan, but the centre-forward deliberately flicked it up over his head with his left foot and, with the same foot, volleyed it home when it dropped in front of him. In one superbly-executed piece of skill Dougan had established an immediate rapport with the home fans among whom, tellingly, were several sporting blue and white scarves. Disillusioned Leicester fans had come to give their former hero their support and send a protest to the Filbert Street board.

The teams that day, Saturday 25 March 1967:

Wolves: Parkes; Taylor, Thomson, Bailey, Woodfield, Holsgrove, Wharton, Hunt (Burnside 59), Dougan, Knowles, Wagstaffe.

Hull: McKechnie; Davidson, Butler, Greenwood, Milner, Simpkin, Henderson, Wagstaff, Chilton, Jarvis, Young

Referee: D Laing (Preston)

Attendance: 30,991

Terry Wharton played his part in Dougan's dramatic home debut – "I made a couple of goals for him that day" – and said the man already carrying a reputation as one of football's most controversial characters did not arrive at the club with any airs and graces. "He was one of the lads. He was just Derek. He was a smashin' chap. The first time I saw him, though, was playing against us in the 1960 Cup Final. I got my letter offering me a contract on Cup Final morning and the club took all us youngsters down to watch the game. Alan Hinton got his letter the same day."

It was something of a shock when after just 13 games back in the First Division, Wharton was transferred to Bolton, but he kept in touch with Dougan. "I always got on well with him. We went down to London Wolves for their 40th anniversary and we had a lovely weekend. They all hung around him and I just had the odd person talking to me. Derek loved an audience." Dougan was the president of the London Wolves Supporters Club and always regarded it as a great compliment and a great honour.

As was the way in those days Hull was the first of three games in a four-day spell over the Easter Bank Holiday. There followed 1–0 wins over Huddersfield at Leeds Road on the Monday and then at Molineux a day later, when 40,939 turned up to watch. Dougan suddenly realised he was with a bigger club than Leicester. However, his next match would see him hitting the headlines for the wrong reasons, though hardly of his making.

Perhaps appropriately it was April 1 when Wolves visited the hostile environment that was then The Den, home of Millwall. Former Arsenal and Nottingham Forest centre-forward Len Julians had given the Londoners the lead early in the second half and they looked to have luck on their side when David Wagstaffe missed a penalty. Dougan denied them victory with a minute left when Scottish international goalkeeper Lawrie Leslie could not hold on to a centre and the centre-forward was on the spot to poke the ball home. As his team-mates ran to congratulate Dougan, a fan ran on to the pitch as if to join in the celebrations. In fact, his intent was far from friendly and he aimed a kick at the Irishman before being restrained. A few days later the 20-year-old culprit appeared before Greenwich magistrates and was fined £5 after admitting using insulting behaviour. The lad, Albert Yates, told the court, "I am sorry for what happened. I'm afraid I got too enthusiastic." Magistrate Alan Stevenson told him, "This is not the work of a sportsman. It never used to happen in the old days."

Just eight games after his transfer, Dougan would help the club clinch promotion, scoring twice as Bury were beaten 4–1 at Molineux. Fans invaded the pitch and there was Champagne for the players in the boardroom afterwards.

The icing on the cake would have been to go up as champions and they should have done, despite losing to title rivals Coventry City a week after clinching promotion. A packed Highfield Road saw Jimmy Hill's side win 3–1 and Dougan met his match for once in the uncompromising shape of the Sky Blues centre-half George Curtis, a man who, alongside John Sillett would manage Coventry to their 1987 FA Cup triumph.

Yet all was not lost and if Wolves won their remaining two matches the title would still be theirs. Dougan did his best to ensure they won the first of those two games, hitting two goals inside the first 25 minutes to set up a 4–1 home win over Norwich. That took Dougan's goals total to nine in nine games and there was good news after the final whistle, too. Coventry had been held 1–1 at Ipswich, so now Wolves needed only to draw their final game at Crystal Palace to go up as champions. Alas, they chose the visit to Selhurst Park to turn in their worst display of the season and were beaten 4–1. Dougan had a poor game, but he was not alone.

Coventry took advantage of Wolves' slip by beating Millwall 3–1 to pinch the title, but Dougan would not have collected a winner's medal in any case as he had only played 11 of the 42 league games. He had every reason to be satisfied with his season, though. His nine goals for Wolves plus his 21 at Leicester represented the highest seasonal return of his career – and would remain so. It also had him top of the Second Division list in the *News of the World Football Annual* even though over two-thirds of his goals had been in the top division. Second to him in the Second Division strikers table was Norwich's Lawrie Sheffield and 13 of his 23 goals that season had been scored for Third Division Doncaster.

On the international front it was not such a successful 1966/67 for Dougan. Northern Ireland's season was limited to the three games in what was still known as the Home International championship. No doubt still disappointed at not making the summer's World Cup finals, Dougan would have loved to put one over on the newly-crowned world champions when England came to Windsor Park in October. It did not work out that way as Sir Alf Ramsey's men won 2–0 with goals from Roger Hunt and Martin Peters. There was early evidence that Dougan was fired up for the match when he clashed with Nobby Stiles. Both were booked. He then brought an early double save from Gordon Banks. Northern Ireland faded after that though near the end Dougan and Willie Irvine created an easy chance for Johnny Crossan which the Manchester City man missed.

At 29, some people might have thought his career was nearing its end, but Dougan was about to prove them wrong. He liked to live well and enjoy life, but his attitude to his profession could not be faulted. He kept himself fit by training hard and it was this dedication which would ensure that far from being finished he was about to enjoy the best years of his football life.

Before he could parade his skills in the top flight once more, he and his Wolves team-mates were about to set off on a memorable adventure on the other side of the Atlantic. They would represent Los Angeles in a USA tournament run by an organisation calling themselves the United Soccer Association.

As Dougan admitted, he could hardly have joined Wolves at a better time. Going to the United States was good, being based in LA was even better. The team were sponsored by Canadian-born multi-millionaire Jack Kent Cooke, who in his time owned the Washington Redskins American football club and the Los Angeles Kings ice hockey team. Married five times he made US history when in 1979 he divorced his first wife with the largest divorce settlement up to that time – 42 million dollars. With such a backer Dougan and the rest were assured of the best accommodation and hospitality. Despite all that, Dougan's abiding impression was of the people's underlying lack of sincerity

The main purpose of Wolves' trip was to promote soccer in the US. Some 40 years later the task was still not complete, but Wolves certainly did their bit on that 14-game trip. In his book *Attack*, Dougan wrote, 'In every game we played superb football. The excitement of winning promotion and going to California charged our batteries.'

The other football ambassadors were Cagliari of Italy, Cerro of Uruguay, Bangu of Brazil, Dundee United, Aberdeen, Hibernian, Stoke, Sunderland, Shamrock Rovers, Glentoran and ADO of Holland. It was against the Dutch in San Francisco that Dougan fell foul of the referee, though, in fairness to the centre-forward, most of the observers felt the refereeing was way below the accepted standard. The official had already sent off an ADO player whose only offence seemed to be to remonstrate with his own full-back for doling out some rough treatment to Wolves winger David Wagstaffe. Both Wagstaffe and Paddy Buckley had to leave the field and go to hospital with a cracked rib and damaged ankle respectively. Then Ernie Hunt was dismissed for retaliating after another tough challenge, before Dougan too got his marching orders.

But it wasn't for any part in the rough stuff that Dougan was dismissed. He was merely doing what he had no doubt done dozens of times back home, namely querying a decision. The referee denied Wolves a penalty when Terry Wharton was upended and as Dougan went to have a word with the official he made the mistake of putting his hand on the ref's shouder. The result was instant dismissal. Manager Ronnie Allen telephoned reports back to the *Express & Star* in Wolverhampton during the tour and told the paper, 'It was just plain ridiculous. The man lost control completely and the game was spoiled in consequence.'

The view on the refereeing was reiterated by chairman John Ireland who arrived home before the end of the tournament and told the paper that unless something was done about it the experiment of trying to introduce football to the American public would fail. 'The whole object of the exercise in inviting foreign teams to the country was to demonstrate how the game can, and should, be played,' said Ireland. 'We all know it is a fine game when properly played but the public are not given the chance to see it, nor the players the chance to demonstrate it. What they could do with is a panel of English referees if they are going to try again.'

Wolves' 1–0 defeat at the hands of ADO was their first in nine games, a sequence that had seen Dougan score in three successive matches – against Hibernian, Sunderland and Glentoran. He was not fit enough to play against ADO in the return game which Wolves won 2–0 and which saw goalkeeper Fred Davies come on as an outfield substitute and score with a header.

That was the only game in the tournament that Dougan missed and he was on target again against Aberdeen in what proved an epic final, played at the Coliseum in Los Angeles. The players went on to the pitch at about 7.30pm and it was well after 11 when they came off. As well as the razzmatazz which slowed down proceedings there was playing time of two hours and eight minutes. Twice Wolves thought they had won it, but a last-gasp goal from Aberdeen's Frank Munro, who would later become a true Wolves great, took the match into extra time at 4–4. Dougan put Wolves ahead with seven minutes left of the extra half hour. Terry Wharton then had a penalty saved by Scots keeper Bobby Clark and Munro scored from the spot at the other end to make it 5–5 with the last kick of the extra period. So the match went into sudden death and after eight minutes of that a Bobby Thomson centre brought an own goal from Jim Shewan which gave Wolves the title.

The trophy was duly presented to Dougan, who skippered the side in the absence of Mike Bailey, absent nursing a thigh injury. Manager Ronnie Allen told the crowd, "I think everybody in the stadium has seen one of the most fantastic games of football that's ever been played."

Dougan had played a part in the game's opening goal when he headed on an overhead pass from Bobby Thomson for Peter Knowles to run through and score. Aberdeen equalised through Jim Smith, who soon afterwards was sent off for a foul on Dave Wagstaffe. The ten men took the lead through a Munro penalty just after the hour to spark a mad scoring spree. David Burnside levelled only for Jim Storrie to make it 3–2 for the Scots. A Burnside header from the 18-yard line quickly restored parity and he completed his hat-trick when a mazy run by Dougan down the left teed the chance up for him. There was more classy play from the Irishman when he made it 5–4. Wharton centred from the right and Dougan calmly beat one player before steadying himself and then blasting the ball high into the net.

Wharton's penalty miss was a unique event in Wolves history. "I told everybody in the world I never missed a penalty until somebody reminded me about that one," he admitted, looking back in 2007. "I'd forgotten that one but I can say I never missed one in this country and that's what I'm proud of."

It was some night and the team were feted at the Sheridan Wiltshire hotel afterwards with the sponsor Kent Cooke well pleased with his adopted team. Dougan recalled, 'The American television commentator was in raptures over the game, said it was the best football match ever played. Two hours and eight minutes were spent playing football and the rest was devoted to entertainment, the interval and presentations. Majorettes and cheer leaders whipped up the excitement but there was scarcely any need as the game itself was full of excitement.'

Dougan enjoyed much of the LA glitz. English entertainer Tommy Steele was over there making a film, *Finian's Rainbow*, and invited the party to visit the set. Dave Wagstaffe also met an old Manchester pal of his – one Davy Jones, a singer with the Monkees, a manufactured pop group, who were then at the height of their fame on both sides of the Atlantic with their TV show. He made the Wolves party guests at the recording of a Monkees show and Dougan loved this unexpected taste of Hollywood glamour. For the match against Shamrock Rovers famous film star Maureen O'Hara was the guest of honour. She was introduced to the teams before the match and then performed a ceremonial kick-off. By that time Dougan had taken on board the laid-back LA style and was sporting a moustache and goatee beard. He jokingly added that there was a touch of the Irish in the fact that Wolves had numbers on the back of their shirts and on the front.

Over the later years of his life Dougan may have gained a reputation as a drinker, but while based at the Sheraton in Los Angeles for two months he is best remembered as a drinker of something non-alcoholic – good old English tea. Dave Wagstaffe explains, "The hotel poolside became the regular meeting place for all the party. It became the place where our own little quartet was formed. The 'Tea Set', as they were dubbed by the rest of us, consisted of Derek Dougan, John Holsgrove, Bobby Thomson and Les Wilson. This foursome when sat at the poolside or round a table were never seen without a pot of tea in front of them. Even after the tour, whenever we played in Britain, Europe or the rest of the world the pot of tea for four was always the first thing to be ordered."

That epic final against Aberdeen was on Friday 14 July, so there was little respite for Dougan and his colleagues, the new English season kicking off just five weeks later. After such a busy summer the players were raring to go and Dougan more than most. He was back in the big time, he had completed ten seasons in English football and was ready to prove that he still had what it took to compete successfully in the top flight.

One of the spin-offs from the American trip was the team spirit that it fostered and typical of the happy atmosphere was a bit of nonsense involving Dougan. This is how winger Dave Wagstaffe recalls it: "Every morning before training there was a ritual. 'Titch' Harding, a well-known ex-referee, used to bring the mail down from the office to the dressing room. Obviously, the Doog got more fan mail than the rest of us and Titch would take the bundle to Derek first. Titch, less than 5 feet tall and Derek, 6 feet 2 inches, would then go through an imaginary tossing-up procedure, Titch pretending to spin a coin and Derek shouting 'heads' or 'tails'. Whichever Derek shouted, Titch would then look up to the tall centre-forward and say, 'Correct.' 'We'll kick that way,' would say Derek. 'OK,' would answer Titch, 'have a good game, gentlemen' and then he would disappear out of the dressing room and back to the office. It was only a harmless bit of fun, but Titch used to look forward to the little ceremony every morning."

Wolves gave early evidence that they could hold their own at the higher level and Dougan was quickly into his stride. The opening day brought a 2–1 win over Fulham at Craven Cottage with the big centre-forward opening the scoring on 33 minutes when he netted from a David Wagstaffe free-kick. Wagstaffe would also create the opening for Mike Bailey to make it two and that set the pattern for this and many subsequent seasons – Wagstaffe the creator for Dougan and a succession of strike partners. A winger in the old style, with the skill to beat a man and send over pinpoint centres, 'Waggy' was as much a hero with Wolves fans in those days as Dougan, Bailey, Richards, Hibbitt and Munro.

Confirmation of Dougan's opening day form came in Phil Morgan's *Express & Star* report, the veteran correspondent writing that Dougan was 'in his element and frightening the home defence every time he went for the high centres from in-form Dave Wagstaffe.'

Over 50,000 packed Molineux for Wolves' first home game of the new season when Ronnie Allen's team were held 3–3 by old rivals Albion in an incident-packed match. It ended with two late goals from the visitors to deny Wolves a win, the second one being fisted home by Tony Brown. Aggressive protests about it saw goalkeeper Phil Parkes sent off and Dougan could hardly have had a more frenzied introduction to the passionate affair that is a Black Country derby.

Three days later came more proof that Dougan could rank with the best strikers of his day when Wolves took on Leeds at Molineux. Under Don Revie, the Yorkshire side would become a power in the land and possessed an all-international half-back line of awesome power. Either side of England World Cup centre-half Jack Charlton were fiery Scot Billy Bremner and hard-tackling Norman Hunter. Yet Dougan took them on and led them a merry dance scoring both goals in a 2–0 win. It was a memorable display and the words of Phil Morgan once more sum it up well. This is some of what he wrote:

'Faced with the third and hardest phase of their three-part First Division entrance exam, Wolves passed with honours, thanks largely to the expertise of soccer graduate Derek Dougan. Widely experienced in this kind of company, Dougan, only 11 Wolves Second Division games away from the top flight last season, seemed to take his colleagues under his wing and usher them through the tests before applying the personal finishing touch with typical goals in the 54th and 66th minutes.

'These moments were the climax, but what had gone before was just as vital since Wolves, urged on by their dynamic skipper Mike Bailey and prompted by the assured know-how of another recent top-class exile Dave Burnside, outplayed their opponents. Among the victims of this runaround were those past masters of the football arts – Billy Bremner of Scotland and Jack Charlton of England. For some reason best known to himself as team captain, Bremner decided to play as a forward. He tried to harass Phil Parkes, but all he got was a wigging from the referee. He tried to do likewise to Les Wilson, stand-in for the injured Bobby Thomson, and only got his name into the referee's book.

'As for Charlton, he happened upon the "Doog" in his most determined mood and had a few lessons in reaching the high ones, let alone a chase or two that left him standing. And when Dougan headed in Dave Wagstaffe's cross in the 54th minute and followed by clipping a short one from Ernie Hunt into the roof of the net 12 minutes later, big Jack was nowhere around. And when Dougan was off the field for a couple of minutes between the goals he was not kidding. He had the stud marks to prove it – and to give extra relish to the shot.'

Those words provide proof to the basic fact that Dougan had sparkled against one of England's most feared centre-halves. Based on those first three games, the prospects for Wolves in general, and Dougan in particular, looked good. It was a false dawn, however. There followed five successive defeats which included the concession of four goals both against Albion, in the return game at The Hawthorns, and Everton at Goodison. The fifth defeat was a humiliating League Cup exit at Huddersfield. By that time Dougan had lost the services of his chunky strike partner Ernie Hunt. Manager Ronnie Allen surprised home fans by selling the ex-Swindon player to Everton for £80,000, promising that a top player would be joining Wolves in the very near future. That player never did materialise, although Hunt's departure allowed Peter Knowles the chance to stake a claim for a first team place once more. This he would do in style.

Dougan gave another virtuoso performance when Wolves ended their losing run with a 2–1 victory at West Ham. The home side paraded their World Cup heroes, Martin Peters, Geoff Hurst and Bobby Moore, but it was Dougan who stole the limelight. As well as nursing along debutant 17-year-old Alun Evans, he found time to score both Wolves goals. He received plenty of verbal abuse from the home fans, but Phil Morgan wrote that he 'positively revelled in the hostility of the crowd.'

It seemed that the greater the reputations of the central defenders who marked him the better Dougan played. Against Arsenal's Terry Neill and Ian Ure he again scored twice, both headers from Wagstaffe corners, and also ran right through the Gunners' defence to lay on a goal for young Evans as Wolves won 3–2 on Monday 23 October 1967.

Two days before that match Dougan had teamed up with Neill as Northern Ireland played a decisive part in the European Championship, or Nations Cup as it was then known. Qualification for the quarter-final stage was being decided over two seasons based on the Home International Championship results. Having memorably beaten England at Wembley the previous season, Scotland were favourites to gain the lone qualification place. However, the Irish spoiled it for them as Dougan had one of his best games for his country in a 1–0 win at Windsor Park, thanks to a goal from Coventry wing-half Dave Clements. It proved Northern Ireland's only win in the qualifying campaign and they finished bottom of the group.

If Dougan and Neill were comrades in the green shirt of their country, they were in opposing camps when it came to the Professional Footballers'

Association. Some might have suggested Dougan was on an ego trip in pursuing a PFA career. He may well have enjoyed the high profile that went with a PFA role, but there is no doubt he also had a genuine desire to improve the lot of his fellow players, especially when it came to the highly restrictive contract system. To his credit, he was not one to perpetually moan about the players' lot and do nothing about it. He WOULD do something about it.

Having joined the PFA committee during his spell at Leicester, Dougan soon made an impression with his enthusiasm for the work and in October 1967 was well in line to get the top job of chairman. The vacancy occurred because former Manchester United captain Noel Cantwell had decided to accept the manager's job at Coventry and therefore had to give up the chairmanship of the players' union. The battle to succeed him was narrowed down to Neill, Dougan and Stoke's former Albion and Manchester United wing-half Maurice Setters.

Setters was the senior committee man, but he was a tough no-nonsense player who had often got into hot water with officials. He knew his disciplinary record was not the best attribute for the role of PFA chairman and decided to rule himself out. Dougan felt Setters was wrong to do so. He did have a bad track record, but he was enthusiastic and dedicated, wanted to improve the welfare of the players and would have made an excellent chairman. Despite Dougan's view, Setters was insistent. He believed the committee would be swayed by the need to have a chairman with the right public image and to save them being put in an awkward position he chose not to run for office. That narrowed the battle down to the Northern Ireland team-mates.

Dougan dearly wanted the position and felt it needed someone with strong views who would not be afraid to express them. He thought Neill would be too weak in the forthcoming discussions with the Football Association and the Football League. However, the PFA committee took the easier option when they met at a Manchester hotel. This is how Dougan recalled the occasion in his book *Doog*:

'We waited in the corridor, making hard work of conversation. When we were called back the expression on Noel Cantwell's face told me I had not been elected. Terry Neill was chosen because he represented what was required, a nice pleasant image. My behaviour on the pitch between 1957 and 1967 had been taken into account and had clearly gone against me. One sending-off at Nottingham when I was with Aston Villa and a number of cautions. My behaviour on the pitch in this period did not relate to my sense of responsibility off it. I was still considered somewhat headstrong when compared with Terry Neill.'

For nearly three more years Dougan would have to mark time as a PFA committee man, no doubt quietly seething at what he saw as Neill's lack of steel in negotiations with English football authorities. Dougan's time would come. It had merely been delayed.

Meanwhile back at Molineux Wolves' form had picked up slightly, though Dougan's pulled muscle after scoring in a a 2–1 defeat at Leeds meant he missed the home and away games with Manchester United over Christmas, which both ended in defeat for Wolves. Clearly the team needed strengthening and Dougan had been frustrated by Ronnie Allen not heeding an earlier suggestion for a signing. The manager did not take his advice to sign England goalkeeper Gordon Banks from Leicester. Dougan knew Banks was willing to move and that Leicester were willing to sell as they had young Peter Shilton waiting in the wings. Though he felt Phil Parkes, then aged 21, had immense promise, Dougan thought the experience of Banks would have been invaluable to the team. He claimed that many years later Allen had admitted to Dougan that he should have listened to him and should have bought Banks, who left Leicester for Stoke City soon after Dougan's departure.

However, that was water under the bridge and Allen would soon start strengthening the squad. The first addition came early in 1968 with the acquisition from Aberdeen of Frank Munro, the man who had scored three goals against Wolves in that epic final in Los Angeles. Then more of a midfielder, Munro would switch to central defence with great success, winning nine Scottish caps on the way. Dougan rated him highly and had urged Allen to sign him. Dougan in later life remained a firm friend, especially when Munro's health deteriorated and saw him having to use a wheelchair.

Munro could not prevent Wolves losing 3–1 at home to Everton on his debut and the arrival of Mike Kenning from Norwich likewise had no effect as Dougan captained the side against his old team Leicester at Filbert Street. Wolves lost that one 3–1 too, with Dougan getting his share of barracking from the fans who once chanted his name in adoration. Dougan was clearly a big name in a struggling team and it was no surprise that there was speculation about whether he would wish to stay at Molineux. It hit the headlines the day after the Leicester match.

Peter Batt, one of the old-style Sunday newspaper sportswriters who would claim to have inside knowledge on what was happening in football, told his readers in the *People* newspaper that Dougan's exit from Molineux was just a matter of time. This is how Batt saw it:

'Bob Dennison, Coventry's new £60-a-week chief scout, was at Leicester yesterday for yet another look at Derek Dougan, 29-year-old Wolves centre-forward. Three weeks ago Coventry failed in a bid to sign Dougan. But they are obviously hoping that a slump in his goal-getting – he has scored only twice since October – may change Wolves' mind. Stoke are also more than keen and are prepared to match the £50,000 which Wolves paid Leicester only nine months ago. You can expect denials from Wolves manager Ronnie Allen, but I understand that as far as the Wolves board is concerned it is now just a question of timing. A recent slump in form – they have won only two of their last ten matches – has put them in relegation trouble. And they may decide it is impossible to part immediately, but you can take it that Dougan will be on the move again before too long.'

Batt's story seemed to leave no room for misinterpretation, but there was an immediate denial from chairman John Ireland who said, "With reference to a report in a Sunday newspaper concerning Derek Dougan leaving the Wolves, and the suggestion that the board would let him go, I have to say there is no question of Dougan leaving the club. I would add he signed a new three-year contract with us on Thursday of last week."

Dougan confirmed this when he told the *Express & Star*, "If my career lasts another ten weeks, ten months or ten years, it will be with Wolves. I signed a contract that will keep me here for the rest of my career and that suits me fine. Let me put it like this, it has taken me five clubs and ten years to find the best club I have ever been associated with and it will take another ten years to leave them."

What bothered Dougan was Batt's report suggesting that manager Allen might deny there was a move in the offing, but the directors might be ready to listen to offers. It struck Dougan as trying to play the manager off against the board and was yet another reason why he built up a dislike for most sportswriters.

Dougan went on, "We have a young manager here and he must be given time to try to do what he aims to do. It is in the very nature of modern football that managers make inquiries about players, but the clubs to whom the inquiries are made should regard such things as compliments since they have players others would like. Perhaps, in Wolves' case some of the speculation has arisen because they have recently been concerned in a number of transfers, but that does not affect my position. I like Wolverhampton and the people and I'm quite happy to stay."

Usually, such transfer stories have a grain of truth in them. If this one had, Dougan would certainly not have been too flattered by interest being shown by Coventry and Stoke. Some might have said they were on a par with, or even better than, Wolves from the playing point of view at this time, but as far as tradition, status and potential were concerned they were a good way below them. Maybe if it had been Manchester United, Liverpool or Arsenal who showed an interest, Dougan's attitude would have been very different. Indeed, in later years, he reckoned he would have gone to Arsenal had he been allowed to and he also maintained that Bill Shankly had wanted to sign him for Liverpool.

To mark his 30th birthday, Dougan found the net against West Ham United at Molineux, but Wolves were beaten yet again, this time 2–1. It would get worse before it got better as a week later Wolves were humbled 1–0 in the third round of the FA Cup by Third Division Rotherham, then managed by Tommy Docherty. Clearly, Wolves needed some new blood and it came first in the shape of Derek Parkin, a highly promising teenager signed from Huddersfield for what was then a record fee for a full-back, £80,000. He would become a Wolves legend, setting a new figure for most appearances for the club. Just 20, Parkin was one of several young players who benefited from Dougan's friendship and advice. Speaking after Dougan's death in 2007, Parkin said, "A lot of people got the wrong end of the stick about him. He was a very thoughtful man and I had a lot of respect for him. I'm sure all the lads feel the same."

It was not only on the field that Parkin received good advice from the Irishman. "He had all the time in the world for people. That's the thing I remember about him as a young player and it always stuck with me throughout my career. After we'd played in the rain, we'd go and shower, have a drink and there would still be supporters outside, wet through from the pouring rain, waiting for autographs. He told me, 'You must always sign autographs' and that's why he was so popular."

A signing soon after Parkin's arrival undoubtedly met with Dougan's approval. At Villa he had hoped they would sign a striker with whom he could link, but the arrival of the man he saw as a prime candidate, Albion's Derek Kevan, did not materialise. At Molineux Ronnie Allen realised Dougan needed a strike partner and signed burly Frank Wignall, a former England international, from Nottingham Forest. It took little time for Wignall to settle in and the partnership with Dougan did more than enough in the end to ensure Wolves' survival.

Wignall's debut saw Wolves beat Sunderland 2–1 at Molineux and he scored his first goal for the club when Wolves won 2–0 against Arsenal at Highbury a week later. As well as the two points, Dougan would have no doubt been sneakily pleased to see the man who had beaten him to the PFA chairmanship, Terry Neill, miss the chance to put Arsenal level after John Holsgrove opened the scoring. Arsenal were awarded a penalty and Neill hit the ball with all he had only to see it hit the crossbar with such force that the ball bounced down well clear of any Gunners players following up.

The Wignall-Dougan double act reached its height, appropriately, against Wignall's old side Forest at Molineux on 6 April 1968 as the recent arrival struck twice and Dougan was credited with a hat-trick in a 6–1 win. The second of Dougan's goals came when a Peter Knowles drive bounced down off the bar and Dougan headed the ball in. Most in the Press box thought Knowles's shot had bounced down behind the line before Dougan made sure. Dougan, not surprisingly, did not concur. The goal which put Wolves 5–1 up came when Parkin's lob appeared to bounce into the net without anyone else getting a touch. Wolves' official verdict was that Dougan had got a glancing headed touch to the ball and so the goal – and the match ball – was his. It was a fitting return to the team for the Irishman who had missed a couple of games because of flu.

Wignall would have a match ball of his own before the end of the season, hitting all the goals as Wolves beat Chelsea 3–0 at Molineux. He scored again a week later as Tottenham were beaten 2–1 at home to see Wolves finish 17th in the table. They had kept their place in the top flight, which was the main aim of that season, and Wignall's contribution of nine goals in 12 games had made the difference just as Dougan's nine in 11 the previous season had given the team that final promotion push.

Before that two-win finale to the season, Dougan had a surprise strike partner in a 2–1 defeat at Chelsea, John McAlle, deputising for the injured Wignall. Later to establish himself as a highly reliable defender, McAlle was one of several young players taken under Dougan's wing. 'The lessons we learned from Derek, as a professional footballer, stood the likes of myself, Derek Parkin and Frank Munro in good stead throughout our careers,' McAlle reflected in the *Express & Star* after Dougan's death.

McAlle added, 'When he arrived in 1967 I had just signed professional terms after my apprenticeship. The Doog was 12 years older than me, but it was just a great feeling to have him in the club. He was a man of strong opinions. If he liked you then you were in. If not, he would ignore you. Simple as that. He was the type of man you needed in a dressing room. Not only was he a really nice guy who could have a laugh, but he was someone you could easily look up to. In training everyone wanted to beat the Doog, probably to try to impress him. We were all trying to keep up with him because he was an incredibly fit guy which was another inspiration to us younger players.'

He may have completed only one full season at Molineux but already the foundations had been firmly laid for The Doog to become a cult figure in a way perhaps never before seen in Wolverhampton. There may have been greater players in Wolves' illustrious past but none had established the special rapport which Dougan built up with the fans. Much of it was down to the man himself. He saw the football pitch as his stage, Molineux as his theatre and the crowd as an audience to be entertained. He knew how to work them, too, but it would have been all in vain if he had not been good at what he did – and he certainly was that.

The faithful loved him because he had not only talent but charisma, too. The name 'Doog' would be daubed on the walls of the subways on the town's ring road and in many other places as well. They would in time sing his praises from the terraces, ranging from simple call and response chants like "What's his name?" "Dougan!" to "Nah-nah-nah-nah, nah-nah-nah-nah, Hey Doog" to the tune of the Beatle's hit *Hey Jude*, the release of which coincided with Dougan's first full season and his rise to cult hero status.

With the Distillery team who won the Irish Cup in 1956.

The fresh-faced lad who became a Wolves idol.

Ready to find fame and fortune with Portsmouth.

Something of a rarity – an almost shy-looking close-cropped Dougan in his early days as a Blackburn Rovers player.

All set for the 1960 Cup Final, Blackburn Rovers in their special Wembley kit. Dougan is third from the right in the back row while on his left is Dave Whelan, the future chairman of Wigan, who was destined to be carried off on a stretcher in the game at Wembley as Wolves won 3–0.

The aftermath of Dougan's shock transfer request on the morning of the 1960 FA Cup final is reflected in the front page headlines of Blackburn's local paper two days later.

Dougan is welcomed to Villa Park by club skipper Vic Crowe.

Opening day of the 1961–2 season and the shaven-headed Dougan trots out at Goodison Park to face Everton and a torrent of Scouse abuse.

Not this time . . . Dougan is thwarted by Charlton keeper Willie Duff at Villa Park in 1962.

Looking through their favourite LPs, Dougan and Jutta soon after announcing their wedding plans.

Smart young couple … Mr and Mrs Dougan guests at a Masonic dinner-dance.

Wedding day for the Dougans with best man boxer Johnny Prescott perhaps showing the Doog what will happen if he does not behave himself.

A typical dad playing football with his boys at their Codsall home as Jutta looks on.

Dougan the family man – carefree days with Jutta and their young sons.

Four Leicester City internationals – four different Home countries. Dougan of Northern Ireland, Gordon Banks of England, Davie Gibson of Scotland and Peter Rodrigues of Wales.

So this is Molineux. Dougan sits in the old Waterloo Road main stand at Molineux shortly after signing for Wolves.

It's a fair cop. Dougan dons a fake police helmet as he helps his sons open some new toys.

The sharpshooters … the fastest goalgetters in the West, Dougan and John Richards.

In action for his country against England but beaten by goalkeeper Gordon Banks.

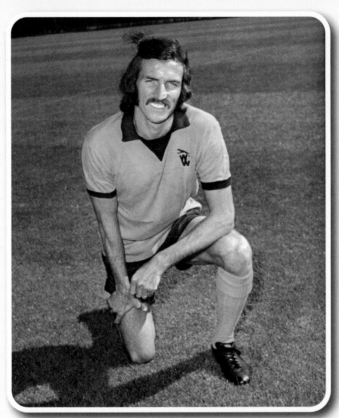

A Wanderer and so a wanderer no more. Dougan pictured in his prime at Molineux, his home for the last eight years of his playing career.

The Dougans' gardener, Percy Duckett, joins them in a 1974 League Cup celebration along with Kenny Hibbitt and John Richards, scorers of the two goals against Manchester City at Wembley.

Get in! Dougan fires home another goal for Wolves, this time against Spurs.

Best restraining influence – skipper Dougan leads George Best away from trouble as Scottish players, led by number-10 Alan Gilzean, remonstrate with the referee during a Home international clash.

Dougan the radio personality – early days with Radio Birmingham.

It's 26 April 1975 and Leeds are at Molineux for the final game of the season. Dougan is substituted for number-10 Steve Kindon so he can make one final League appearance before his adoring Molineux fans.

Happy times … Dougan smiles for the camera while George Best and goalkeeper Pat Jennings share a joke as Northern Ireland players relax. Jimmy Nicholson is on the right. Soon Doog would be shunned by his country's selectors.

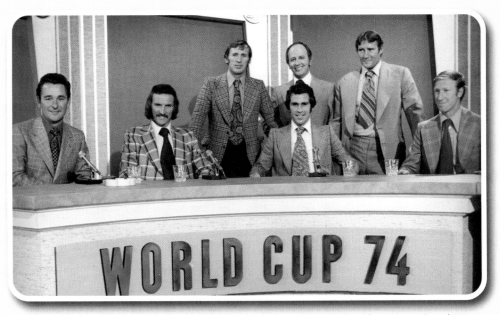

The 1974 World Cup panel which helped continue Dougan's role as a national TV personality. Seated (left to right) are Brian Clough, Dougan, Newcastle defender Bobby Moncur and Jack Charlton. Standing are Pat Crerand, anchorman Brian Moore and Malcolm Allison.

Still the fans' hero, Dougan is chaired from the field at the end of his testimonial game.

Great PR from Wolves' new chief executive and managing director ... Dougan joins the fans to watch the opening game of the 1982–3 season.

Is that a vulture I see circling? New manager Tommy Docherty poses for the Press with Dougan in June 1984. Within a year both would be gone.

Managing director and chief executive Dougan welcomes new boss Graham Hawkins to Molineux.

Jutta sparkles in her trouser suit.

Jutta looking equally good in a stunning dress.

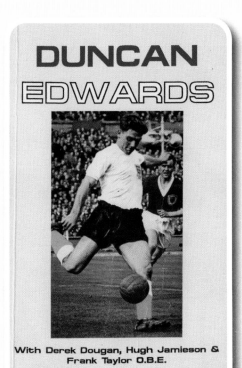

The front cover of the book launched to help raise cash for the ill-fated Duncan Edwards medicine centre appeal...

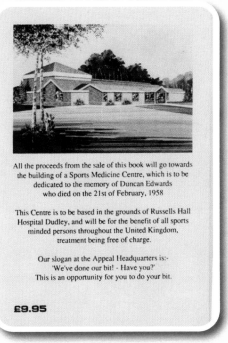

... the back cover of the Duncan Edwards book – many volumes of the publication were just binned.

The Dougans and their sons with Jutta's mum, Elisabeth.

Now make sure you look smart . . .
Jutta helps Dougan prepare for
a night out.

Nice shirt, shame about the tie!

(Above left): A special couple, the Dougans all dressed up for another black-tie occasion. (Above right): Showing why Tailor and Cutter named him best dressed man.

The Dougan family.

A 1980 snap of Derek and his sons with his father-in-law Franz Xaver.

Dougan, Gerry Armstrong and Billy Bingham help carry the coffin at George Best's funeral.

Proud parents with Alexander at Coventry Cathedral after he had collected his law degree.

Sons Nick and Alex with former Wolves director Doug Hope help carry Dougan on one last journey in a coffin bearing his familiar number-10 and signature.

Chapter Seven

You're Banned

AFTER THE EXCITEMENT OF THE previous summer in Los Angeles, 1968 was a genuine close season for Dougan and it may have been during this time that he began work on the first of several books which bore his name, his autobiography *Attack*, published by Pelham Books. Dougan's literary career owed much to his good fortune in becoming friends with feature writer Ray Seaton, who was first on the *Leicester Mercury* and then moved to the *Express & Star* in Wolverhampton. Seaton's interests were many and varied. He loved film and theatre and old-time comedians, being responsible for biographies of two of Britain's legendary funnymen, Will Hay and George Formby. Seaton was one of life's eccentrics. After his death, Gerry Anderson, another *Express & Star* legend, summed him up beautifully in his obituary by saying that Seaton was the sort of chap who could tell you who played second lead in a 1933 B movie, but could not tell you where he had parked his car that morning. Luckily for Dougan another of Seaton's passions was football.

In Dougan's first and subsequent books one could detect the hand of Seaton and it is pretty certain that the bulk of the writing was done by him with Dougan providing the facts and anecdotes. In *Attack*, which Dougan dedicated to his wife Jutta and sons Alexander and Nicholas, there is a page at the beginning, carrying the words 'My thanks to Ray Seaton for helping to prepare this book.' To be fair, Dougan was an intelligent man with no shortage of opinions, but one suspects he was happy to let Seaton put them down on paper. Seaton, too, it has to be said, was only too happy to help, but many of Seaton's colleagues felt he never got the credit he deserved for Dougan's literary work

Bill Smith worked for many years in the *Express & Star* features department alongside Ray Seaton. "I think Ray and Derek first met when Ray was on the *Leicester Mercury* and Derek was with Leicester City," Smith confirmed. "Ray idolised Derek and I know he virtually wrote his books and his newspaper articles. I got on with Derek very well and I said to him that he ought to mention that Ray was his collaborator and he said, 'Well, I do when I talk to people.' Derek did add that he thought Ray was one of the best journalists in the world and I think he did credit him in some of his books. I don't know what Ray got for helping him. I think he gave him a Humber Sceptre car once, or else sold it him very cheaply. I eventually bought it off Ray for £120.

"I remember when Ray had a hair weave and Derek did as well. I'm not sure who did it first. The difference was that Ray was virtually bald. Derek was always a larger than life character. Many years later I used to see him from time to time as he lived near me. He would often wear a big black leather hat. It was not a Stetson, but it had a big brim. He also had a long coat almost down to his ankles. He liked to be noticed, did Derek. I'd often bump into him in the paper shop at Birches Bridge and he'd be putting £20 on the Lottery. It was usually £20 or so."

Veteran Wolverhampton freelance sports journalist Ron Warrilow recalls seeing Seaton in Queen Street, near the *Express & Star* offices and Seaton was proudly sporting a smart pair of shoes. Warrilow said Seaton was doing a little dance, shuffling his feet to show off the shoes, and Warrilow asked him where he had got them and was told, "Derek gave me these for writing his last book."

Another who would later help Dougan was Percy M Young, who was a musicologist, composer and conductor as well as being director of music at Wolverhampton College of Technology. Born in 1912, Young loved football and as well as writing biographies of Handel, Schumann and Elgar he also wrote histories of Wolves and Bolton Wanderers. It was *Express & Star* Wolves reporter Phil Morgan who introduced Dougan and Young and they became firm friends, Young writing the foreword for his 1972 book *Derek Dougan, The Sash He Never Wore* and probably providing a lot of assistance with the writing. One could say it was a cynical move by Dougan to befriend people like Seaton and Young, as they could help him with his books, but there is no doubt he genuinely enjoyed their company and they his. Indeed, both would probably have actively encouraged Dougan in his literary efforts and been happy to help.

Although the initial work on *Attack* may have been done during the summer of 1968, the book was not published until the following year after Wolves had again failed to make a big impression, but had at least kept their place in the top flight. That 1968/69 season proved another good one for Dougan, but not for the manager who had signed him, Ronnie Allen. Dougan would be saddened at Allen's departure which would make way for the arrival of a man who would slip easily into Dougan's growing list of 'Managers With Whom I Did Not Get On'.

The campaign began stutteringly for Wolves, with three defeats and only two wins in the opening six games. Dougan was on target in both victories, 3–1 at home to QPR and 1–0 at home to Leicester. The latter saw Dougan outshine City's costly signing from Fulham, £150,000 Allan Clarke, only for he and the rest of the Wolves forwards to be denied a hatful of goals by young Peter Shilton in the visiting goal. A Mike Bailey long throw-in saw Dougan finally break the deadlock with a header on half-time. Dougan then sustained a foot injury and had to limp off 20 minutes from the end of that game. Alun Evans was substituted for him and when Dougan was not fit to face Stoke a week later it was Evans who deputised. After such a promising start to his Wolves career, Evans had become the target of the Molineux boo boys. As Wolves stuttered to a 1–1 draw with the Potters Phil Morgan reported, 'Alun Evans must have thought the whole business a nasty dream, especially when the crowd picked on him.' That was to be the last first-team appearance for Evans. He would soon leave the club and return to haunt them and figure in a match which would put the writing on the wall for Ronnie Allen.

Bill Shankly had seen potential in Evans and took him from the jeers of Molineux to the cheers of Anfield, making him Britain's first £100,000 teenager. The transfer went through on 16 September 1968 and 12 days later Evans returned in triumph to score twice as Liverpool put six goals without reply past Alan Boswell, a goalkeeper Allen had signed from Shrewsbury a few days before selling Evans. Many reckon this defeat was what clinched Allen's departure, but Wanderers played nine more matches before the managerial axe fell.

Dougan quickly helped Wolves banish the Liverpool blues when a week later he scored the only goal of the game against Coventry City at Highfield Road. He sank almost to the ground in order to head the ball in after David Woodfield had nodded it on and that, said Phil Morgan, was 'a noble effort to round off perhaps the Irishman's most efficient display this season.' When Wolves won 2–0 at Sheffield Wednesday with Dougan winning a penalty for the opening goal by Peter Knowles and then scoring the second, John Dee wrote in the *Express & Star* that Dougan was man of the match.

Wolves' results were picking up, apart from a shock League Cup exit at the hands of Blackpool, and Dougan was on target again as they earned a 1–1 draw at Burnley. He headed in a Mike Kenning corner for the equaliser, his status at the club having been confirmed beforehand when Allen named him skipper in the absence of the injured Mike Bailey. Allen said after the game, "We let them off the hook, Burnley were lucky to get a point." He would be making no more post-match statements as a Wolves manager. He was sacked four days later, on Wednesday 20 November 1968. Dougan wrote about the day of Allen's dismissal in his book *Attack*:

'We were to have had a day off, to relax and play golf. There were moans and groans when we were called to the ground. One player had announced in the Press that he was seeking a transfer and we suspected that this was the cause of our being asked in, to be warned against speaking out of turn to the Press. Or perhaps we were required for special training. None of us thought it was to be told that the manager had been asked to resign. Ronnie Allen came to us and said, "Well lads, from today I'm no longer manager." That was all, simple and to the point. He told us in a matter-of-fact way that must have concealed some emotion. We did not know what to say. None of us had paid much attention to the rumours. Ronnie Allen's departure was sudden and without fuss. He made no complaint, did not hurl brickbats in Press statements and accepted the board's decision with commendable grace and dignity. He went with the satisfaction of having taken Wolves back to the First Division.'

His successor was already lined up – Bill McGarry, manager of Ipswich Town. Wolves had tried to get him in September 1965 after caretaker boss Andy Beattie resigned, but had been told by the Portman Road board that they could not talk to him. That refusal allowed Allen to continue as coach and later be appointed manager. This time Ipswich agreed McGarry could leave for Molineux. Ironically, he and Allen had played in the same Port Vale team for several seasons immediately after the Second World War. Both had gone on to play for England, McGarry winning the first of his four caps in the 1954 World Cup finals in Switzerland. He had been a hard man as a player and was the same as a manager. He was still only 41 when he joined Wolves. Dougan's initial reaction in *Attack* was basically to reserve judgement. 'The Press had built him up into some kind of managerial ogre, describing him as a hard disciplinarian,' wrote Dougan. 'He can be tough, severe when he feels it necessary, but he is direct and I have heard more than one player describe him as a man's manager.'

It seemed as if Dougan was giving McGarry the benefit of the doubt. It would not take too long before his views would change dramatically. In later life his remarks about McGarry were scathing. To say there was no love lost between them is putting it mildly. Yet McGarry would be the manager under whom Dougan served longest. Many thought Allen's brand of football was more subtle than McGarry's, but the latter definitely took Wolves to greater heights and made them into a side who were among the best in the top flight. Maybe Dougan's dislike of the manager was tempered by the fact he was playing in a very useful team, which would eventually bring Wembley glory back to the club.

Sammy Chapman, who twice took over the managerial reins at Wolves during the dark days of the mid-1980s, has his own take on the Dougan-McGarry relationship. "I think he and McGarry had respect for each other in football terms," says Chapman. "McGarry knew Derek could play and Derek knew McGarry could manage. You don't have to get on outside the club, you don't have to like each other as long as you have that respect.

"There's an old saying in football – 'I've never seen a coach make a player, but I've seen a player make a coach.' And Derek was a very good player. McGarry, I am sure, realised that. Derek could see things around him. He may not have put as much store on scoring as he should have done. He was happy to make goals for others, though he still scored his fair share. He loved the whole arena, loved the crowd, loved to show them what he could do. He was probably a better left-sided midfield player. He loved the idea of playing there and he could see a pass and run any distance, but I suppose people saw his physique and automatically thought centre-forward."

If, as Chapman suggests, there was a grudging respect between McGarry and Dougan then it had run its course by the time Dougan published his book, *Doog*, in 1980. By then retired, Dougan was far less circumspect in his description of McGarry's arrival. It had, he said, a touch of farce with an opening scene that would have better suited Brain Rix, famous star of the farces which were regularly staged at the Whitehall Theatre in London. All the players were assembled in the dressing room when McGarry made his entrance. The door burst open and he walked in wearing a tight-fitting light blue tracksuit. The suit was so tight that when McGarry lifted his leg and tried nonchalantly to put his foot on the seating which ran around the room, he missed and stumbled. He carried on as the players stifled their giggles and told them, "I am the manager and I don't give two ***** if you don't like me. I don't want you to like me." Dougan reckoned that seven years later he was still taking McGarry at his word when it came to that last statement. McGarry concluded his introduction by telling them what they would do and how they would do it. Some of the younger players may have been impressed by the tough-guy approach, but Dougan had heard it all before.

Changes soon followed McGarry's arrival. Greater emphasis was put on physical fitness, with the manager leading by example. Dougan conceded that the boss was fit for his age, but then so was Dougan. He may have been the oldest player on the books, but he was among the fittest, though not quite so fanatical as young centre-half David Woodfield who would walk several miles from his home to Molineux each day for training and then walk back again.

An early alteration to the way of things at the club was that the general office was out of bounds to all players, apart from skipper Mike Bailey. It was just a petty rule, as far as Dougan could see, to let them know who was boss. The office staff did not have a problem with players calling into the office as it saved them work. The players would pop in to collect any mail or messages and to buy tickets for matches. The decision to make the office out of bounds affected Dougan more than the rest in view of his work with the PFA and the need to contact fellow officials or to be contacted by them. There were no such things as mobile phones in those days.

Before the new regime took effect Wolves welcomed McGarry with a 5–0 home win over Newcastle. Some said this scintillating display was more a tribute to the departed Ronnie Allen than a welcome to his successor. Despite the scoreline, one of Wolves' best players that day was goalkeeper Phil Parkes, keeping Newcastle at bay after Peter Knowles had scored on 11 minutes. Frank Wignall made it two before the break and as the Geordies faded in the second half Knowles scored his second, sandwiched between two from Dougan. All three of the second-half goals came from centres by Dave Wagstaffe, who was in sparkling form on the left wing.

Results were mixed after that, a defeat at Old Trafford being followed by a 2–0 win over Spurs at Molineux during which Dougan showed McGarry what he could do with a man-of-the-match display that saw him score from a half chance after 63 minutes and then make a slide rule pass from which Wignall made it two. After a 1–1 draw at Chelsea and a dismal 3–0 home defeat by Sheffield Wednesday, the scheduled Christmas games were postponed, so that Wolves welcomed 1969 with a trip to Boothferry Park to face Hull City in the third round of the FA Cup. It was a trip which earned a place in Wolves folklore, but not for the result, even though Wolves won.

This was the first occasion since McGarry's arrival that an away game had been deemed worthy of an overnight stay. After some days training in Southport the squad travelled to a hotel near Hull on the Friday before the game. At the evening meal defender John Holsgrove, down to play centre-half next day, ordered himself a prawn cocktail as a starter. McGarry heard him and hit the roof. "What do you think this is, Butlin's?" roared McGarry, who reckoned that such food was bad for footballers.

Dave Wagstaffe remembers it well. "We all sat there absolutely amazed, looking down like chastised school kids. McGarry walked over and stood at the end of the table. 'I'll tell you what you can fucking eat,' he growled. 'Soup to start, steak or chicken for the main course and fresh fruit salad for dessert.' Believe it or not, that menu of soup, steak or chicken and fruit salad was to stand wherever we went in this country or in the world for the whole of McGarry's days as manager of Wolves. It was pre-ordered whenever possible when the hotel rooms were booked."

The Hull incident was always recalled when Wolves players of that era got together. The story was often re-told by Dougan himself. So much so, that after Dougan died, Bobby Gould, in paying tribute, mentioned it but reckoned it had been Dougan who had dared to order prawn cocktail.

Whatever Dougan had dined on the evening before it certainly did not affect his display in the Cup tie as Wolves came back from an early goal by Hull striker Chris Chilton to win 3–1 with Doog twice on target. His first was typical Dougan. A long ball by Mike Bailey found him running free down the middle of the pitch and he took two or three strides before hammering the ball past goalkeeper Ian McKechnie. After Frank Wignall had made it 2–1, Dougan collected his second when he headed home a Les Wilson cross, goalkeeper McKechnie slipping as he came out.

Dougan may not have been the man with a taste for prawn cocktail, but he did eventually have problems with McGarry over one aspect of his diet. Dougan did not like sterilised milk and so after a match would go to the tea-room where the women there would give him a mug of tea made with pasteurised milk. Sometimes he would send an apprentice to fetch it or former trainer Jack Davies, who still helped out at the club, would bring it in for him. McGarry never commented until one day he was in a bad mood after a poor display against Burnley and laid into Davies when he brought in Doog's beverage. "Get that fucking tea out of here," he yelled, adding that the tea the rest of the players drank ought to be good enough for Dougan.

Younger players might have said nothing, but Dougan took McGarry to task, asking why he was taking out his anger on old Jack and pointing out he had been drinking tea with pasteurised milk ever since he had joined the club. Only reply from the manager was, "If it's good enough for me to drink, it's good enough for you." Like most bullying types, McGarry, Dougan found, was a different proposition if one stood up to him. After the tea incident he marched into his office to have it out with the boss who quickly saw the mood Dougan was in and admitted he had been out of order. "I was wild with my defence for letting them through so many times," was McGarry's excuse.

The main Burnley tormentor that day had been Steve Kindon, a fast rampaging tank of a player, and Dougan believed it was that display which caused McGarry to sign Kindon as Dougan's likely replacement. A good honest player, who had begun as a winger, he was not at that time in the Irishman's class. Maybe he was happy to drink his tea with sterilised milk, though.

Tottenham abruptly put an end to any premature hopes of a Cup run, beating Wolves 2–1 at White Hart Lane, and within a few days a new strike partner arrived for Dougan. Hugh Curran was signed for £65,000 from Norwich and would eventually become the first man to win a Scottish cap while at Molineux. McGarry may well have signed him as security in view of Peter Knowles's threat to turn his back on football because of his Christian convictions as a Jehovah's Witness. In their first game together Dougan and Curran both found the target at home to Manchester United only for Bobby Charlton and George Best to cancel out the goals in the second half.

The partnership looked promising and Dougan was still a dangerman to most defences. After a 0–0 draw at Molineux, Southampton manager Ted Bates explained his team's cautious approach by reasoning, "You cannot take too many chances with a man like Derek Dougan around." There was a similar result when Leeds, on their way to winning the title with a then record 67 points, visited Molineux and Phil Morgan wrote, 'Derek Dougan was once again too much for big Jack Charlton.' Later a 3–1 home win over FA Cup finalists Manchester City had Morgan reporting that 'one of Dougan's incredible bursts of speed' had taken him past the visitors' defence before centring for Peter Knowles to score.

Dougan was clearly a man well able to hold his own with the best in the land, though the team had still not made an impact after their return to the top flight and that win over City was their lone success in the final 11 games of a season which saw them finish 16th in the First Division. Internationally, Dougan had a successful start to the season. He scored in Northern Ireland's 3–2 friendly win over Israel in Jaffa and again when they beat Turkey 4–1 in a World Cup qualifier at Windsor Park. The return game in Istanbul brought a 3–0 win and for the first, and only, time in his international career Dougan had played in three successive victories.

After that early-season success, Dougan and his Irish team-mates must have been looking forward to the Home International tournament which, for the first time, was being condensed into one week at the end of the season. At home to World Cup holders England, Northern Ireland started like a whirlwind with Dougan and George Best creating a succession of chances. Unfortunately for the Irish, Burnley's Willie Irvine wasted three good opportunities to score before Martin Peters headed home a Francis Lee free- kick to put England ahead. An Irish rally brought an equaliser for Eric McMordie, but two late goals earned England a 3–1 win. By holding Scotland 1–1 in Glasgow and then playing out a goalless home draw with Wales, the Irish might have felt they were heading in the right direction. Sadly for Dougan another World Cup campaign would end in disappointment.

There was no time for him to reflect on the Home International campaign as he had to catch a plane to join Wolves in the United States. Two years after their previous successful excursion to America, the team were representing Kansas City in the North American Soccer League. Dougan, did not fancy the long flight after an arduous season and wasn't looking forward to another dose of US razzmatazz, for which he had no appetite. His protests were in vain and Bill McGarry told him in no uncertain terms that he would have to join the squad as soon as the internationals were over. Wolves had won three and lost one of their first four games when Dougan arrived for the match with Aston Villa, representing Atlanta. Dougan made an immediate impact. He hit the winning goal in a 2–1 win after Brian Godfrey had cancelled out a Peter Knowles penalty.

While Dougan enjoyed the game and the atmosphere something annoyed him greatly. Before kick-off Peter Knowles, apparently because of his Jehovah's Witness beliefs, refused to stand for the playing of the national anthems. The other players told Dougan that this had been going on since the start of the tour. When Dougan asked Bill McGarry to make Knowles stand, the manager would not – or could not. Reflected Dougan in Doog, 'A little of my respect for both of them died out there. So much for McGarry's authority.'

In the next match Dougan was credited with two goals in a 3–0 victory over Kilmarnock in St Louis. The first was definitely his, but reports back to the *Express & Star* from McGarry suggested a Dave Wagstaffe lob had gone directly into the net even though Dougan was on hand to harass the goalkeeper. "Dougan said he got a touch but we all thought it was Waggy's goal," said McGarry. Dougan was never slow to claim a goal as his, no matter how slight a touch on the ball might have been. He was not alone in that, merely doing what all great strikers have done over the years.

Dougan was on target again when Wolves beat Villa 5–0 in Kansas to clinch the tournament and he scored two more when the final match was lost 3–2 to Dundee United in Dallas. The final report on the trip credited Dougan with five goals not six, so his claim for that extra one in St Louis seems to have been rejected.

McGarry's insistence on Dougan jetting to the USA to join what was hardly the most important of ventures was another nail in the coffin of their relationship and so Doog was all ears when his old Peterborough boss Gordon Clark called him unexpectedly. Clark was by then chief scout with Arsenal, then under the managership of Bertie Mee. The prospect of a move to Highbury really excited Dougan. True, he had pledged his future to Wolves, but that had been under Ronnie Allen, a manager with whom he got on and whom he respected. Wolves under McGarry was another thing entirely.

With Dougan keen to move and the relationship with McGarry poor the deal ought to have gone through. However, nothing came of it and Dougan was never told why. He could only assume that McGarry had dug in his heels because Arsenal were above Wolves in the table and managers were usually unwilling to sell players to better clubs. It might have been because McGarry knew there would be an outcry from the fans, though he was the sort of hard-nosed character who would not have been too bothered by a bit of criticism from supporters. If these were not the reasons then it might just have been bloody-mindedness on McGarry's part to deny the player a dream move. It would have been a dream move, too, as the Gunners were on the verge of great things. Within two years they would be celebrating having become only the fourth team in English football history to do the League and Cup double. Dougan could have been part of that. He may have been 31, but he would still produce five more vintage seasons, so Arsenal's loss was Wolves' gain.

There was time in the summer of 1969 for Dougan to assemble some thoughts on the new Molineux regime for the *Park Drive Book of Football*. He wrote of the contrast between the regimes of Ronnie Allen and Bill McGarry. 'Ronnie gave us a fairly free rein,' wrote Dougan. 'Players were encouraged to express themselves individually. Bill McGarry has a different approach. He believes in all-purpose, non-stop play and stresses the importance of teamwork. In the old days when football was a more casual sport, training was often nothing more than a few laps around the pitch, followed by a quick fag and then a kick-about. A famous international player left a club because he knew this approach was wrong. His team-mates scoffed and said he was being superior. They were finished before they were 30 and he was still at his peak at 35.

'At Molineux we have a circuit of about 20 exercises including weight-lifting. At first we spend 40 seconds on each exercise, with an eight-second interval between. Then we complete the circuit again, in 20-second sessions. Trainers used to stand and watch. Now they compete, demonstrating as well as promoting workrate, a professional term that commentators now regularly use and which one even hears on the terraces. Leeds and Liverpool are outstanding examples of teams that have made workrate a fine art. But sometimes I wonder if trainers are going overboard with their stop watches, graphs and diets. There is a danger, however remote at present, that one day we could be turning out machine-made footballers, players technically conditioned to such an extent that they have no individuality and no personality in their game.'

Dougan added that, 'Wolves train much harder than any of the other five clubs for which I have played' and he must have benefited from it as he was at an age where he needed to be at peak fitness to prolong his career. It had not always been that way as he recalled ruefully. 'If training is overdone it can tire players so much that they are not fit for strenuous matches. This was what was happening to me at Portsmouth, before my physique had fully developed. I was put on weight-lifting and at the time it took so much out of me that my playing suffered. By Saturday I felt on the verge of exhaustion.'

After their American success Wolves hit the ground running when the 1969/70 season began. McGarry had added Scottish international Jim McCalliog to their ranks and he would settle in well, helping the team begin with four successive wins, Dougan marking the opening-day 3–1 win over Stoke at Molineux with a couple of goals. However the third game of their campaign saw Dougan land in hot water as Wolves won 3–2 at Sheffield Wednesday on Saturday 16 August. He and Wednesday's Peter Eustace were given their marching orders by Harlow referee Arthur Dimond after 75 minutes, despite Dougan protesting his innocence. This was how Phil Morgan saw it in his *Express & Star* report:

'There was an air of mystery about the incident because I could find nobody who saw it all. Dougan declared himself blameless – and wished there had been a TV camera to prove it – while Wednesday made allegations of kicks and counter kicks. As the ball was cleared from the Wednesday goal area, I saw Dougan fall backwards. There was a scuffle and referee Arthur Dimond went to the scene. He spoke to Eustace, who left the pitch, and when Dougan got to his feet he followed the Wednesday man from the field. A sad end for two who had done so much for their teams. Dougan, leading Wolves with all his well-known efficiency, caused near havoc in the Wednesday defence and Eustace was one man who looked as though he might achieve something for Wednesday.'

Dougan's pleas of being the innocent victim may have helped him when he came before the FA disciplinary committee who gave him a 14-day suspended sentence. In other words, he would not be banned, providing he behaved himself. That proved to be asking too much.

The winning run ended with a 0–0 home draw with Manchester United when Dougan was kept under tight control by his old adversary Ian Ure. After the inevitable departure of Peter Knowles into premature retirement because he could not reconcile playing football with being a Jehovah's Witness, Leeds' former England winger Mike O'Grady was signed, so Dougan had a second new player with whom to get in tune. Knowles's final match had seen Dougan and his strike partner Hugh Curran, who scored twice, give Wolves a 3–0 lead against Nottingham Forest. However, they surrendered it and ended up drawing 3–3, leaving fans more concerned with the throwing away of a point rather than the exit of Knowles.

The new formation seemed to work out well, but Dougan's role in steering Wolves to better things would soon be curtailed – and it was all his own fault as he made headlines for the wrong reasons. Knowing he needed to behave, Dougan should have kept his fiery temperament in check. It was a task that proved beyond him and he let his temper boil over with severe consequences when Everton visited Molineux on Saturday 4 October. The Merseysiders, who went on to win the title that season, were leading 2–1 when the game erupted as Dougan remonstrated with a linesman and was sent off for the second time in two months. Dougan, it was claimed, had sworn at the linesman, but the fans still reckoned he should not have been sent off and the atmosphere was so volatile that the police on duty at the ground lined the perimeter of the pitch to ensure there were no invasions. Once again, let Phil Morgan tell the story:

'Wolves and Everton were putting on a lively and entertaining show for an hour. Then, suddenly, there was near pandemonium and things were never the same again, not even Wolves' home record, which went by the board. Derek Dougan, arguing with a linesman, taking the long walk to the dressing room, the crowd erupting at the back of the North Bank; the crescendo of protest against referee Keith Walker, the second penalty, the third booking and the scene had changed from the pleasant to the best-forgotten.'

Referee Walker needed a police escort from the field at the end. As well as sending off Dougan he had awarded two penalties, Joe Royle putting Everton ahead from the first on 15 minutes and Hugh Curran firing home the second on 66 minutes to make the final score 3–2. The official also booked the visitors' John Hurst and Alan Ball. It was nothing new for Walker. A week earlier he had needed a police escort from the Hawthorns pitch after Liverpool had equalised against Albion six minutes into time he had added on 'for time-wasting and gamesmanship.' There was no fourth official in those days to work out the minimum time to be added on. After the Wolves incident it got even worse for Walker. The Express & Star reported on its front page on the Monday after the match that he had been asked to leave his Maidstone flat by his landlord who feared possible reprisals from disgruntled football fans.

With a suspended ban hanging over Dougan's head the club and fans knew the outcome would be a suspension, but they could not have guessed it would be a monumental one. The FA disciplinary committee met on 29 October at the Dominion Hotel, Lancaster Gate, London, Dougan looking the epitome of sartorial elegance in a smart suit with a handkerchief in his top pocket. The six-man commission, chaired by Vernon Stokes and including FA secretary Dennis Follows, came down on him like a ton of bricks. They banned Dougan for 56 days. It meant he would miss eight games and would cost him probably £800 in wages.

After the hearing Bill McGarry described the decision as 'vicious' while chairman John Ireland said, "Justice at any level should be for the punishment to fit the crime. But for a non-violent crime on the uncorroborated word of one linesman a sentence of this kind seems to me poor justice."

PFA secretary Cliff Lloyd, who represented Dougan at the hearing, said he associated himself with everything Ireland had said. Lloyd was instrumental in getting a BBC film of the Everton incident shown and pointed out that while the linesman's word was uncorroborated, Dougan had two witnesses, Sandy Brown and Colin Harvey of Everton, giving evidence on his behalf, along with Wolves captain Mike Bailey. Lloyd said that quite apart from the general implications of the disciplinary committee decisions, there was an urgent need to get uniformity on law interpretation, especially on the question of bad language, which was the complaint against Dougan. Lloyd said, "The laws of football refer to 'foul and abusive language', but even in this respect it is difficult to find a hard and fast rule. There are referees who swear at players – and it is accepted – but others merely hearing a swear word might threaten a sending-off."

There was some suggestion that Wolves might take the FA to court claiming restraint of trade, but it never happened. Dougan had no alternative but to take his hefty punishment. Asked for a comment by Phil Morgan after the hearing he said only, "The club chairman has made a statement with which I am in agreement but beyond that – nothing. I have even turned down requests today to appear on television and radio programmes because I think this is best at the moment."

However, the ever vigilant Morgan was able to quote from Dougan's book *Attack*, which was due to be published in a few weeks' time and in which Dougan called for radical changes in the disciplinary process. Wrote Dougan, 'These hearings give me an impression of a Star Chamber with a bucket of whitewash on one side of the bench and a bed of nails on the other. Most players would prefer an independent tribunal with much wider representation, including the Professional Footballers' Association. Why are players not legally represented at these hearings? They are not always articulate or confident enough to press their own cases. If a player is in danger of being suspended or fined he ought to have legal representation, preferably a solicitor engaged by the PFA.'

His last game before the suspension took effect was against Albion at Molineux on 1 November, Wolves winning thanks to the only goal of the game, by Mike O'Grady 13 minutes from time. Ray Matts reported in the *Express & Star* that 'all eyes were on the Irish international as he turned on enough talented showmanship to keep his fans and the club counting the days till his eight-week ban ends.' During his absence Paul Walker, Bertie Lutton, Les Wilson and Frank Munro wore the number-nine shirt.

Dougan's return to action came in a 3–0 third-round FA Cup defeat at Burnley, which Wolves promptly avenged a week later by winning 3–1 at Turf Moor in the league. However, the comeback was brief and by coincidence was ended in the return League game with Everton at Goodison. In a game Wolves lost 1–0, Dougan was hurt in a 59th-minute clash with England full-back Keith Newton. He was so badly injured that he had to be carried off on a stretcher and was checked in to the Queen Victoria Nursing Institution in Wolverhampton and three days later needed an operation on his cheekbone. It was a nasty injury and would sideline him for another seven games, an absence which helped widen the gap between him and McGarry.

Dougan had been trying to flick the ball on with his head not realising how close Newton was to him and he had hit the Everton man's head with terrific force. So bad were his injuries that the Everton club doctor wanted him to be admitted to a hospital in Liverpool rather than travel back to Wolverhampton.

However, Dougan wanted to be close to home and travelled back on the Wolves coach in some considerable discomfort. Despite this, McGarry did not speak to him or come to his seat to see how he was feeling. Evidence of how bad was the injury was the fact Dougan needed 30 stitches to the side of his head, under his eye and in his mouth. Doctors had to wire the bone via his mouth. He was in a bad way, but being in the QVNI, as it was known, he was able to have visitors at any time. Team-mates duly came to see him, but not once did McGarry call to check on him. The club sent a basket of fruit, which was the usual thing when a player was in hospital, and there were inquiries from chairman John Ireland and assistant secretary Jack Robinson, but nothing from McGarry.

Eventually, Dougan got bored with hospital and discharged himself so he could be at home. He recalled in his book *Doog*, 'I tried to busy myself at home and did not go near the ground. I waited in vain for a phone call from Molineux. No-one rang to inquire about me. I was a forgotten man. This may seem incredible, but this is how it was.'

When Dougan was feeling a bit better and able to go out he and his wife Jutta decided to visit the Sir Tatton Sykes pub in the middle of Wolverhampton for lunch. It was run by one of the town's best-respected landlords, Bill Hancock, whom Dougan had known for many years. As he arrived at the pub who should be on his way out but McGarry with journalist Hugh Jamieson, newly arrived in the Midlands to work for *The Sun*. Dougan felt like hitting the manager, but Jutta calmed him down. Let Dougan take up the story:

'Bill McGarry had a habit when talking of keeping his gaze fixed towards the floor. I can only remember him ever looking at me directly a few times and this wasn't one of them. As we met in the pub entrance he said, "How are you?" looking down at my feet. I should have said "They're all right," meaning my feet, which he appeared to be addressing. I said, "I'm a little better, thank you." That was all. End of conversation. He did not ask when I expected to be back in training or what the doctors had told me. Just a casual "How are you?" that did not carry with it the anxiousness of a manager without his leading goalscorer. The brief encounter destroyed my appetite for lunch. I sat at a table wondering if he was peering from behind the door to make sure I did not order a prawn cocktail!'

The Sir Tatton Sykes was a meeting place not just for Wolves players. Hancock used to love the company of football people and his pub was a popular meeting place for the game's officials and Pressmen. Bobby Thomson, Dougan's Scottish-born team-mate at Villa, confirmed this. "You'd see Noel Cantwell and Malcolm Allison in there, people like that. I should think more transfers were made at that pub than anywhere else in England."

Jamieson would get to know both Dougan and McGarry well during his time in the Midlands. He wrote after Dougan's death in 2007, 'McGarry, a manager of the old school, was always suspicious of having what he termed "a barrack room lawyer" in his dressing room – especially one so outspoken as Dougan! Dougan, for his part, relished the situation, but in the end both helped to fashion a top-four Wolves side, playing an exciting brand of football.'

Dougan's absence from the side led to McGarry giving a debut to a young Warrington-born striker who would eventually have his name for ever linked with that of Dougan. John Richards made his bow in the famous gold shirt in a 3–3 draw with Albion at The Hawthorns on Saturday 28 February 1970. After four games he had to make way for the fit-again Dougan, but at the end of the season the two would be on the field together for the first time and the seeds of a special partnership were sown.

In the game before Dougan's horrendous injury at Goodison Park, Wolves had beaten Ipswich 2–0 at Molineux thanks to goals from Dougan and Hugh Curran. That left Wolves still riding high in the First Division but they would fade dramatically from then on. Not one of their final 13 league games was won and eight of them were lost as Wolves finished 13th. It was their best position since returning to the top flight, but they had looked like finishing far higher.

It would probably have suited fans and players alike if the season had ended there, but Wolves had been chosen to represent England in a new competition, the Anglo-Italian Cup, along with Sheffield Wednesday, Albion, Sunderland, Middlesbrough and Swindon. It was a fairly mean-ingless tournament, but it did enable a little piece of Wolves history in providing the first occasion on which Dougan and Richards were on the pitch together. Having beaten Fiorentina 2–1 at Molineux, Wolves then entertained Lazio on Saturday 9 May 1970. Richards, still only 19, was substitute and came on for Paul Walker. Thus Richards and Dougan were on the field together. How long that was is not recorded in Phil Morgan's match report of Wolves' 1–0 win, thanks to a Mike Bailey goal. Morgan could not be expected to realise the significance of the occasion and was far more concerned with the ill-tempered goings-on which boiled up in the final minutes of the match. The Italians had claimed goalkeeper Phil Parkes had dropped the ball over his line. The Italian referee said no and no doubt understood the expletives used in the protests made heatedly to him, with Giorgio Chinaglia the ringleader. The upshot was Chinaglia's dismissal and a scuffle in the tunnel as he left the field. Police had to step in to calm him down. The referee also made three Wolves bookings – Hugh Curran and Dave Wagstaffe. The latter was booked twice, but in those days it did not mean an automatic sending-off.

A week later, Wolves played the return game with Fiorentina in Florence and Saturday 16 May 1970 was an historic day in Wolves annals. Richards and Dougan started a game together for the first time and both scored. The Italians took the lead through Brazilian Amarildo, but on 38 minutes Richards collected his first senior goal for Wolves. The Italians failed to clear a long ball and Richards was on the spot, as he would be so often in future years, to fire the loose ball home. Hugh Curran put Wolves ahead in the second half and then laid on a goal for Dougan. Richards wore the number-eight shirt and Dougan the number-nine. Richards and Dougan also lined up together five days later when Wolves lost 2–0 to Lazio. At that stage Curran was still thought of as Dougan's strike partner and it would be another season before the name of Richards became synonymous with that of Dougan.

Indeed the battle for the strike roles in Wolves' attack would leave not only Richards sidelined, but Dougan battling for his place as McGarry decided he needed to strengthen that department. Ironically, bearing in mind that Arsenal had been interested in signing Dougan a year earlier, it was to Highbury that McGarry turned. He signed one-time Coventry striker Bobby Gould for £55,000. Still only 24, Gould had lost his place at Arsenal to John Radford as Bertie Mee shaped the side that would in 1970/71 have one of the greatest season's in Arsenal history. However, Dougan had other things on his mind during the summer of 1970 . . .

Chapter Eight

CHAIRMAN AT LAST

FAILURE TO BE APPOINTED chairman of the Professional Footballers' Association in 1967 had rankled with Dougan. He found it exasperating in the extreme. While he had every admiration for PFA secretary Cliff Lloyd, he felt Terry Neill as chairman was far too weak when it came to negotiating with the Football League and the Football Association. The players were battling for some important changes in their working conditions and were doing so against football authorities who still showed a somewhat condescending attitude to them. Dougan believed tough, but respectful, talking was needed and found himself and Lloyd doing most of the negotiating at meetings. He may have enjoyed having his say, but knew that his words did not carry the same authority as they would if they had come from the chair. He desperately wanted power because he genuinely felt he could do a better job than Neill. As he put it in *Doog*, 'Chairmanship of the PFA, I knew, would give me an extra dimension in which to express myself on behalf of the association which had become my way of life. That is why I was so exasperated at times in negotiations and wanted to put words into Terry Neill's mouth.'

Neill's desire to go into management finally allowed Dougan the chance he longed for. Neill was in June 1970 appointed player-manager of Hull City and so would have to give up his PFA appointment. Dougan duly succeeded him and according to his recollection in *Doog* 'the committee agreed unanimously that I should be the next chairman. Although Bobby Charlton, who had the cleanest possible record, even cleaner than Terry Neill's, was on the committee, my name was the only one proposed, in spite of my having been sent off twice only nine months previously.'

Terry Neill remembered the incident differently. In his book, *Revelations of a Football Manager*, Neill wrote, 'At the meeting to choose my successor I wanted to have the thoughts of Bobby Charlton, but because of club commitments Bobby wasn't present. He was a marvellous ambassador and I thought it important to find out if he was interested in the position. Derek Dougan, who clearly wanted the job himself, was most upset. "He's not here, so we can't consider him," he said heatedly. "All right," I said, "I nominate you." And he got the job.'

Bobby Charlton would certainly have been a fine ambassador for the PFA, but Dougan's view was that this was not an ambassadorial role. There was vital business to be done if the players were to gain the sort of freedom that people in other professions enjoyed. It is difficult to argue with Dougan's view. The players had far more chance of bringing about change with the eloquent and determined Dougan as their leader than they would with 'Gentleman Bob' at the helm.

After Dougan's death in 2007, Neill paid him generous tributes but added, "On occasions he and I, shall we say, agreed to disagree, which was not uncommon. We were both from east Belfast and similar backgrounds and we didn't see eye to eye. But my overall thoughts now are that Derek should be remembered for what a great footballer he was – and he was a great footballer."

Neill and Dougan had been allies in the Northern Ireland side during 1969/70 but once again the bid to reach the World Cup finals ended in failure. In the three-country qualifying group, the Irish had begun well with those two wins over Turkey, but the main obstacle were the USSR and they proved too good. Despite the presence of Best in the side, Northern Ireland were held 0–0 in Belfast and without him went down 2–0 before 103,000 fans in Moscow a week before Dougan collected his eight-week suspension. At the end of the season the Irish decline continued as they lost all three Home internationals in an eight-day spell. Dougan played in the first two, a 1–0 home defeat at the hands of the Scots and a 3–1 defeat by England at Wembley before injury ruled him out of the game against Wales in Swansea which the home nation won 1–0.

Rather than PFA politics, Bobby Charlton had more pressing matters to consider that summer – the little matter of the World Cup finals in Mexico and trying to help England retain the trophy they had won so dramatically four years earlier. Northern Ireland may have failed to qualify, but Dougan's profile would be lifted greatly during the tournament thanks to his part in a ground-breaking innovation on ITV – the panel of experts. The brief was to be controversial and they could hardly have had better ingredients for ensuring that was the case than Dougan, Manchester United's Scottish wing-half Pat Crerand and Manchester City's outspoken assistant manager Malcolm Allison. Bob McNab completed the quartet, but it was the three larger-than-life characters who made the panel compulsive viewing. Michael Parkinson, then a columnist with the *Sunday Times*, wrote that Dougan, Crerand and Allison were the most entertaining trio since Wilson, Keppel and Betty. For the uninitiated, Wilson, Keppel and Betty were an old-time music hall act who specialised in doing the sand dance. The television people wanted outspoken views and they got them. Dougan described the German and Italian teams as 'peasants' because they employed a sweeper system and when there was a discussion about the merits of Total Football he brought the panel down to earth with "I keep hearing about total football but what is it? All I know is Total petrol!"

If PFA work and TV work were not enough, Dougan was also carving out a career in local radio with a regular show on Radio Birmingham, the station which later became Radio WM. Cutting his teeth in broadcasting in those days was one Denis MacShane, later to become a Labour MP and a minister in Tony Blair's government

This is how MacShane remembers those days. "When the BBC launched its local radio service for the West Midlands in 1970, Derek and I worked as presenter and producer of a lively Friday programme on sport. As a brand new BBC journalist and apprentice soccer reporter I was in awe of the legendary Doog. A great Wolves striker, a Northern Ireland international, and someone who lifted television coverage of the 1970 World Cup to new heights with his brilliant commentary and cross-chat. Derek single-handedly helped shape a model of getting players to comment on games that has hardly changed since those great days except that he had a brain to match his boots. His wit, incisive comments and a warm Ulster generosity about players made listening to his comments an essential part of watching the World Cup.

"At the BBC he had the best contacts book in the business. A call from Derek and the top stars of football, rugby, cricket, athletics were ready to come and be interviewed and take part in studio discussions. I travelled with him as we went to talk to sports men and women and he loved the business of reporting and trying to dig new information out of people in a way that journalists who have never played high level sport cannot quite manage. He was generous with tickets for matches and everyone at the BBC in Pebble Mill loved to see the lanky fella with the smiling face as he came into the news room and other offices for a chat.

"Derek was more than a player, broadcaster and personality. He began his career when the maximum wage rule still limited players' earnings. By the time I got to know him footballers got their share of the money that their talent earned for the owners of clubs and the broadcasters. Derek took his work as chairman of the PFA very seriously. In addition to my BBC work I was already involved as a trade union activist in political work and Derek and I spent hours talking about how social justice could be delivered to a wider community. It was not just wages. Again and again, Derek urged young players to get a trade or some other qualification so that when their playing days were over they would have an income. He was always going to be a star as a broadcaster, getting involved in business or a much-desired speaker on the after-dinner circuit. But most players did not have his fluency or his all-round business acumen and he worked hard to persuade his fellow professionals to think beyond their days in the game.

"Derek loved political engagement. In 1978, the World Cup was played in Argentina where an evil military junta had seized power and imprisoned thousands of trade unionists, socialists and journalists. I was then president of the National Union of Journalists and Derek came with me to the Argentinian Embassy in London where we handed in a football covered with the names of some of the victims of South American fascism. Derek's politics were not mine, but he understood the need to stand up against injustice and was not afraid to be counted. My life led to work in Europe and then to become an MP and minister. Derek stayed in his beloved Wolverhampton and did not retire to some sunny resort as do so many sports stars. Derek had an energy and love of life that was bigger than most. Not everything he did worked out and not everything he said was thought through. But he engaged with the world and showed how his football genius was located in a much bigger mind and a great generous heart. I can honestly say that the years when I collaborated with Derek Dougan were the warmest, wittiest and very often wisest moments I have to look back on."

As with his books, Dougan needed a helping hand with his broadcasting and was fortunate to have a future radio legend working with him at Radio Birmingham – Tony Butler. Butler eventually pioneered the football phone-in, but in Dougan's early broadcasting days he worked more behind the scenes. "Derek was the first presenter of Radio Birmingham's Friday night sports programme," says Butler, "and I had to write the script for him. You would have thought he would be able to interview people for himself, but he couldn't. I had to write the questions for him. Derek was great if you fed him the questions but as a journalist he was the world's worst. I mean, you could not have sent him out to a football match and asked him to do a live report."

Butler still has fond memories of those pioneering local radio days. "We had a legendary station manager Jack Johnson and I remember once one of

Derek's programmes included a write-in competition. Jack said we'd had a great response and opened a bottle of Champagne to celebrate – he did not need much excuse. At some stage I asked Jack how many letters we'd had and he said, 'About three!' I think I eventually said to Jack one day that I was fed up of having to write scripts for Derek Dougan and he threatened to sack me. Derek thought he needed only to come in, sit there and open his mouth and that was all he had to do.'

While Dougan did not carve out a lengthy radio career, Butler was still broadcasting in 2007, the year he received a Sony Radio Award for lifetime achievement. His nightly football phone-in programme on Radio WM is still compulsive listening .

Dougan in 1970 was truly a national figure, but he had endeared himself to people in and around Wolverhampton, too. Phil Morgan, in the *Wolverhampton Wanderers Football Book*, which was published at the end of the season, tried to sum up the appeal of the man who had achieved something close to cult status. 'Why is the Doog a household name?' asked Morgan. 'Why did an eight-year-old boy on the Low Hill council housing estate in Wolverhampton who had never seen a football match, throw himself on the floor at home and cry when he heard on television that the Doog had been suspended for eight weeks? Why did two teenage girls write to say they would not attend another match at Molineux until he returned? This is the sort of adoration that used to be reserved for film celebrities and is now lavished on pop stars. He has the easy bravado, the genial flamboyance and the extroverted charm of a pop star. But that combination is but a part of his popular appeal.

'Before I met Derek Dougan on his arrival in Wolverhampton from Leicester City, his reputation had preceded him,' continued Morgan. 'Somebody suggested a reputation is what is ascribed by others; character is what belongs to oneself. It was the Doog of the popular image that we knew, the devil-may-care rebel, the striker of attitudes, the upstart who would not play ball if he did not feel like it. And that image, it seemed after getting to know him, was not a distortion but a fabrication. Articulate, generous and considerate, it was impossible to reconcile the image with the man.'

Morgan also mentioned Dougan's charity work. As Wolverhampton chairman of the Mental Health Research Fund, he had raised more than £1,000 to buy a coach for mentally-handicapped children and this work said Morgan was not compensation for self-indulgence but an awareness of his public responsibility. This was how Dougan explained it to him, "A player who has enjoyed success in the game and who is in the public eye owes a great deal to the public. He has to give something back. I don't mean that I feel an impersonal obligation to help various charities. I have a particular interest in those with whom I am associated. I mean that a player who has a personal following ought to look around and see how he can respond straight from his heart. This isn't sentimental; it's what I mean by responsibility. If you just sat back and lapped up all the praise and compliments, wallowed in your fan mail and bought the papers just to see your name in the headlines, you'd be a big-headed fool with an irresponsible outlook on life."

With the enigmatic Danny Hegan added to their squad, Wolves had a fine 1970/71 season, which also saw the emergence of Kenny Hibbitt as a force, after being manager Ronnie Allen's last signing. However, the campaign got off to a poor start with three successive defeats, but a run of six League wins during September and October showed the team were on the up. The possession of three experienced strikers seemed to work to Wolves' advantage, though it was Gould who made the most League appearances with 34 to his credit while Dougan made only 23, four fewer than Hugh Curran. The three contributed between them 45 of the team's 64 League goals and at one stage it looked as though Wolves might have an outside chance of the title, though they eventually finished 13 points behind champions Arsenal. When the sides met at Molineux at the beginning of March, however, Wolves were on 38 points and Arsenal 42. The Gunners won 3–0 and Wolves eventually had to be content with fourth place.

Having to share the striking duties with Gould and Curran led indirectly to Dougan making an unexpected first team appearance at centre-half, the position to which he had always maintained he was best suited. He was named as substitute for the League game against Stoke City at Molineux on Saturday 5 September 1970 and when central defender Frank Munro sustained a thigh injury Dougan got his chance to roll back the years. He was sent on for the second half and acquitted himself well in the middle of defence. As Phil Morgan put it in the *Express & Star*, 'At the interval Munro, his thigh bandaged, dropped out to let Derek Dougan get off the subs bench and have a go at defence with just the right air of aplomb.'

As well as Munro, other central defenders were sidelined. John Holsgrove was unfit and David Woodfield recovering from a cartilage operation. Wolves had a second-round League Cup tie at Oxford United four days after the Stoke game and manager McGarry was cagey about who would play, saying only, "I would not hesitate to use Dougan again at number-five if the occasion arises – and it might very well." The boss must have known what he had in mind and with none of his three recognised centre-halves available he duly gave Dougan a defensive role. There was no fairytale ending to the story as the Second Division side scored an upset win thanks to the game's only goal through Dick Lucas on 16 minutes. Phil Morgan made no criticism of Dougan or anyone else, preferring to note that only goalkeeper Phil Parkes emerged from the game with any credit. Morgan added, 'In their vain effort to save the game, Wolves towards the end thrust Derek Dougan up front after his spell at centre-half and put on Danny Hegan in place of Bobby Gould. But these moves, born of desperation, achieved little.' Dougan was never called upon to play centre-half again. Enough said!

That high League finish in 1970/71 brought the prize of a place in the inaugural UEFA Cup, introduced to replace the Inter Cities Fairs Cup. However, there was some welcome silverware for Dougan when he helped Wolves win the Texaco Cup, a competition for clubs from England, Scotland and Northern Ireland. Remarkably, in the four rounds of this cup, Wolves won every away leg but only one at home. Dougan's only goal in the competition came in the 3–0 victory at Morton in the first leg of their second-round clash. He came on a substitute for Hugh Curran in the first leg of the final when Wolves beat Hearts 3–1 and was in the starting line-up for the return when the Scottish side won 1–0 at Molineux. The semi-final had brought a trip back to Ireland to play Derry City and before the game there was a stay in a Belfast hotel where winger Dave Wagstaffe came face to face with some Dougan bravado.

Belfast during the Troubles could be an unnerving city to visit and Wagstaffe said the players were reassured by Dougan who promised, "Stay by me and you'll be OK." Wagstaffe said he, Dougan and John Holsgrove took a late evening stroll down to one end of the street outside the hotel. Returning to the hotel they debated whether to walk to the other end of the street, but thought better of it as it was getting late. There was then a loud explosion. A bomb had gone off, but when a shaken Wagstaffe pointed out, "That was where we were about to walk." Dougan remained calmness itself and straight-faced said, "I told you, stay by me and you'll be OK."

Dougan's status in his home land had been increased by his taking over the captaincy of Northern Ireland. He could not inspire them to victory, however, in a difficult opening game in the European Nations Cup qualifying group. They were beaten 3–0 by Spain in Seville, but fared much better against the group minnows Cyprus. Dougan was a scorer as the Irish won

3–0 in Nicosia and again when they won 5–0 at Windsor Park. Those goals took his total to eight in 33 internationals. He would play 10 more times for his country but, despite his continued scoring success at club level, would not score again in an international. Although Northern Ireland lost at home to England, Dougan had the satisfaction of leading his team to a rare victory over Scotland, 1–0 at Hampden Park, and a 1–0 home win over Wales.

Hampden saw Dougan in opposition to team-mate Frank Munro for the last 19 minutes when Munro came on for Frank McLintock. There was time enough for Munro, winning his first cap, to show some of his skill at Dougan's expense. He took the ball on his chest on the edge of the Scottish penalty area and then took it past Dougan. Recalled Munro, "He chased me for 15 yards and just hacked me down. I said, 'What are you bloody doing?' and he said, 'There are no friends in this game.' The Doog had the last laugh, though. His shot was going out until it hit John Greig's heel and went into the other corner." The goal, on 14 minutes, was indeed credited to Greig as an own goal.

The trip to play Cyprus was recalled by George Best in his book of anecdotes, *Scoring at Half-time*. He and Dougan were among a group of players who enjoyed a drinking session in a little taverna in Nicosia. This is how Best remembered it: 'The bar owners were nice people and kept our drink flowing. They kept tabs on our spending quite informally by chalking up the number of beers we had on the bar. They were doing this by marking five lines and a sixth line striking through it to signify every sixth drink. It was agreed at the end of the night we'd settle up according to the totals. The Doog had other ideas and each time he went to the toilet he licked his fingers and rubbed one of the boxes away. He thought this was hilarious until one of the waiters noticed and took him to task. Derek was having none of it and denied he had done this and, before we knew it, the excitable little Cypriot and the towering Irishman were rolling around on the floor fighting. Between us, the players and the taverna staff, we managed to break them up, settle the bill and get out before things really turned nasty. Derek is a nice man and, true to form, he went back there alone some hours later to apologise and ended up having a friendly nightcap with all the staff.'

It was a season of great progress and a fine Wolves side was taking shape. Frank Munro had established himself in central defence with John McAlle alongside him and Hibbitt and Jim McCalliog were looking good with Mike Bailey in midfield while Dave Wagstaffe was still parading his special skills on the left wing. Dougan had passed the age of 33 during the campaign and some may have wondered whether his days at Molineux were numbered, especially as Gould and Curran had youth on their side. However, things change quickly in football and Dougan would show the doubters that he was far from being a spent force.

McGarry, for all the antagonism between them, must have rated Dougan as he decided to sell Bobby Gould to West Bromwich Albion very early in the 1971/72 season and also made it clear Hugh Curran no longer figured in his first-team thoughts. Dougan, despite being reinstated as a first- choice striker, got off to a slow start in scoring terms before hitting hat-tricks in successive matches at the end of September. The first three-timer came in a 4–2 home win over Nottingham Forest and the next treble was also at Molineux four days later as Academica Coimbra of Portugal were beaten 4–1 in the second leg of their first-round UEFA Cup tie.

His final goal was special. A long kick from goalkeeper Phil Parkes saw two Academica defenders collide with each other as Dougan pulled away from them and he hit the ball with all he had got. 'I never saw it beat the goalkeeper,' Dougan recalled in *Doog*, 'I knew it was on its way into the net when I turned to receive the acclaim of my team-mates. I had not scored another goal quite like it in my career. It was one of those shots you know is goalbound the moment it leaves your foot.'

Six goals in two games meant Dougan was feeling on top of the world, but his remarkable performance merely served to highlight the bizarre man-management of McGarry. 'Afterwards there was no word of compliment from Bill McGarry; not a single word.' wrote Dougan in 1980 Strangely, over 20 years later when being interviewed for the book *Running With Wolves*, Dougan remembered it differently. "That was the only time in eight years he said to me 'Well done'," Dougan told author Peter Lansley.

Before his hat-trick double, Dougan had again done battle at international level with the USSR in the European Nations Cup, as the European Championship was then still known. Northern Ireland did well in losing only 1–0 and that through a penalty by Muntian. The return in Belfast three weeks later saw the Irish held 1–1 and so fail to make qualification. Dougan had an unusual strike partner in that match – Terry Neill, who switched from central defence. Neill remembers the game well. "Doog and I played as twin centre-forwards and it was an education to play with him up there, to realise just what a great player he was."

As well as being reluctant to give praise to Dougan, McGarry would exert his authority in other ways. The ban on players using the general office at Molineux caused problems for Dougan, in the days well before mobile phones, when he needed to make an urgent call to PFA secretary

Cliff Lloyd. That left him with a dilemma as players late for the 10am start to training were fined and Dougan knew that Lloyd did not arrive at the PFA office in Manchester until 9.45. There would have been no problem if he had been allowed to use the office phone at Molineux. He rang McGarry and told him he needed to speak to Lloyd on an urgent matter which could not wait until after training. McGarry showed no sympathy for his problem, merely reminding Dougan of the consequences of being late for training. Dougan's solution was to hurry to the ground, get changed and then use a public telephone at the nearby Wolves social club.

There was no explanation as to why McGarry would not allow him to be a few minutes late for training. As far as Dougan could see it was just a case of the manager showing him who was boss and being bloody-minded. It merely served to lessen even further what little respect Dougan retained for McGarry. Apart from skipper Mike Bailey, McGarry treated the other players the same way as he did Dougan and in a perverse way it probably helped squad morale in that they were all united in their dislike of him. To his credit, Dougan never allowed the poor relationship to affect his displays on the field.

Without doubt, Dougan had become a cult figure in Wolverhampton. The word 'Doog' was prominent among graffiti around the town in places like the ring road pedestrian subway. Even in the glory days of the 1950s no one player had been singled out for such adulation. As John McAlle put it many years later, "On the pitch his rapport with the supporters was as special as it was instant. He just had that way about him – real charisma. I can close my eyes now and see him perhaps missing a chance and looking at the North Bank with his arms raised as if to say 'I can't believe I missed that one.' And they loved him for it."

Chapter Nine

EUROPEAN GOAL KING

THE UEFA CUP CAMPAIGN WAS a marvellous one for Wolves in general and Dougan in particular. He scored in the first four games, having begun with a goal in the first leg of the Academica tie when Wolves won 3–0 in Portugal. The second round saw Wolves beat Dutch side Den Haag 3–1 away and then 4–1 at home with a Dougan goal in each leg, the strike in the Molineux game being the only one by a Wolves player. The Dutch managed to concede three own goals.

For a third successive round Wolves had to play the first leg away and for a third time they won on opposition territory. This time time it was John Richards who scored, the only goal of the game against Carl Zeiss Jena in East Germany. Dougan scored twice when Jena were beaten 3–0 at Molineux and so had a personal tally of eight goals in just six European games. That set up Wolves' most difficult task so far when they were drawn against Italian giants Juventus. By that stage an injury to Mike Bailey had let the enigmatic Danny Hegan into the team. He had made the most of his chance to play in central midfield. In Dougan's eyes, Hegan, a colleague of his in the Northern Ireland side, should have retained the place in midfield at Bailey's expense the following season. However, McGarry showed loyalty to Bailey, his skipper, and Dougan felt it misplaced. Hegan was always prone to go off the rails and to turn up late for training after a drinking binge, but Dougan felt he might have changed his ways if he had been given the incentive of a permanent place in midfield.

For the latter half of that 1971/72 season and the UEFA Cup closing stages, Hegan was, like Dougan, in top form and nullified the Italian club's dangerman, Helmut Haller. In Italy, Wolves earned a 1–1 draw. Juventus and Wales legend John Charles had been asked to accompany Wolves as an ambassador and interpreter and it proved a master stroke. Not only did he ensure Wolves were welcomed everywhere they went in Turin, he also gave them valuable advice. After the game he correctly forecast that after being held at home, Juventus were as good as beaten in the tie. He said most of the Italian side's players would have no appetite for the match in Wolverhampton and so it proved as Wolves won 2–1 with Hegan and Dougan hitting the goals. It was the sort of win to rank alongside the epic Molineux floodlit friendly wins over Honved, Spartak and Real Madrid.

A wonderful adventure continued with semi-final success over Ferencvaros, when yet again Wolves had to play away in the first leg. They drew 2–2 in Hungary and won the return leg 2–1, goalkeeper Phil Parkes stealing the limelight with a penalty save in both games. The reward for Dougan and Co should have been a final against one of Europe's giants. Instead they had to face Tottenham, who were probably equally disappointed at having to face English opposition. It was the first and, so far, only time two English clubs had met in the final of a major European competition. In those days it was played over two legs. A one-off game at a neutral venue would probably have given it more impact.

Spurs had also put out one of Italy's top teams, AC Milan, in the semi-final and maybe if the Italians had triumphed they would have been more glamorous opposition in the eyes of Wolves fans. A big centre-forward would dominate the first leg of the final, but it was not Dougan. Spurs' England star Martin Chivers struck twice as the Londoners won 2–1 at Molineux. Thanks to a Dave Wagstaffe goal to cancel out one by Alan Mullery, Wolves drew 1–1 at White Hart Lane where Dougan was replaced by Hugh Curran late in the game, but try as they might they could not find the equalising goal and Spurs lifted the trophy 3-2 on aggregate.

Teams in the final:
Wolves: Parkes; Shaw, Taylor, Hegan, Munro, McAlle, McCalliog, Hibbitt, Richards, Dougan, Wagstaffe. In the second leg Bailey and Curran came on as subs for Hegan and Dougan.
First leg scorer: McCalliog, second leg, Wagstaffe.
Tottenham: Jennings; Kinnear, Knowles, Mullery, England, Beal, Gilzean, Perryman, Chivers, Peters, Coates.
First leg scorer: Chivers 2, second leg, Mullery.
Molineux attendance: 38,362, White Hart Lane, 54,303.

Yet another example of McGarry's iron rule came after the second leg. Hugh Curran had not got on the coach as it set off, but it was quickly realised and driver Sid Kipping was ready to turn back as he was only about 20 minutes into the homeward journey. McGarry told him to drive on and Curran could make his own way back. Dougan found this succession of petty incidents difficult to accept, but rather than let them get him down, Dougan's remedy was to throw himself more and more into the community. He had grown to like Wolverhampton and its people. He was busy helping raise money for the Mental Health Research Fund, much in demand for other fund-raising events as well as being invited to speak at local clubs or appear on sports forums. There was also his TV and radio work, all of which helped him put out of his mind the eccentricities of McGarry's reign.

So Wolves had missed out on a major honour, but the 1971/72 season had been a memorable one for Dougan. He was top League scorer for the club with 15 goals, two more than John Richards. More significant than the goals each had scored was the forging of a partnership which would continue to flourish in the next two seasons. They were like the sorcerer and his apprentice, Dougan the wily old pro and Richards a natural goalscorer who benefited from Dougan's knock-downs and lay-offs. It took nine games for Richards to collect his first League goals of the season. He hit both when Wolves beat Derby County 2–1 at Molineux on Saturday 13 November 1971. A week later came another of those matches which have become etched on the memories of all Wolves fans who saw it. Double holders Arsenal were the visitors to Molineux and looked like taking the points when Ray Kennedy gave them a 1–0 half-time lead. On a snowy winter's day Wolves turned things around gloriously in the second half, Dougan scoring twice as they ran out 5–1 winners. Fortunately the game was featured on the BBC's *Match of the Day* programme and a so fans elsewhere around the country could see for themselves the heights Wolves were then reaching. That game was the second in a ten-match unbeaten league run. Alas, Wolves faded in the later weeks of the season, eventually finishing ninth, with Dougan scoring only twice in his final 15 League outings. The second of those goals came in Wolves' final First Division fixture and what a match that was!

Five days after Wolves had played the home leg of their UEFA Cup final, they had to face Leeds. It was Monday 8 May 1972. This was the great Leeds side, which under manager Don Revie were on the verge of glory. Two days earlier, they had won the FA Cup by beating Arsenal at Wembley and a win at Molineux would make them First Division champions and only the fifth side ever to do the Double. It seemed unfair to ask them to play just two days after a Wembley final, but they were favourites to win at Molineux as Wolves' thoughts were very much on the second leg of their European final. Professional pride would still have made Wanderers do their utmost to deprive Leeds of this place in football history in any case, but they were given extra reason to play above themselves by murky goings-on in the days leading up to the game.

Allegations that offers were made to Wolves players to enable Leeds to win are well documented. There are members of the team who will always steadfastly maintain that they were asked directly to do things to help Leeds' cause. And it was not the only occasion that these sordid accusations were levelled at a Don Revie team. The evidence is credible, if furiously denied by Leeds. Word of the approaches was relayed to Bill McGarry and the manager decided he needed to address the players on the morning of the match. He called them out to the centre circle of the Molineux pitch as if he feared the dressing room might have been bugged. Then he told them in no uncertain terms that if any player gave the impression of not giving 100 per cent that night, they would never play for Wolves again.

Whether it was McGarry's threat or the insult to their professional integrity, but something fired up Wolves on a memorable evening when Munro and Dougan gave Wolves a 2–0 lead with a Billy Bremner goal the only Leeds reply. A crowd of 53,379 saw the match with thousands locked outside. Wolves' win meant Brian Clough, another who had enjoyed with Dougan sudden fame as a TV pundit during the World Cup summer of 1970, learned while sunning himself in the Scilly Isles that his Derby County side had thus became First Division champions. For not only had Leeds lost, but Liverpool, who could also have taken the title, failed to beat Arsenal at Highbury on the same night.

Wolves skipper Mike Bailey, speaking after Dougan's death in 2007, rated that season, and the UEFA Cup campaign in particular, as being Dougan's best time as a player. "He really came alive in those European games. He and John Richards were a real handful and at times defenders would be watching Derek which allowed Richie the chance to score and vice versa. He was very fit and took his training very seriously. He could run all day." Full-back Derek Parkin reckoned the Dougan-Richards partnership was probably the best in Europe at that time. "They frightened the life out of people, not just in England but abroad, too."

Dougan had no time to dwell on Wolves' failure to beat Spurs in the UEFA final, for three days later the Home International Championship began. Northern Ireland disappointingly lost 2–0 at home to Scotland in Belfast, but on Wednesday 23 May 1972 came one of the highlights of Dougan's career when he helped his country win 1–0 at Wembley. It was Northern Ireland's first win there for 15 years and Dougan well remembered that previous occasion, having at the time just started his career in

England at Portsmouth. The goal that brought victory came after 33 minutes from Terry Neill. Danny Hegan, showing the sort of form that had so impressed Dougan at Molineux, was one of the Irish stars that night and it was from his corner that goalkeeper Peter Shilton dropped the ball and the ensuing scramble ended with Neill scoring from a few yards out. The Irish kept England at bay to ensure unhappy England debuts for Colin Todd, the Derby defender, and Tony Currie, Sheffield United's mercurial midfielder.

Although Dougan and Hegan could not inspire their country to a home win over Wales in the final match of the Championship – they were held 0–0 in Belfast – they were in great spirits when soon afterwards they flew out to join the Wolves party who were on a lengthy summer tour of North America, Australia and New Zealand. They had played Aberdeen four times in exhibition games, in San Francisco, Seattle, Vancouver and Los Angeles, and the Irish pair teamed up with them for the arduous Australasian section. Dave Wagstaffe remembers Hegan and Dougan arriving to link up with rest of the party. "They were in high spirits after Northern Ireland's win over England, the emphasis being on spirits after a 12-hour flight with the bar open. Danny was even carrying a small Irish flag." The rest of the tour down under was long and gruelling and by the end of it the other Wolves players felt they knew every kick of the game in which Northern Ireland had beaten England.

Although he may not have won any on-field trophies in 1972, Dougan did collect an award outside football. It was evidence of his high profile outside the game that he was named the year's best dressed man by the magazine *Tailor and Cutter*.

Dougan and David Wagstaffe could have been forgiven for thinking Bill McGarry had signed a potential successor when he splashed out £100,000 to get the fast-raiding Steve Kindon from Burnley. Dougan was 34 when the 1972/73 season opened while Waggy would reach 30 during it. Yet both were far from finished and McGarry was merely strengthening his squad in adding a player who could play out wide or as a striker. Kindon's appearances were limited as Wagstaffe showed he was still at his peak, while Dougan spent the season creating a Wolves legend in the shape of his partnership with John Richards.

In their first full season together, the pair had been in the starting line-up on 40 occasions and those matches brought a total of 30 goals between them. Now they would start 48 games together and those would produce 50 goals. In other words it meant that on average every time the two were in harness that season they produced a goal. Of those 50, Dougan would score only 16 and Richards 34. If statistics can ever prove anything it seemed to show the way the pairing functioned, with Dougan the creator and the elegant Richards the finisher. Against Kilmarnock in a Texaco Cup game at Molineux in September each scored twice in a 5–1 win. In the same month a 5–3 home win over Stoke saw Richards hit three goals and Dougan one. When Manchester City visited Molineux in March they accounted for all the home goals in a 5–1 success, Dougan this time grabbing a hat-trick. In that game Wolves' goals came between the 21st and 57th minutes. Dougan opened the scoring and Richards then hit two, Dougan laying on the second. Early in the second half Richards could have had two more. Each time, City's bulky goalkeeper Joe Corrigan turned his shots aside only for Dougan to score from the rebounds.

John Dee wrote in the *Express & Star*, 'Goal power returned to Molineux as Wolves ruthlessly destroyed Manchester City. All five came in a 36-minute spell which saw Wolves produce vintage attacking football that ripped through City's defence with the precision of a surgeon's scalpel.' He added that Dougan was showing a new lease of life, while Richards's control was impeccable and his speed from static positions like that of a greyhound. Dee was merely confirming that this was a strike force made in heaven or, to be more precise, Molineux. For some fans around that time they were one and the same thing! This was the season that really marked down the twin combination as something very special. Wolves fans would not see their like until Steve Bull teamed up with Andy Mutch and, though that pairing produced more goals, Dougan and Richards did the business at the very highest level.

Dougan missed the opening game of the 1972/73 season through injury, but the fourth game of the campaign saw him open his scoring account and reach a notable landmark as Wolves beat West Ham 3–0 at Molineux, His goal was the 200th he had scored in the Football League, making him, proudly, the first Irishman to reach that figure. He was made to wait for his goal, but went close earlier in the game as John Dee reported in the *Express & Star*, 'Dougan, showing the enthusiasm of a teenager, raced through the West Ham defence and fired in a fine shot only to see the ball strike an upright.'

He was not to be denied and Dee described his special moment, 'Sunderland picked up the ball in midfield, slammed a great cross to Dougan's head and there it was, his 200th League goal. The crowd rose to the big Irishman, the North Bank chanted his name until the echoes could be heard miles away and Dougan, the hero of so many games, was over-awed by it all as he saluted his adoring fans in his usual style with arms out-stretched.'

In all, Wolves played 60 matches that season, the main reason being a twin assault on Wembley which ended in double failure and double dismay for Dougan who must have wondered if time was running out for him to make a second cup-final appearance at the famous old stadium and, most important, to make up for the dismal day there with Blackburn in 1960. It all looked comfortable in the League Cup as Orient, Sheffield Wednesday and Bristol Rovers were seen off at Molineux in the first three rounds, Dougan scoring in each game. A place in the semi-finals looked a formality with a fourth home draw and mid-table Second Division side Blackpool the visitors. However, the Seasiders held Wolves 1–1. They must have had visions of an upset, but the replay saw Dougan score the only goal of the match to set up a two-leg semi-final against Tottenham, the side who had ruined their bid for a European trophy the previous season. There was more heartache for Dougan as Spurs won the first leg 2–1 at Molineux and then clinched a final place with a 2–2 draw at White Hart Lane, the game going to extra time. Few would deny that Wolves had the better of the two games, but Dougan's compatriot Pat Jennings stood between them and a place at Wembley. As Dougan reflected, 'The difference between Wolves and Spurs was Pat Jennings. One man does not make a team, but a world-class goal-keeper can seal the success of a good side.' Dougan added ruefully, 'It was by no means a new experience for me to be in a side whose full potential was not grasped at the vital moment.'

One route to Wembley had been ended, but Dougan and Wolves still had the twin towers in their sights thanks to the FA Cup where, just as in the League Cup, they were drawn at home in each of the four rounds on the way to the semi-final. Manchester United, Bristol City and Millwall were sent packing, each 1–0 and then Coventry 2–0 to set up a semi-final clash with Leeds, the side whom Wolves had deprived of the Double a year earlier. Dougan nearly missed the game against Coventry. It was on March 17, St Patrick's Day, but there was no luck of the Irish when during the warm-up a shot from substitute Steve Kindon knocked him out. The kick-off was delayed as Dougan received treatment and Kindon received a verbal blast from a fuming Bill McGarry. The incident is often re-told with a smile by the players from that time. Kenny Hibbitt recalled it in fan Clive Corbett's lovingly-compiled book *Those Were The Days*, saying, 'The fans were chanting "Dougan, Dougan" and he always responded by putting his arms up. As he was doing so, Steve just blasted one and hit him full on the back of the head. He's out cold needing the smelling salts. I remember McGarry racing on ranting.' Derek Parkin told Corbett, 'You can imagine McGarry's reaction, can't you? He went ballistic.' Happily for Kindon, Dougan recovered fully and it was his flick-on which enabled John Richards to open the scoring.

The semi-final was an epic encounter at Maine Road, Wanderers being hampered by not having skipper Mike Bailey fully fit, even though he was able to come on as substitute. There was an early miss by young Barry Powell from a Dougan flick-on and one defensive lapse saw Billy Bremner make Wolves pay. John Richards, who had scored in the three previous rounds, hit a post late in the game. It was little consolation to Dougan that Leeds would go on to be the victims of one of the FA Cup's biggest upsets when they lost to Second Division Sunderland in the final.

Dougan played in two Northern Ireland World Cup qualifying matches during 1972/73, a 3–0 defeat at the hands of Bulgaria in Sofia and a disappointing 1–0 defeat by Cyprus in Nicosia. He may have thought he was still able to cut it at international level at 35, but actions during the summer would make any arguments on that score null and void. Dougan involved himself in organising a special game which is still recalled with fondness in Ireland, but which ultimately finished his international career.

With the Troubles at their height, Dougan first came up with the idea of a pre-season tournament featuring Manchester United, Leeds, Liverpool and Wolves. The quartet all signalled they were willing to take part. If four English football giants were prepared to play in Belfast it would not only lighten the gloom in the province, but also show others that it was a safe place to visit. Dougan's idea seemed a good one, especially as proceeds would be split between two worthwhile sporting projects. One was the proposed new athletics track to be named after Mary Peters, who had won pentathlon gold at the 1972 Munich Olympics, and the other was to help pay for much-needed new floodlights at Windsor Park.

The pre-season tournament plan excited Dougan, but then another proposal came along that had him even more enthusiastic. Enterprising FIFA agent Louis Kilcoyne, whose family were involved with top Southern Ireland club Shamrock Rovers and who was the brother-in-law of Leeds star Johnny Giles, had pulled off a great coup in persuading star studded world champions Brazil to play a match in Dublin as part of their build-up to the 1974 tournament in West Germany. Who would provide the opposition? This was where Dougan's enthusiasm reached new heights. He was skipper of Northern Ireland and Giles was captain of the Republic of Ireland. Why not pick an All-Ireland side to play the Brazilians? It was a dream Dougan had always held and now it could happen. Before his side's trip to Cyprus for that ill-fated World Cup game, the squad met at a hotel in London and Dougan arranged to meet Irish FA president Harry Cavan and secretary Billy Drennan.

He had a double whammy to present to them – the pre-season tournament and a game against the best team in the world on Irish soil. Would they share his enthusiasm? The response surprised him, depressed him and eventually isolated him. He described the moment in his book *The Sash He Never Wore . . . Twenty Five Years On*:

> 'Here in the face of what was for me the greatest moment in my footballing life, I was confronted by a cold and stoney silence. For me the idea of an All-Ireland team created the possibility of contributing to the healing of division, perhaps. Certainly, people would come together and in a society in which neighbours were rent apart by the bigatory and hate of the Irish situation, a temporary sporting unity would be a major achievement. The response of Harry Cavan to the news I brought was precise and well focused. He informed me, tersely, that he would put the discussion to members of the Irish Football Association. Mr Drennan warmly told me he would be in touch and would let me know what was happening. When we met in London that evening I was captain of the Northern Ireland team and had been for four years. We went to Cyprus, played the game, came home and went our separate ways, but the issues raised that night in the hotel have never been discussed again to this day. Neither man came back to me.'

If the pre-season tournament had to be scrapped there was no way Dougan was going to miss out on the chance to field a side against the mighty Brazilians. After much to-ing and fro-ing and being told what they could or could not do, a team chosen from Northern Irish and Republic of Ireland players duly took the field at Lansdowne Road, Dublin on 3 July 1973. They were not allowed to call themselves All-Ireland. They were labelled a 'Shamrock Rovers Select XI.'

The occasion was still further undermined by an instruction that only a Brazilian flag could be flown and only their anthem played before kick-off. This, however, did not stop the St Patrick's Brass and Reed Band playing

A Nation Once Again to the packed 34,000 crowd towards the end of the pre-match proceedings.

Brazil won 4–3 in a match which fully lived up to expectations. They were 4–1 up thanks to goals from Paulo Cesar (two), Jairzinho and Valdomiro. In the final minutes Dougan tapped in a Terry Conroy cross and then his header across goal enabled Conroy to score. It might have been 5–3, but Pat Jennings saved a late penalty from Paulo Cesar, whose spot-kick success had begun the scoring. The teams were entertained well at the Gresham Hotel afterwards and the match passed into history – and so did Dougan's international career.

Years later he reflected, 'After it, I probably had a couple of my best years at Wolves, but I never played for Northern Ireland again. I finished up with 43 appearances, seven short of my second gold watch.' That was a reference to the watch he said he received for being a part of the 1958 squad who reached the World Cup quarter-finals.

Teams on that special occasion:

Shamrock Rovers XI: Jennings (Tottenham), Craig (Newcastle), Mulligan (Crystal Palace), Hunter (Ipswich), Carroll (Birmingham), sub O'Kane (Nottingham Forest) 66, Giles (Leeds), Martin (Manchester United), O'Neill (Nottingham Forest), Conroy (Stoke), sub Dennehy (Nottingham Forest) 88, Dougan (Wolves), Givens (QPR), sub Hamilton (Ipswich) 66.

Brazil: Leao; Ze Maria, Luiz Pereira, Piazza, Marco Antonio, Paulo Cesar, Clodoaldo, Revelinho, Valdomiro, Jairzinho, Dirceu.

It was getting on for five years since Brazil had last conceded three goals in a game – against Yugoslavia in a 3–3 draw in Rio in December 1968 – and the point had been made about the prowess of an all-Ireland side. Recalling the game, Terry Conroy told *Scotland on Sunday*, 'It was at the height of the Troubles and we wanted to come together and make a statement that people at this level could get on.' He added that the players had indeed got on famously.

Cavan, the man who did his best to get the match stopped, informed national manager Terry Neill not to select Dougan again. Many years later Dougan stressed, 'There was no hidden agenda that day, as far as I was concerned. I just felt it would be a unique opportunity for us bearing in mind the Brazil we were facing were the bulk of the 1970 World Cup-winning side. The only three who were missing were Pelé, Gerson and Tostao. I never realised that I would not get to play international football again. Harry Cavan tried to get the match cancelled purely and simply because he felt that it was going to be a precedent, that the north and south was going to come together after that. It was very selfish.'

Dougan went on, 'I was on a TV show with Sir Stanley Rous (president of FIFA) before the Brazil match and he made a beeline for me after it. He said to me, "What are you doing upsetting Cavan? He is on the phone to me constantly trying to get the Irish match called off." Cavan was trying to stop progress, but for a trade unionist and former secretary of a white-collar union, he did very well out of the game and had a tremendous lifestyle. I always believed people who do well out of the game should be more charitable, but he wasn't. He may have changed the name of the team, but what he couldn't do was take away that memorable day. No Irish team before or since has scored three goals against the Brazilians and I don't think any will.'

It was hardly surprising that no Irish team had ever scored three against the Brazilians – the countries had never met! A year after the Shamrock Rovers game, the Republic met Brazil for the first time and were beaten 2–1 in Rio. Brazil beat them 7–0 in 1982, but lost 1–0 in Dublin in 1987 and drew 0–0 there seven years later. Northern Ireland have met Brazil only once, the South Americans winning 3–0 in the 1986 World Cup.

An all-Ireland team would remain a Dougan dream and his 1981 book *How Not To Run Football* had him asserting that the lack of such may have contributed to George Best's waywardness. Wrote Dougan, 'If there had been an all-Ireland side I am sure that George would not have gone off the rails. His erratic behaviour was sometimes caused by frustration. Here was an absolute genius without the international showcase he needed. Restricted by nationality, he remained an outsider, never able to reach the centre of the top international footballing events.' It was a controversial opinion, almost as controversial as the book's cover which showed an image of Best nailed, Christ-like, to a cross.

Dougan's exile from the Northern Ireland side began even before the game against Brazil and one effect of it was to deny him what would have been a special moment – playing in same international as his partner-in-goals John Richards. The continuing troubles in the province meant the Irish team's home game against England in the Home International Championship was played at Goodison Park, Liverpool. Sir Alf Ramsey gave Richards his first and – disgracefully, in the eyes of Wolves fans – only full cap, playing out of position wide on the wing. If it had not been for the activities which had incurred the displeasure of the Irish FA, Dougan would surely have been playing opposite his Wolves team-mate. International football had ended for both men but at least Dougan had 43 caps to his name.

It was quite a summer for Dougan as he had also spent six weeks in South Africa as a guest player for Arcadia Shepherds in Pretoria. It was there he spotted a young English centre-forward whose potential he rated highly. So much so that when he returned home he recommended that Bill McGarry give the player a trial with Wolves. After failing to break through with several English clubs he had gone to South Africa to work as an electrician and play part-time football. Dougan saw in him the type of player who might one day take over from him as spearhead of the Wolves attack. His name? Peter Withe. Dougan's judgement was spot on and Withe went on to achieve great things, though not with Wolves.

McGarry told Dougan after a few weeks' trial that he did not think Withe had what it took and he would not be signing him. Before he was told the news Withe played in a practice match between the first team and the reserves, which the latter won 4–0, Withe scoring all the goals. That changed McGarry's mind and he did sign him, but never really rated him nor gave him an extended chance. Withe would leave Molineux only to win championship medals with Nottingham Forest and Aston Villa, with whom he also scored the winning goal in the European Cup final. He also won 11 England caps. Not for the first time, Dougan was proved right and McGarry wrong.

Semi-final defeat at the hands of Leeds did enable Wolves to take part in an unusual match at the beginning of the 1973/74 season against Arsenal, the other beaten semi-finalists, to decide who had officially finished third in the FA Cup, as if that would be consolation to either side! The match at Highbury was won 3–1 by Wolves with an in-form Dougan giving home centre-half Jeff Blockley a difficult afternoon and scoring two goals. He might have expected to be skipper in that game with Mike Bailey absent, but Bill McGarry gave that honour to Danny Hegan, the player who had caused him so much trouble by missing training frequently and then disappearing from his home for days at a time. The hope was it might get Hegan to knuckle down. It was a good idea, but Hegan did not mend his ways and after a few months he would be transferred to Sunderland. It meant that Hegan's English career had turned full circle – he was signed by Sunderland in September 1961 for £4,000 from Albion Rovers as an 18-year-old, but did not break into the first team before moving to Ipswich.

Soon after the match with Arsenal Dougan wondered whether he would be next to be on his way from Molineux and he put it down to more bloody-mindedness by the manager. McGarry ordered the players back for extra training on the Thursday afternoon, something senior players only did when they were recovering from an injury. The trouble was that Dougan had agreed to appear at a local store as part of a promotional campaign. A large advert in the *Express & Star* on the Wednesday night invited youngsters to meet Dougan at Owen-Owen in the town's Mander Centre. He would be promoting some boys' shoes called 'Clarks Attackers' and the ad proclaimed it 'a terrific opportunity to get autographs, talk to a star footballer and look at our exciting shoes.' Dougan was probably the best known person in Wolverhampton at the time and felt he could not possibly disappoint the fans who would turn up to see him, not to mention letting down the store. Dougan decided to skip the extra training and fulfil his obligations, even though he was fully aware it could mean him parting company with Wolves. It would be a mighty wrench, but he had made up his mind the time had come.

Before going to Molineux on Friday morning he rang assistant secretary Jack Robinson and told him to get his insurance cards ready for him. He told Robinson the reason – that he had finally had enough of McGarry. He knew the assistant secretary was duty bound to tell the manager. When he arrived at the ground Dougan actually put his boots into a bag, collected his post and even said cheerio to the players. This was it. Goodbye Wolves.

McGarry asked "What's your problem?" and when Dougan told him he thought it was incredible asking him back for training when he knew he had an important prior commitment, McGarry pleaded innocence. Although Dougan did not believe him, McGarry insisted the extra training had nothing to do with Dougan's high profile appearance at Owen-Owen. Dougan expected to be fined for missing training, but he was not. He walked from the office the incident closed. Back in the dressing room he remarked to Dave Wagstaffe, "I must have set a record for the shortest retirement in the history of the game – 20 minutes!"

Although there was no doubting Dougan's determination to walk out if the confrontation had gone the other way he would in seven months' time be thanking his lucky stars that he was still wearing the famous gold and black.

Two goals at Highbury not only showed the Arsenal hierarchy what they had missed when that proposed deal fell through a few years earlier, but it gave Dougan a flying start to the season. He scored twice more in the opening League game, a 3–1 home win over Norwich City and also netted in each of the next three. Five games and seven goals, he had never had a scoring spell like it in all his years at Molineux. In stark contrast his strike partner John Richards was having one of those sequencess that hit all goalscorers when chance after chance goes begging.

Richards, who had hit 36 goals the previous season, was without a goal in his opening eight matches and Dougan was angry that manager McGarry was not reassuring the young player and giving him some encouragement. It came to a head when Wolves opened their UEFA Cup campaign, made possible by their fifth-place finish the season before. The match was against Belenenses in Portugal and there was speculation in newspapers that Richards might be dropped. McGarry had done nothing to reassure Richards, and Dougan believed this was the manager's misguided way of trying to motivate the striker. That tactic might work with some players, but not, Dougan believed, Richards and it all came to a head on the morning of the game. When Dougan went down to breakfast he deliberately ignored the manager and chose not to sit at one of the vacant places on McGarry's table. When the boss asked Dougan why he had sat by himself, that was his chance to let off steam. According to Dougan, in his book *Doog*, this is what he said:

'I don't agree with the way you are treating John Richards. His confidence is sagging and I'm doing my best to keep him going. If he's out it will affect me. Instead of the goals being shared, I'm getting them at the moment. But it could easily be the other way round. You're taking it out on him, so I'm taking it out on you. He's too nice a kid to be treated like this. He's never given you a problem on or off the pitch all the time he's been at the club.'

Apart perhaps from skipper Mike Bailey, only Dougan would have dared speak to McGarry in that tone. After his pre-season showdown it was clear that Dougan was not prepared to bite his tongue any more. Whether Dougan's words had any effect or whether the manager had planned to play Richards anyway, Dougan never found out. However, Richards did play and duly ended his drought by scoring the opening goal in Wolves' 2–0 win that evening. Almost inevitably, Dougan scored the other one. Richards untypically lost control later in the game. He got involved in a rumpus with a Portuguese player, aimed a blow at him and was sent off.

If McGarry resented Dougan's fame and popularity, he was no doubt annoyed even more when Eamonn Andrews greeted Dougan with his famous big red book and announced "This is Your Life". This episode went out early in 1974 and was yet more evidence that Dougan was a personality of national stature. Even then the manager had tried to use the pogramme to turn Dougan's team-mates against him. They travelled to London for a midweek game and when told they would have to stay overnight, the players were far from happy. They usually travelled back straight away after a match in the capital, even a night one. When skipper Mike Bailey was delegated to ask if McGarry would scrap the overnight stay, the boss surprisingly agreed. So they duly made the coach trip home only to be told by the manager when they arrived in Wolverhampton that they must be at the ground smartly dressed at 9.30 next morning. The following day they arrived at Molineux and were taken by coach back to London, McGarry explaining that they were returning there to take part in Dougan's special programme. Had McGarry explained the real reason for the planned overnight stay there would have been no objection from the players. The whole business appeared to be motivated by McGarry's dislike of Dougan's celebrity status plus a desire to drive a wedge between the Irishman and the rest of the squad. If the latter was the case, he failed miserably.

When the programme had been broadcast, this was how Dougan's good friend Ray Seaton reviewed it in the *Express & Star*, 'Derek Dougan was so surprised when he stepped out of a taxi to be confronted by Eamonn Andrews and then the Uncle Tom Cobleys of football that for once he was almost speechless. Thames TV cameramen followed him in action, concentrating on him pulling up his socks. The cameramen should have pulled up their own socks and showed him at his best, heading goals or laying them on for John Richards.'

While it said much of Dougan's profile to be included among the long-running programme's subjects, Seaton was clearly not impressed.

Chapter Ten

WEMBLEY GLORY DAY

LEEDS, FOR A SECOND SEASON RUNNING, ended Wolves' FA Cup campaign, though this time in the third round. However by then, early 1974, Wolves had their sights firmly set on Wembley via the League Cup. They were in the semi-final and favourites to beat Norwich. The roles were now back to normal up front with Dougan the provider and Richards the more frequent scorer. It was Richards who had hit the only goal of the game when Liverpool were beaten 1–0 at Molineux in a game that had to be played on a midweek afternoon because of power restrictions during the miners' strike. And it was Richards who struck in the first leg of the semi-final as Wolves drew 1–1 at Carrow Road. He was on target again as Wolves completed the job with a 2–1 win at Molineux. At last! Dougan was back in a Wembley cup final and at 36 he knew this was almost certainly his last chance to win a major trophy.

Unlike his appearance at the home of English football 14 years earlier everything was right this time for the veteran Irishman. He was fully fit, he was content with his life and happy in the town whose club he was playing for. There was a similarity to the 1960 game in that he was playing for the underdogs even though Manchester City were not quite the power they had been a few seasons previously. With Francis Lee, Colin Bell, Rodney Marsh, Mike Summerbee and the veteran Denis Law in their line-up they would, most experts thought, have too much class and experience for Wolves. There was also the fact that Wolves' regular goalkeeper Phil Parkes had been injured since the semi-final and Gary Pierce, on his 23rd birthday, would be in goal in only his 14th first-team game for the club. As well as Pierce, Wolves had inexperience in the shape of full-back Geoff Palmer and midfielder Alan Sunderland, but all of them would rise magnificently to the occasion.

A typically sunny cup final day saw Wolves and City, both in tracksuits, walk out side by side. Leading the Manchester team out was manager Ron Saunders, the man whose arrival at Portsmouth had hastened Dougan's departure from Fratton Park. There were formal introductions before kick-off to guest of honour the Duke of Kent and to Alan Hardaker, the Football League secretary, and Bob Lord, the feisty Burnley chairman who was the League's vice-president. It was noticeable that the longest conversations were with Dougan and there was no doubt some good-natured banter between the PFA chairman and two of the Football League's stalwarts.

Many, looking back on the final, which Wolves won 2–1, would have an overriding impression that Dougan did not have a great game. It's true to say he did not have one effort on goal, but on re-watching a video of the match one is struck by the amount of attention City paid to him, usually in the shape of Tommy Booth and Mike Doyle, two no-nonsense defenders. It seems obvious they were aware of the dangers of the Dougan-Richards combination and the need to keep Dougan quiet and thus lessen the danger of his strike partner. This apparent pre-occupation with Dougan probably allowed other Wolves players like Mike Bailey, Alan Sunderland and Kenny Hibbitt a little more freedom

The Dougan danger was evident as early as the ninth minute. A trade-mark Wagstaffe long centre started a spell of pressure as Dougan nodded the ball from the far post only for Alan Sunderland to have his shot blocked. A similar move saw Sunderland's shot half-blocked by Tony Towers and the ball spin in an arc and almost drop under the bar. Sunderland, within minutes, had another shot deflected on to a post. Dougan was then the subject of four fouls in the space of ten minutes. Doyle and Booth bowled him over for the first, then the centre-forward nut-megged Booth on the right of the penalty area only for the City centre-half to stamp on his foot. When Dougan turned up on the left it was full-back Glyn Pardoe who barged into him and the fourth free-kick came when Dougan leaped to try to reach a Frank Munro clearance only for Booth to climb all over him in winning the header.

Ironically, the worst challenge went unpunished four minutes before half-time when Doyle kept on running with arms flailing after Dougan had parted with the ball. The big man had obviously been caught in the face and went to the ground in some pain. This was no forerunner of modern-day play-acting but a genuine injury. Trainer Sammy Chung had to give him attention and when Dougan got to his feet he shook his head vigorously. He was still groggy. This time, however, there was no free-kick.

The tough treatment went on in the second half. Another Booth barge into Dougan had the Irishman rubbing his head and there was a joint tackle on him by Doyle and Towers on the left touchline which brought yet another free-kick as Towers kicked out and caught Dougan again. All this rough stuff was taken with unbelievable restraint by Dougan. In his younger days he may have retaliated but, older and wiser, he no doubt realised that City were ruffled by him and the free-kicks they conceded did them no favours. Although Dougan did not have a dramatic influence on the match he did have a minor role in the build-up to both Wolves goals.

Wolves took the lead just before the break after Dougan had harassed Booth into conceding a throw-in on the left touchline. Wagstaffe threw the ball to Hibbitt who turned it infield to Bailey who then pushed it out to the right for Palmer to set Sunderland free. Sunderland checked and returned the ball to Palmer who crossed towards the back of the City penalty area. John Richards's attempt to make contact failed and the ball reached Hibbitt who was able to hit home a looping volley despite appearing to miscue his shot.

Colin Bell equalised for City on the hour, but Wolves won the match with seven minutes to go. Luck was on their side as McGarry was preparing to substitute Barry Powell for Richards, but then Wagstaffe pulled up and clearly could not carry on. So Richards remained on the pitch and would win the match with a flourish. The build-up was a deep cross from the left by Hibbitt. Dougan, as ever, was there to nod the ball back. It might have come to Sunderland had not Towers intervened to head it behind. Booth headed out Hibbitt's resultant corner only for Bailey to put Sunderland away to the right of the penalty area. His cross hit the heel of Rodney Marsh, deflecting the ball enough to put it straight into the path of Richards. From near the penalty spot he drilled the ball home. Dougan, finally, had some silverware, not a medal but the tankard which went to winners of the trophy.

After collecting his tankard, Dougan gave a hug to chairman John Ireland who was at the front of the royal box. Like other Wolves players, Dougan had the greatest of respect and affection for Ireland. That was why when in charge at Molineux several years later he would make Ireland club president and re-name the Molineux Stand the John Ireland Stand.

In a memorable pose during the on-pitch celebrations after the cup had been lifted and acclaimed by the massed Wanderers supporters Dougan sank to his knees, hands together as if saying a prayer of thanks. A major trophy winner at last.

Dougan told ITV commentator Brian Moore afterwards, "It's been like a fairytale come true. The seven years I've been at Wolverhampton Wanderers – it's been like a honeymoon." He paid tribute to the side's younger players, but thought goalkeeper Gary Pierce had probably been man of the match. "He's had 14 games and he's got a major honour. I've had to wait 17 years." He added that walking out and seeing 100,000 people, a sea of faces, had been a fabulous spectacle. "It gets you inside. You realise that all the sweat, toil and tears is worth it. I would personally soldier on another 17 years if I thought that was at the end of it. It's a wonderful feeling."

Moore asked Dougan if it was the greatest moment of his career and the reply was, "The greatest moment of my career was when I was made chairman of the Professional Footballers' Association four years ago, but, in footballing terms, it makes up for 14 years ago when I was in a losing side. I know what it's like to be on the losing side at Wembley. The other fellas haven't experienced that."

He was also touched by the spirit in which the game had been played. "I was talking to Denis Law and Mike Summerbee and I think they were delighted – really – for us. If only the supporters could see the enthusiasm from Manchester City afterwards for our team – it was a wonderful sight. I really do believe there's an awful lot of good feeling in football among footballers, contrary to what you read in the media." Considering the tough treatment City had meted out to him, these were generous comments indeed.

Teams at Wembley on Saturday 2 March 1974:
Wolves: Pierce; Palmer, Parkin, Bailey, Munro, McAlle, Hibbitt, Sunderland, Richards, Dougan, Wagstaffe (Powell).
Goals: Hibbitt, Richards.
Manchester City: MacRae; Pardoe, Donachie, Doyle, Booth, Towers, Summerbee, Bell, Lee, Law, Marsh. Sub: Carrodus.
Goal: Bell
Referee: E Wallace (Crewe). Attendance: 97,886

Richards's injury would put him out of action for the rest of the season and in the League game a week after Wembley Dougan's new strike partner was the man he had brought over from South Africa – Peter Withe. Both scored in a 3–1 home win over Ipswich. They played a couple more games together, but for the final eight games of the season the twin strikers were Steve Kindon and Alan Sunderland. McGarry was clearly looking to the future and it was Richards and Sunderland who were paired together in the opening six games of 1974/75. The manager eventually had to turn to

Dougan's experience and he played in both legs of the UEFA Cup clash with Porto, when Wolves lost 4–1 away and won 3–1 at home to go out 5–4 on aggregate. Dougan scored in the Molineux leg and three days later he came on as substitute for Kindon and grabbed Wolves' consolation in a 2–1 defeat at Middlesbrough. It would prove to be his last goal for the club.

A Richards injury saw Dougan make one last start towards the end of the season and it looked as though he would be allowed to slip quietly from the scene of his triumphs after confirming he would retire at the end of the campaign. However, several Press reports suggested that it would be wrong to let such a fans' favourite disappear in low-key fashion. Supporters made their views clear, too. McGarry bowed to the pressure and named him as substitute for the final home game of the season – against Leeds on Saturday 26 April 1975. He came on late in the match to a great ovation. He was also granted a testimonial game later that year.

Dougan may not have been wanted at Molineux, but there were reports that he would be welcome at arch rivals West Bromwich Albion – as manager. The Hawthorns club, who were then in the Second Division, had parted company with their boss Don Howe with just a few matches of the season to go. The *Express & Star* reported on 8 April that Dougan's name had been linked to the Albion vacancy, but he told the paper, 'In the past couple of years I have been connected with at least a dozen clubs in respect of vacant managerial posts, but there have been no approaches from The Hawthorns.' However, the story would not go away and national newspapers speculated that Dougan was a popular choice among several Albion players. Two days after their first story, the *Express & Star* had to kill the rumours once more with a back page lead story headlined 'Doog for Albion? It's just not on.' The report written by the paper's Albion reporter Bob Downing said:

'Reports that Derek Dougan is the players' choice to take over the manager's chair at The Hawthorns will not affect the club's decision. This was made clear by chairman Bert Millichip today as he described these reports as complete wild speculation. "The job has been advertised and I have no idea whether Dougan has applied," said Millichip'

Downing finally put the lid on the story when he wrote, 'Despite discussions among the players my information is that Derek Dougan will not be applying for the job.'

If Dougan had been given the top job at The Hawthorns, one of his first moves could well have been to scrap their famous shirts of navy blue and white stripes. He thought them old-fashioned as he explained in his book

Attack, when trying to fathom why the club did not attract larger crowds. 'I don't think the striped jerseys help.' he wrote. 'It is not an attractive strip and prevents players from exuding the indefinable glamour that is always associated with a popular team. Striped jerseys belong to the past. I think West Bromwich could increase attendances by a few thousand simply by adopting plain-coloured jerseys.' It was an interesting theory and he had a point. No team wearing striped shirts have won English football's top division since Sunderland in 1935/36.

As it happened, the Albion job did go to an Irish legend well into his 30s – Johnny Giles, a key figure in Leeds United's rise to prominence during the late 1960s and early 1970s. Dougan was never slow to air his views on the game, but even he would have been hard-pressed to predict the way the 1975/76 season would go. Giles, as player-manager, guided Albion back to the First Division and Wolves were relegated, costing Billy McGarry his job. Dougan may have been sad to see his old club demoted, but would have shed no tears for the departing manager, especially as he received a £32,000 pay-off. That really annoyed Dougan, who still had a year of his contract left when he decided to retire and had been initially offered just four weeks' wages as a pay-off. He reckoned he was entitled to £6,000 in basic salary if he had hung around for that final year. After some haggling, Dougan eventually received £1,000.

A happier event in the 1975/76 season was a last hurrah for Dougan in the shape of a testimonial game at Molineux when Wolves played an International XI. Testimonials are usually carefree and goal-laden, but the game, on 21 October 1975, amazingly ended 0–0. The main thing was that Dougan took centre stage and had the chance to take a proper final bow before a large crowd. The *Express & Star* reported: 'It was a night charged with emotion as 25,658 fans packed into Molineux to say their final farewells to Derek Dougan – their admiration and respect for one of football's great characters being amply mirrored by such a magnificent turnout. Fast-talking, long-striding, goal-scoring Doog took the centre of the stage. But what a pity the final curtain came down on Doog's career without a goal provided by Wolves and an International XI.'

Nearest Dougan came to a scoring goodbye was a header which had 'goal' written all over it before Stoke and England full-back Mike Pejic cleared the ball off the line. Wolves' average home league attendance that season was just below 23,000, so the gate said much for the affection in which Dougan was held.

Teams:

Wolves: Pierce, Palmer, Parkin, Bailey, Munro, McAlle, Hibbitt, Carr, Richards, Dougan, Daley (Farley).

International XI: Shilton (Stoke), sub Parkes (QPR), Gidman (Aston Villa), sub Whitworth (Leicester), Pejic (Stoke), Thomas (QPR), Watson (Manchester City), Dodd (Stoke), Worthington (Leicester), Bell (Manchester City), Gerry Francis (QPR), Bowles (QPR), Hudson (Stoke), sub Kendall (Birmingham).

He may have been out of top-flight football, but Dougan's views on the game still carried weight. He had been asked to write a column in a national newspaper and in those days of strong unions, to do so he needed to be a member of the National Union of Journalists. He duly applied to the Wolverhampton branch of the NUJ and the debate over accepting him was long and sometimes heated, many knowing that his column was almost certainly written with much help from Ray Seaton. The general consensus of opinion among members was that it was better to welcome a new member rather than argue the merits of his work. The fact was a newspaper was willing to employ him and he was willing to become a union member. His application was eventually accepted.

Respected freelance photographer Stewart Perkins, then an *Express & Star* staffman, has been an NUJ official for many years and thought it ironic that the branch meeting had attracted a large attendance for once though the issue that prompted it was trying to STOP someone joining the union. "He squeaked in by a whisker," said Perkins. "The argument was about recently retired footballers doing trained NUJ members out of work, so it was quite a cogent, well-defined one and I think we had a pretty good debate about it."

Dougan, having obtained his 'passport' to be a journalist, could easily have left it at that. Attendance at NUJ branch meetings was always very low, except during industrial disputes and no-one seriously expected Dougan to take an active part. However, once in he made a point of attending meetings, not just attending but often dominating and ensuring meetings lasted much longer than they had previously. It was typical of the man. He loved an audience and here was another, no matter how small.

Perkins recalls, "He was once asked to remove his feet from a table where a female member was sitting and he apologised to the 'little girl' if he was causing her offence. I remember there were newspaper reports at the time that he and Rodney Marsh had fallen out because Rodney thought

Derek was a bit of a male chauvinist. Actually I don't remember him being that offensive. He just used to come along a bit tanked up occasionally. I used to like Derek, though. He used to attract trouble, but he wasn't a bad member. I never quite knew what his politics were. I know that he ensured that he had nothing to do with the successful campaign to stop a freelance photographer in Wolverhampton, Som Raj, from being deported, though I asked him for his help on a few occasions. He was, I think, happy to lend his celebrity status to other worthy causes.

"He always attracted attention though. I remember when my mother decided to do her bit for Sicilian street urchins by being one of the volunteers at our church to give one a home for a few weeks. This little lad called Antonio was allocated a dream break away from the slums of Palermo, and instead spent six weeks on our rough council estate on the outskirts of Birmingham. Anyway, he was a football fanatic, so my brother and I took him to see a Baggies-Villa game at Villa Park. The Doog was playing for Villa then, and had shaved his head. This little lad was immediately transfixed by Derek and couldn't stop talking about him. I think that when he returned to Sicily the only British footballer he remembered was the Doog."

Perkins also tells a pithy tale which highlights the McGarry-Dougan relationship. "I was covering training with the Wolves squad at Dunstall Park racecourse. At one point McGarry became quite animated. He called out to Dave Wagstaffe 'Waggy, I want to do something slightly different now. I don't want you to take it right to the byline. I want you to take it before you get to the area from Mike (Bailey, I think), take a few steps as though you're going to run, and then hit it to the near post. John, you'll be lying deep at first, and I want you to take that ball at speed at the near post. Oh, and Dougan. . . I want YOU to stay out of the fucking way.'"

Dougan did not stay too long out of football at the sharp end. He decided to go into management at non-league Kettering Town and would make waves as he had done at almost every football club he had been with. In doing so he was proving that he was ahead of his time. He was one of the first to realise the potential to clubs of carrying advertising on their shirts.

His predecessor at Kettering was a certain Ron Atkinson, who had left to join Cambridge United. Dougan had strong views on how football should be run and on how the game could make more of its commercial possibilities. One of the first things he did on being made chief executive at Rockingham Road was to start talking to local firm Kettering Tyres about a sponsorship deal. Part of the deal would be the ground-breaking move to have the sponsor's name on the team shirts. It had taken years, after the idea was first suggested, even to have numbers on shirts and the English authorities seemed to have an in-built resistance to change. Shirt sponsorship had been agreed elsewhere in Europe and Dougan knew it would be only a matter of time before it was accepted in England.

Dougan was prepared to take on the Football Association and on Saturday 24 January 1976 Kettering Town ran out on to their home pitch to face Bath City in the Southern League Premier Division with the 'Kettering Tyres' name boldly emblazoned across their shirts. Rather than commend Dougan for his initiative, the FA came down heavily on him and did so quickly. It took only four days for them to inform Dougan that the logo had to come off the shirts. He maintained that though the FA had banned sponsorship nothing was in writing.

The shirts with 'Kettering Tyres' on were never worn again, but Dougan was not going to submit to the FA without a fight. He changed the logo on the shirts to 'Kettering T' and maintained that T stood for 'Town'. He got away with it for two more months before the FA decreed that if they did not remove 'Kettering T' from the shirts they would be fined £1,000. Dougan had to give in. At the height of the dispute Dougan told the Press, "I could finish up in Sing Sing or Strangeways, wherever the food is better. I find it inconceivable that petty-minded bureaucrats have only this to bother about."

Dougan had secured a place in football history and he got backing from Bolton and Derby in officially proposing that shirt sponsorship be allowed and in just over a year the FA accepted the proposal. Not for the first time, Dougan had pointed the way. Ironically, once the FA had agreed to it, Kettering could not get a sponsor for the 1977/78 season, by which time Dougan had left the club. He had ambitious plans to take Kettering forward and these included ground improvements, but he resigned on 23 August 1977 saying he was disheartened by the lack of response to his appeal to support the re-building fund. Dougan's brief flirtation with managership included a return to playing and, to prove – in his own words – that he could still be 'deadly from one yard', he scored the winner against Third Division Oxford United at the Manor Ground in an FA Cup first round replay in November 1976. Kettering then beat Tooting and Mitcham to reach the third round, but were beaten 3–2 at home by Colchester.

While the shirt sponsorship saga had been going on Dougan had something to celebrate as PFA chairman when the chairmen of the 92 Football League clubs agreed in principle that players should have freedom of contract. That was at the annual general meeting of the Football League, but the clubs were not going to concede easily and the negotiations with the PFA dragged on. A year later the League's AGM deferred the whole freedom of contract issue for three months. League secretary Alan Hardaker insisted the door had not been shut. Dougan's comment was, "We have spent 26 months of negotiations to arrive at this position and the game cannot afford to miss the opportunity."

Dougan was backed by a PFA committee of top men equally as determined as he was, notably Gordon Taylor who would become the PFA's chief executive, Terry Venables, later to manage England, and Bristol Rovers forward Bruce Bannister. Add to them the tenacious secretary Cliff Lloyd and it was a combination who would not take 'no' for an answer. When an agreement had finally been reached on how compensation fees would be arrived at in transfer deals the Football League at last agreed to freedom of contract at an extraordinary general meeting in April 1978. Dougan, as with shirt sponsorship, had helped change the face of the game.

Taylor led tributes to Dougan's PFA work after Dougan's death in 2007. "I was proud to have served with him and worked under him." said Taylor. "I had eight years under him as chairman and he led the PFA, along with my predecessor Cliff Lloyd, all through negotiations in establishing a constitution and a collective bargaining agreement, which have stood the test of time. He led as chairman and that brought in the players' right to move in 1978 which was the forerunner of Bosman." Brendon Batson, former PFA deputy chief executive, added, "He was a great champion of players' rights and conditions and was an integral part of current terms players enjoy now. For many years players were treated like cattle. But he was very outspoken in saying that players had an important role to play and they deserved to be free and masters of their own fate."

While freedom of contract was the major achievement of Dougan's PFA work he also helped lift the profile of footballers when he played a leading role in setting up the annual PFA awards. There had been a Footballer of the Year award, voted for by journalists, since 1948, but the new awards would be made by the players themselves. Not only this but the winners would receive their trophies at a gala dinner given even higher profile by television coverage. The first PFA Player of the Year was Norman Hunter of Leeds in 1974, followed by Colin Todd of Derby in 1975 and Pat Jennings of Tottenham in 1976. However, the awards of 1977 saw Andy Gray, then with Villa, voted both Player of the Year and Young Player of the Year. That was not so much a problem as the fact that his team had been held 0–0 by Everton at Wembley in the League Cup final and the replay was four days later.

Gray had injured his ankle at Wembley and rather than stay in London he had returned to Birmingham for treatment. Manager Ron Saunders then put his foot down and said there was no way Gray would be allowed to travel back down to London for the awards ceremony as the journey might aggravate the injury. Gray believed the real reason Saunders said 'no' was to assert his authority, but the player was amazed at Dougan's suggested solution to the situation. Dougan needed the main award winner at the dinner and when he could not make Saunders change his mind he telephoned Gray asking him if he would surrender one of the awards so someone who was able to attend the dinner could collect it in front of the TV cameras. Recalled Gray in his book *Gray Matters*: 'I was staggered. I couldn't believe he'd asked me that. I told him the PFA's members had voted for me and that what he was proposing was a fix purely for the benefit of the TV cameras. It stank and I wanted no part of it.'

Ever resourceful, Dougan then suggested a camera crew go to Gray's home in the Midlands to do a live link from his living room where Villa skipper Chris Nicholl handed over the awards. The saga, if nothing else, showed Dougan's determination to make the PFA awards a success and their Player of the Year accolade is probably now rated more highly than the Footballer of the Year.

Chapter Eleven

WOLVES AT THE DOOR

IT WOULD HARDLY COVER THE COST of an average Championship striker in the modern game, but back in the late 1970s the £1.5million outlay on the new Molineux Stand plunged Wolves into a cash crisis that would lead the club through the most traumatic decade in their history. It was built to replace the crumbling but long-beloved Molineux Street stand and was the brainchild of former chairman Harry Marshall. Far from being a structure that would signal a new era of success for Wolves, it was a millstone that would drain the life of the world famous club and drag them to the brink of extinction. 'Marshall's Folly' as it became known, landed Wolves with a bank loan that they were still struggling to pay off three years after its official opening in 1979. By the summer of 1982 it had triggered off a bitter battle for control of the club. It brought chairman Marshall into direct conflict with most of the town's establishment as he tried to cling on to power.

Roger Hipkiss, a Wolverhampton-born insurance broker, rallied a group of so-called rebel shareholders in a bid to topple Marshall. The well-being and future existence of the club he had supported since he was a boy was Hipkiss's prime motivation. However, he also harboured deep resentment for Marshall, the man who had ousted the previous chairman and lifelong friend John Ireland seven years earlier. Ireland himself had achieved his own notoriety as the chairman who sacked legendary Wolves manager Stan Cullis in 1964. He was also the driving force behind the signing of Dougan when the striker moved to Molineux from Leicester.

Dougan was a peripheral figure in the Hipkiss campaign to overthrow Marshall, but had his own personal reasons for wanting the club to be in new ownership. He was interviewed by Marshall for the vacant manager's job in 1978 and always resented him for the dismissive way he dealt with his applicaton. The Doog later discovered that the job had already been promised to John Barnwell and his interview was, according to the former striker, a farce. "I went through the charade of a boardroom interview because I was under pressure from supporters to apply," Dougan said at the time, "It was a farce really, but I had to honour the fans' expectations."

The prospect of Dougan returning to haunt Marshall loomed when his name was proposed as a replacement Wolves director during the Hipkiss-led revolution. His name was initially meant to appear on a resolution to be put to an extraordinary general meeting held on 8 June 1982, but was removed for fear of adversely affecting the vote to remove Marshall. Dougan had upset sections of the local establishment in the past with his outspoken views and the rebel group could not risk losing their key support. He attended a meeting with Hipkiss and chief shareholders Mitchells and Butlers and the *Express & Star*, who asked that Dougan should leave the discussions and his name be deleted from the resolution or they would withdraw their support.

The EGM was an angry and acrimonious showdown between Marshall, by then an isolated and desperate figure, and his growing army of opponents. Former Aston Villa chairman Doug Ellis and ex-Wolves goalkeeper Malcolm Finlayson were presented as the potential saviours of Wolves and were to be elevated to the board if Marshall and his 80-year-old vice-chairman Wilf Sproson were voted out of office.

There was insubordination from within the Molineux ranks with one director, George Clark, a board member for 15 years, telling the meeting of shareholders, "I will not tolerate Marshall Law any longer. The chairman is no longer going to dictate to me. I have no confidence in him any more. Unless he is removed from the chair Wolves have no chance." However, Marshall came out fighting. He insisted it was only the goodwill generated by himself that was keeping Wolves afloat and that would disappear if he was dislodged as chairman. He claimed Birmingham City headed a queue of creditors who were willing to call in a receiver over the non-payment of the balance of a £350,000 transfer fee for defender Joe Gallagher the previous summer.

The battling chairman painted a grim financial picture, admitting that Wolves had debts of £2 million and were losing £5,000 a week. He depicted Doug Ellis as a "buccaneer who moves from club to club". Marshall then presented his own rescue plan, which involved selling off an office block in the Molineux Stand to Walsall FC chairman Ken Wheldon for £500,000, the sale of Andy Gray to the highest bidder and the possible development of the historic Molineux Hotel into a supermarket. A show of hands at the EGM voted massively in favour of the rebels and for the removal of Marshall, who immediately called for a ballot box vote of all shareholders.

That gave the chairman the majority he needed to stay in power, but it was a close call. He edged the vote by 4,211 to 4,107, but the rebels were not satisfied with the outcome and claimed some 500 votes were invalid.

Marshall by then had recruited the full support of Walsall chief Wheldon, a successful scrap metal dealer, who later bought Birmingham City. When it was hinted that Wheldon could join the Wolves board, Dougan announced he would put together a consortium to take over Walsall!

Events were unfolding at breakneck speed and when the Hipkiss rebels issued a writ to overturn Marshall's ballot box victory, the chairman claimed there was a personal vendetta against him. However, on 16 June Marshall resigned. He claimed he could have answered the accusations, but the whole saga was now preventing the club from operating properly. Doug Ellis became the new chairman with Malcolm Finlayson alongside him, but their tenure was to be short-lived. A fortnight later Ellis asked Lloyds Bank to appoint a receiver after a thorough examination of Wolves' books revealed debts of £2.5million. The bank was owed £1.8million and interest charges alone were costing the club £1,000 a day. In a lengthy statement to supporters Ellis said, "You will appreciate that it is with deep sadness that this course of action had to be taken, but you may rest assured that I and fellow directors will do everything within our power to assist the receiver and to ensure that League football will continue to be played at Molineux if that path is available to the receiver or in accordance with his wishes."

Fortunately there existed then no penalty for the club in terms of points being deducted from their league total, but the stark reality for Wolves was plain and chilling. Unless the receiver could find new owners who would clear the debts to his own satisfaction and provide a guarantee that football could continue to be played, the club would be shut down after 105 years.

The would-be purchasers were soon jockeying for position. Ellis and Finlayson were the early front runners, with Wheldon not far behind and there was also a declaration of interest from Anton Johnson, a nightclub owner, chairman of Rotherham and a self-styled 'King of Clubs.' Ellis later insisted that he was never really interested in buying Wolves, but was merely acting as a 'caretaker' to ensure the club stayed in existence. "I attended a couple of meetings with a man called Sidney Shore who was the regional head of Lloyds Bank," says Ellis. "He was clearly concerned about the plight of Wolves and contacted me because of my experience of running football clubs. I explained to him that I was a Villa man, but I would do everything I could to help. Once Mr Marshall had resigned I got my people thoroughly to investigate the club's finances and I am afraid that it was not a very good situation. Wolves could not continue trading as they were. In the end it was Lloyds Bank who appointed the receiver and I stepped back having completed the job I had been asked to do."

Finlayson, who is still running a successful steel stockholding business in Kingswinford in the West Midlands, pulled out all the stops to keep Wolves alive – as befitted the man who was a fearless goalkeeper who won an FA Cup winners' medal with the club in 1960. "I put £370,000 into the club as a loan before the receiver came in," he revealed. "I did it to give Wolves some breathing space and relieve some of the interest they were paying on the debt. I could have dropped a real clanger there and lost it, but fortunately I had a solicitor who was sensible enough to ring-fence it and make sure I got it back before the receiver was appointed. We did the same thing with around £70,000 that had already been received in advance season ticket sales so that the supporters would not lose out.

"But eventually it got to the stage where Lloyds Bank wanted the whole overdraft paid off by nine o'clock next morning. I was disgusted with them and withdrew all my business interests with them immediately. I worked hard to try to get a successful consortium together. Ken Wheldon approached me, but I knew a bit about his business background and didn't want to go in with him. I tried to get Sir Jack Hayward (Wolves' saviour in later years) but I couldn't persuade him. He seemed to be already involved in some way with the Wheldon group.

"I was aware that Derek Dougan was involved in a consortium, but I wasn't sure who his partners were. I am not sure whether even he did at that particular stage. I had known Derek for a while. When he was a player I would often give his family a lift to matches. Derek was a man with a lot of bonhomie. But there were a lot of layers to him. However many you stripped away you never quite felt you got to the heart of him."

The onus was on the receiver, Alan Adam of Birmingham accountancy firm Peat, Marwick, Mitchell, to find someone with the financial clout and expertise, not just to satisfy the demands of Wolves' creditors but to satisfy the Football League they could run the club effectively. Quietly and secretively, another consortium was gathering momentum. It was put together by Wolverhampton-based Scot, Doug Hope, who had developed successful businesses in car sales and property. He was also a long-time acquaintance of Dougan. In an exclusive interview for this book, Hope has talked for the first time about how he developed the proposal and carried it through to a successful takeover of Wolverhampton Wanderers.

Hope says, "It all started rather obscurely when I put an advert in the local paper, the *Express & Star*, for a Rolls-Royce I had for sale. A guy rang up in response to the advert. His name was Mike Cornwell and he said he had this property for sale near Wolverhampton Ring Road. It was a black and white half-timbered house. I ended up doing a swap deal with him for the property and the Rolls-Royce. His parting shot to me was that if I ever got any property deals that might interest him, I should get in touch. When Wolves were in danger of going out of business I contacted Mike and told him what the situation was. I explained there was a development potential in place for anyone who could save the club from extinction. Otherwise, it was in danger of being sold off piecemeal. He put me in touch with someone called Mike Taylor in Manchester who was friendly with an architect called John Starkey who in turn was involved with a firm called Allied Properties.

"I had already known Derek Dougan socially for a long time. Everyone knew Derek back then. Everyone felt he was their friend. His name immediately came into my mind when I started developing this idea of a takeover of Wolves. I told Derek I knew of this group who were interested in buying the club, but they had no experience of running a football club. For that matter neither had I. I suggested they got together for a chat and that's how he became involved. We had meetings with Mike Taylor, John Starkey and another Allied director Mike Rowland and then eventually we went up to Manchester to meet the principals, the Bhatti Brothers, Mahmud and Akbar. We met them at a very luxurious portakabin. They had a business called Grosvenor Aviations, which was based on a factory estate at Manchester Airport. That was the only time I saw the Bhattis dressed in traditional Arab dress. Derek talked to them at length and told them what he had in mind and what he could do for the football club. He stressed all along that if Wolves could be saved, there was a property deal there and we were looking at the land on the North Bank car park as a possible supermarket site.

"The elder Bhatti was Mahmud – he was only about 30 – and it was strange really because he seemed star-struck by Derek. Needless to say, he was very impressed by what Derek had to say. After we had been there for several hours we went for something to eat at the Four Seasons Restaurant in Wilmslow. Mike Rowland was continually up and down taking phone calls and it was becoming clear we had a positive response to our plans. Derek had demonstrated to them he could run the business successfully and the property side all seemed to stack up. He kept on stressing how 105 years of history and tradition could go to the wall if we were not successful. They took it on board. Rowland, in particular, was very keen on it. But it all had to come together very quickly. The Football League had put a deadline of 30 July on any takeover being accepted by the receiver. In the end we put it together in three to four weeks from a standing start.

"A lot had to be taken on trust. We assumed the Bhattis had got the money. In the end it transpired they put in around £500,000 of their own cash and the rest they borrowed from Lloyds Bank against the assets of the football club. Wolves were the first big club to find themselves in receivership, but the receiver could not act on sentiment alone. It was his job to get the best deal possible for the creditors. So who knows what would have happened if Allied Properties had not had their bid accepted. When Doug Ellis got Lloyds Bank to call in the receiver, I think he expected to get it for a pittance. He thought he would be the only game in town. In the end we paid £2,050,000 for it. Doug offered £1.8 million and Ken Wheldon, apparently with some backing from Sir Jack Hayward, bid £1.65 million.

"What was obvious at the time was there was a lot of huffing and puffing from the majority Wolves shareholders, like Mitchells and Butlers and the *Express & Star* and other local establishment people. There was a lot of gnashing of teeth, but they were not prepared to put in any money. They all cried crocodile tears about the sad plight of Wolves, but wouldn't put their hands in their pockets. Otherwise, the likes of Derek and I, with the backing of Allied Properties, would not have needed to get involved in it.

"On the day of the Football League deadline, Derek and I were ensconced in Peat Marwick's office in Birmingham and going backwards and forwards between there and the Grand Hotel. There were so many hiccups along the way. At one point it was all going to fall apart because someone needed the services of a Liberian company lawyer. Don't ask me why. We eventually tracked one down in New York. Derek was becoming very excited about the thought of being involved with Wolves again. We really had thrown caution to the wind in doing all this. At the last minute, when everything seemed to have been agreed, the Football League said they were still not satisfied. They said they wanted guarantees from the directors that Wolves would be able to fulfil their fixtures. So Derek and I each had to sign £50,000 guarantees to the League. It all finished at 4.57pm on Friday 30 July with three minutes to spare. Victory was ours.

"I wasn't about to gloat, but I could not help but think back to a meeting I had earlier that year in May with Harry Marshall. I was involved with Mike Cornwell in trying to buy the new stand and rent it back to the football club to help them through their financial problems. It was clear the stand had become an albatross to Wolves because of the debt incurred in building it. I walked into the meeting with Marshall and offered my hand to him. He said, 'I am not shaking hands with you. You have been involved in those meetings with Roger Hipkiss.' I let it pass, but obviously he didn't want to do any business with us. It's never a good idea to be arrogant to people you think are irrelevant. They have a habit of popping up to haunt you. Within six months I had done just that. Harry Marshall was in complete denial. He thought it was all going to come out in his favour, even when it was collapsing around his ears. His arrogance cost him in the end. If he had been prepared to negotiate with any of the people who wanted to help the club he would have survived."

Dougan was ecstatic as he took the centre stage at a Press conference to announce the successful takeover. He would become the chairman/chief executive with Hope as vice-chairman and soon he had supporters rallying to the cause as he addressed them with an almost religious fervour. "In the space of a few weeks, a miracle has happened at Molineux," he declared, "and it was worked with only three minutes to spare. That was how close Wolves were to going under and Doug Hope and I are proud to think that we have played our part in securing the well-being of a club which is very close to our hearts. We will welcome with open arms the support of anyone to keep the club on an even keel. The people who have backed the survival of the club have stated their wish to remain anonymous and that is something I hope everyone will respect. All I can say is that they are Mancunians who feel a very close affiliation to Wolves. I will be chairman and chief executive of the new company and for that I will be paid nothing. I will have total control of the club, but I have no desire to influence whoever is in charge of the playing side, whether it is in team selection, training or recruitment of players.

"There has been a lot of speculation already about the future of Andy Gray. I am a great admirer of the qualities he has to offer and nothing would please me more than to see him score 30 or more goals for us in the new season. But if the Manchester United manager Ron Atkinson wants to start negotiating for him I am ready to start talking to him in terms of £1 million. Or if he wants to offer Norman Whiteside, Lou Macari and Garry Birtles plus a cash adjustment in Wolves' favour I would be delighted to hear from him."

Dougan was back – typically full of bluster and bravado and the fans lapped it up . However, soon the rhetoric would have to be supported by financial acumen, solid management and good judgement. Wolves fans were overjoyed that the miracle had been performed and there were more to follow. The Doog would make sure of that. He was their Special One long before a certain Chelsea manager had laid claim to that self-imposed title.

Chapter Twelve

HOW NOT TO RUN FOOTBALL

IN ONE OF HIS MANY autobiographical works, entitled *How Not To Run Football*, Dougan set out his own vision of how the game should be given back to the fans. He wrote, 'Football clubs are reacting to their financial problems as if bitten by a rattlesnake they did not see coming . . . While the present system remains and perpetuates itself, the game will continue to decline, as supporters drift away to find other diversions. Football has failed to keep pace with social change.'

Now Dougan had the chance to turn his ideas into reality. At the forefront of his mind was a strong desire to embrace the local community and make them feel part of their club. He had criticised the building of the Molineux Stand because no provision was made to combine it with a multi-sports and recreation centre for families. As chairman and chief executive of Wolves he now had the position of power to implement these revolutionary plans. He had a captive audience. There was no doubting that. The belief that the Doog would deliver his promises was not an issue as far as Wolves fans were concerned. Hope and expectation were in abundance.

However, what supporters failed to realise was that there was a mountain of practical problems to overcome. Saving the club with three minutes to spare was a monumental achievement. Putting the club back together from the ruins of the summer of '82 needed more money and expertise. Dougan's first decision on Day One of the new regime was an inspired one. By recruiting Eric Woodward as his general manager he brought on board a man of substance and stability who had helped Aston Villa rise from the ashes in the 1960s. With that experience supporting him, the new chairman and chief executive was free to go and meet his people and convince them he could walk on water. He was preaching to the converted when he called a public meeting at Wolverhampton Civic Hall a week after his anointment.

More than 2,000 people greeted their saviour and in return he pledged to deliver them to the Promised Land. "Give us your support for a year and judge us after that," he urged his enthralled audience. "We have taken the first step and created the miracle by keeping Wolves alive. Now it is up to you to take the second step and get behind us. If I don't implement or provide 50 per cent of the things that you have suggested, then I couldn't possibly face you in 12 months' time. I will promise you one thing – if anyone at Wolves is discourteous to you and doesn't treat you with the respect you deserve they won't be working with us very long."

John Ireland was now back in the fold, having returned from self-imposed exile. He made his first appearance on a public platform since he was removed by Harry Marshall and promised he would now start attending matches again as club president. In the months ahead, the Molineux Stand would be renamed the John Ireland Stand – a symbolic gesture and the final removal of the vestiges of Marshall Law. Ireland told the public meeting, "Derek has played some wonderful games and scored some marvellous goals, but he never scored a better one than when he reached an agreement to save the club with three minutes to spare. I would like to put on record my personal appreciation for the tremendous effort these young fellows have put in to keep Wolves alive."

The gathering left the Civic Hall feeling Wolves had been given a fresh start by Dougan and his backers. However, that was not enough for one fan who had bombarded the Doog with a list of questions and demands. "Is there anything else you want?" asked Dougan. "Yes, I would like your tie," replied the North Bank regular. It was an expensive silk Christian Dior tie, but Dougan removed it from his neck and handed it to the startled supporter. Here was a man who seemed ready to give them all they asked for. If only delivering football success was that easy. Dougan would ultimately discover it was not.

There was a distinct shortage of courtesy and respect when it came to dealing with the management team left behind by the previous owners. Manager Ian Greaves and commercial manager Jack Taylor, the former World Cup final referee, were both asked to resign in the first week and when they refused they were sacked. Phil Shaw, the club secretary, lasted slightly longer, but only because he had been on a three-week family holiday in Florida. He was dismissed after serving the club for 33 years.

"It really was an amazing period," recalls Doug Hope. "The whole of the country seemed to be talking about what was happening at Wolves. We even replaced the Falklands War as the main item on some news bulletins. I remember getting home late one night and my then wife Shirley asked me who was this 'millionaire property developer Doug Hope' they had been referring to on television. Derek went through the place like a whirlwind.

He wanted people around him whom he could trust and who would do things the way he wanted. We were all happy to go along with him.

"The number of departures shocked a lot of people. There was even a cartoon in one paper with the caption, 'Dougan sacks himself.' Eric Woodward was the calming and guiding influence which Derek needed and he was also a man of great experience. Derek had very clear ideas. Don't get the idea he didn't know what he was doing. In the past he had run Kettering Town and had been chairman of the PFA for eight years and 12 years on their executive.

"But there were day-to-day issues to be resolved. We did not have a physio or a club doctor. A guy called Dennis Conyerd wandered in off the street, having read an item in the local paper, and announced to us he was a physio. Derek simply said to him. 'When can you start?' He proved to be a very popular guy in the dressing room. Then we recruited Doctor Bill Tweddle, a wonderful John Cleese-type character, who was another great addition to the team. We even had the old coach driver from Derek's playing days, Sid Kipping, back on board. He used to do all the odd jobs, like making Derek copious amounts of tea and toast. Right down to old Reg, the doorman, there was a great deal of togetherness and optimism. There was a feeling that we had our backs to the wall, but that made us all the more determined to succeed."

The whirlwind had left a trail of debris in its wake, but Dougan continued at a frantic pace. His most important appointment was a team manager to replace Ian Greaves. His successor surprised most Wolves fans. When he disappeared from Molineux one afternoon, accompanied by Doug Hope, he was seen heading towards Shropshire and it was widely assumed he was to offer the job to Shrewsbury Town manager Graham Turner, who eventually became manager many years later when the club had plunged into the Fourth Division. However, on 4 August Graham Hawkins was named as new Wolves boss. The newspapers next day greeted the appointment with the headline 'Graham Who?', but diehard fans knew who Hawkins was. He was a playing colleague of Dougan's back in the '60s before leaving to have a successful career with Preston and Blackburn. He had cut his managerial teeth as assistant at Port Vale and more recently alongside Turner at the Gay Meadow.

Hawkins faced the most difficult task of all. He had to assemble a squad in time for the season's kick-off against Blackburn Rovers on 28 August. He had very little to work with apart from disillusioned seasoned professionals like Andy Gray and Joe Gallagher, loyal stalwarts like Mel Eves, Wayne

Clarke and Geoff Palmer and a bunch of enthusiastic, but totally untried and untested youngsters. If saving the club was a miracle, the job Hawkins did in steering Wolves to promotion that season was more akin to discovering the Holy Grail and the meaning of life put together. It is an achievement often forgotten in the history of the club. He began by putting out a team on the opening day which included four teenage debutants, Ian Cartwright, Paul Butler, Billy Livingstone and David Wintersgill, who was a 16-year-old straight from school.

After Dougan had pulled off another incredible public relations coup by spending the whole game watching from the terraces among the hard core fans, Wolves beat Blackburn 2–1 with both goals from Eves. It triggered a run of nine unbeaten games and suddenly the prospect of promotion from the Second Division was being whispered. Despite the hint of big investment on new players from the Bhattis, all Hawkins had to spend was £141,000 with which he astutely acquired goalkeeper John Burridge from QPR, defender Alan Dodd from Stoke City and, towards the end of the campaign, goalscoring midfielder Billy Kellock from Luton.

Hawkins had been in the thick of pre-season training at Shrewsbury when he got a phone call out of the blue from Dougan. He was blissfully unaware of the events at his former club and was happy in his role as number-two to Turner.

"I hadn't followed any of what was going on at Molineux when Derek got in touch with me," recalls Hawkins. "I hadn't spoken to him for such a long time and wondered what he wanted me for. We were old team-mates and I shared a room with him when we went out to America to play as the Los Angeles Wolves. I think I was the only player who was prepared to put up with all of his talking.

"Anyway, when he rang me, he asked me if I wanted to go and work for him. I said, 'Where and what as?' I honestly didn't know he had taken over at Wolves. When he told me he wanted me as his manager, it was quite a shock. The answer was obviously 'yes'. I was thrilled and honoured. I was full of pride for myself and my family who all grew up as Wolves fans. They had always been my team. I had stood and watched them as a kid on the South Bank when I would be one of the first through the turnstiles every Saturday.

"When the newspaper headlines came out next day asking 'Graham Who?' it didn't bother me. I wasn't the best-paid manager in the game and didn't even negotiate a bonus for winning promotion. That didn't concern me either. I was just delighted to be given the job. All I asked was that I would be able to get on with the job without any interference from Derek or anyone else. I had not had the experience of working with players like Andy Gray and John Richards, but I was straight and fair with them and respected what they had achieved in the game. I suppose I was a bit naïve, but I was full of enthusiasm and adrenaline and that made up for the fact that there was not much money for players.

"We had to throw the young lads in and they ran their socks off for us. I don't think it did too much for their careers in the long term, especially the young lad Wintersgill, who was only 16 when he made his debut. I don't think it was fair on him to throw him in at that age, but I didn't have a lot of choice. As for me, I didn't fear anything. I was on such a high.

"Playing that first game of the season against one of my former clubs Blackburn was a good thing because I knew a fair bit about them and what their weaknesses might be. I pointed out a few things in my team talk which turned out to be spot on and led to us scoring two goals through Mel Eves. I think that helped me to establish myself with the players, though to be fair we could have lost by ten goals that day.

"Derek was fine to work for. He was very much a technical director and that was way ahead of its time. He never interfered. We would get together for a scotch on a Friday afternoon and I would tell him what my team was for the next day. He would ask me why I was doing this or that and questioned a selection here and there, but he never tried to get me to change things. He always supported me – unless he was doing things behind my back and I doubt that very much. He would come into the dressing room and have a chat with the players sometimes, but I didn't mind that because we were very much a family club. Derek wasn't a coach and he knew that, so all he wanted to do was give the lads a bit of extra motivation. He never put any pressure on me and in fact I think he kept a lot of pressure away from me.'

Promotion was finally secured as runners-up to Chelsea with a 3–3 draw with Charlton and the return to the top flight of English football within 12 months of the life-saving takeover by the Bhattis led Wolves fans to believe that there were even brighter days ahead. Dougan, as ever, was not shy to emphasise his own importance in the promotion campaign. However, in later years he would revise his opinion of the Bhatti brothers whom he originally defended to the hilt and described as men of honour and dignity.

"Within three or four weeks (of the takeover), we were told we would have to have an overdraft of £1.5 million for a month which the Bhattis got off Lloyds Bank," Dougan told Peter Lansley, author of the book of

Molineux heroes *Running With Wolves*. "I had money to spend on players and the tragedy for me was that we all knew Graham (Hawkins) was a fine manager and a fine bloke. It was my role to produce the resources for him to strengthen the squad. Mike Rowland told the Press I had £1 million to spend. I got promotion that season on £141,000 with which John Burridge, Alan Dodd and Billy Kellock were bought. That's something Sir Jack Hayward has never been able to do. We had a better than average side – Mel Eves was still young, although John Richards was finished. Andy Gray was a wonderful fellow, John Humphrey was a talented full-back and those three signings just took us above that.

"You wouldn't believe the problems I inherited from the previous regime. I had a direct line to the Bhattis and we'd talk 20 times a day. They'd ring me up about everything and anything, if they saw a snippet in the papers. They got carried away with the excitement of being top of the table and would come to a board meeting practically every Monday, which was always professionally run. But the problems I had to deal with off the pitch . . . unsecured creditors, people coming in late for the money owed to them. The club had been very badly run. It all happened so quickly, I didn't have time to look into the Bhattis' family background. It took me six months to walk around the ground. I was in from 7.30am and I spent more time with Mrs Clamp, the cleaner, than anyone else as she would offer me a cup of tea when everyone else had gone home.

"Mahmud Bhatti would tell you everything in the garden was rosy. Akbar, at 20, was chairman of Allied properties. They didn't actually say they were from the Middle East. They didn't actually say they were well connected in Saudi Arabia. But when you went to their offices in London and saw all these pictures on the wall of princes and King Faisal and heard talk of all their friends in Saudi, you assumed that's where they were from. Basically, they were a couple of Pakistanis from Manchester. They had bought Allied properties for £10,000 the year before and blew it up through a couple of property deals in London. They sweet-talked Lloyds Bank into getting a £2 million overdraft, so it was pretty convincing. I started getting bad vibes, about Christmas."

Always there was money due to be invested into the club from off-shore sources. That was the party line repeatedly being fed to the local Press. It never arrived. The Bhattis remained hidden from public view and were only exposed as the men behind the takeover in a front page exclusive by the *Express & Star's* then chief reporter Derek Tucker after months of painstaking investigations. In truth, Wolves' future prosperity hinged on the granting of planning permission for a superstore development on land owned by the club behind the North Bank end of the ground. The application was refused by Wolverhampton Council and gradually the financial situation worsened as Wolves, at first buoyed by that unexpected promotion, began their slide from the First to Fourth Division in successive seasons.

Doug Hope recalls, "Before the takeover was completed there were meetings with Wolverhampton Council who intimated that they were in support of the supermarket development. I think there was a conspiracy against us because the local establishment resented the fact that outsiders had got control of the club. Manders, the company who owned the town centre shopping precinct, had a lot to lose if the development went ahead and they didn't care about the well-being of Wolves. I firmly believe they led the opposition to our plans.

"When things started to turn against us, the Bhattis pulled their money out. They felt the council had reneged on the verbal agreement. They stood to make a lot of money out of the development. When permission was eventually granted for a supermarket to the club's subsequent owners in 1986 I am led to believe the development company, the Gallaghers, made millions out of it. That sort of money would have enabled us to build Wolves into a real force. After we had won promotion in the first season the plan was to buy some high profile players to establish us in the First Division. Graham Hawkins identified the players we needed. They included Republic of Ireland defender Mick McCarthy (later to become Wolves' manager), future England striker Gary Lineker, who had agreed to join us for £100,000, Micky Gynn from Coventry (an FA Cup winner in 1987) and a goalkeeper from Peterborough called David Seaman, who also went on to play for England. We identified the players we wanted and I reckon we would have got them if the money had been there. We would have easily established ourselves as a First Division club.

"It didn't help the Bhattis' cause that they refused to speak to anyone. The only time they were spotted at the club was when the *Express & Star* got a picture of them sitting in the directors' box at one of our home games. On a personal level they were fine, but they didn't want a public profile and you couldn't get away with that in football. As things went from bad to worse our financial plight got pretty desperate and I was on the phone constantly to Gordon Taylor at the PFA for help. On one occasion he lent us £20,000 to pay the players' wages on time."

Roger Hipkiss became a Wolves director soon after the takeover and he describes the slow and painful collapse of the Bhattis' project as a betrayal of the brothers by the local council. He is convinced there were devious forces at work in the refusal to grant planning permission. He said, "It wasn't obvious and, of course, no-one would admit it, but I reckon there were racist undertones. Don't forget Wolverhampton was the constituency of Enoch Powell, author of the famous 'Rivers of Blood' speech and I believe there was still an element of those sentiments, prevailing throughout the town. They were dark-skinned outsiders and a lot of people in the community didn't like that. The Bhattis had a raw deal – no question about it. They had been promised everything and ended up with nothing. They couldn't keep putting their own money in and getting nothing in return. There were no television deals then and no knights in shining armour coming forward with big sponsorship contracts. To this day Allied Properties have never been paid money held and owed to them by Wolverhampton Council. I believe with compound interest this amounts to £3 million-plus."

Hope, Hipkiss and Dougan all ended up putting in their own money – amounts up to £50,000 each. In the statement of affairs for Wolverhampton Wanderers (1982) Ltd Dougan was showed to be owed £21,000 which he never got back. Hope recovered his loan because he proved he was a creditor of Wolves when they went back into receivership in 1986 and not Allied Properties. Hipkiss is still fighting for his money.

One of the first casualties of the tumultuous 1983/84 season was manager Graham Hawkins as relegation from the First Division became more of a certainty. Without money to invest in his struggling team, he was left with a hopeless task. The team began without a win in their opening 14 League matches. The fact they broke their duck with victory over old rivals Albion at The Hawthorns did little to lift spirits. Andy Gray had been sold to Everton by then and Ken Hibbitt, Mel Eves, Peter Daniel and Wayne Clarke left during the summer. Hawkins's departure came a few weeks before the end of the dismal campaign, Jim Barron acting as caretaker for the remaining games. Amazingly, the team did that season what no Wolves team had done since December 1950 – beat Liverpool at Anfield.

The decision to sack Hawkins not only left the likeable Black Countryman heartbroken, it also left him jobless, penniless and in total despair. There was no money in the kitty to pay him any compensation and he had to sign on the dole. "Winning promotion in that first season was a great achievement, but we knew there needed to be some changes if we were to take the next step up," Hawkins said. "My assistant Jim Barron, youth coach Frank Upton, chief scout Sammy Chapman and I all knew we had to have a major influx of players. I went to a board meeting that summer and said it would take between £750,000 to £1million to get Seaman, Grimes, Bracewell, McCarthy, Gynn and Lineker. That was the quality we needed to move forward. But the money was never there. I said to Derek, 'If we don't sign players, we are in trouble.'

"Then I went on my family holiday to Greece and while I was away I found out we had signed a winger, Tony Towner, from Rotherham for around £100,000. I knew about him as a player, but had never seen him play. He would have been about number-45 on my lists of targets. I think Derek saw him as the new Waggy."

Dougan had virtually blown the whole transfer budget in one outrageous, ill-judged swoop and left Hawkins to soldier on against impossible odds. Gradually the manager felt his future was being placed under increasing pressure. He knew there were moves from within the boardroom to allow Dougan to become more involved on the playing side – though he never sensed they came from the chairman himself.

Hawkins remembers, "I attended a board meeting and it was the Bhattis who indicated they wanted Derek to play a more active role with the team. Derek didn't say anything, but I don't think he wanted that. I said to them if that was what they wanted, they should pay up my contract and I would walk away.

"When it was obvious we were going to get relegated I got the phone call to say I was being sacked. I was expecting it. I can't even remember who made the call. There had been a meeting in London. It was the way it was done that most upset me. I was told to clear my desk and leave the ground. I was so distressed I couldn't even speak to the players before I left. I was disappointed Derek didn't make that call to me. I think he would have been concerned about how it was handled. There was no agreed settlement and it left me in serious financial trouble, I had taken on a bridging loan and the club had agreed to service it. I had two houses because I had been unable to sell one of them, so I took on a loan with big interest charges.

"I said to the club, 'Pay off my mortgage and I'll leave it at that.' They offered me £10,000 and I said 'No'. I ended up having to sign on the dole. I had no money and no job. I had to go to the dole office and sign on every other week. I got offers from newspapers to sell my story which would have helped, but I didn't want to throw any dirt at the club. I took it to an industrial tribunal to get my compensation and its chairman said: 'You have won your case, but I don't know whether you will ever get your money.' In the end it took me seven years to get my £20,000."

Hawkins eventually took on a coaching role in Bahrain where, contrary to opinion, he did not earn a fortune from the oil-rich Arab state, but gained a lot in terms of quality lifestyle and job satisfaction. Ironically he was offered a job by Graham Turner as his assistant manager at Aston Villa, but had already agreed to go to Bahrain and refused to break his word. After scouting for another former club, Blackburn Rovers, he accepted a job in Kuwait, just as Saddam Hussein's tanks were about to roll into that country so that bit the dust. After running his own pub and working for a pottery company, Hawkins later became the highly respected head of football development for the Football League.

"I never saw Derek for ages after I was sacked by Wolves," Hawkins says. "But gradually we got in touch and would ring each other. He came over to see me in Shropshire when I was running the pub. I got a call from him after he had read a thesis written by my son Richard on health and safety regarding sports injuries. He was interested in it because of the work he was doing getting a better deal for retired players. He asked me to go over to his place in Wolverhampton for a meal. He was in great spirits and although he looked a bit drawn, it was the same old Derek. That was just a couple of weeks before he died. I don't know whether that was fate or not.

"Despite what happened at Wolves I always regarded Derek as a friend. He gave me the chance to manage Wolves, my club. I admired the work he did for the PFA and the way he would challenge the establishment on behalf of players who had football related injuries. It was a crusade for him. He didn't mess around. He went straight to the people at the top to get things sorted out."

Dougan hated the fact that he was a party to the sacking of Hawkins. "Derek found that very difficult to do," recalls Hipkiss. "Graham was very much a part of the Wolves family, but it was felt he had lost his way. Everything was in decline, but it wasn't all down to Graham. The ground was falling into disrepair and attendances were falling fast. Graham needed better players to turn things around but the money just wasn't there."

Hawkins's replacement was a shock appointment. The Wolves board interviewed Alan Mullery, Don Mackay, Alan Durban and former players Mike Bailey and John McAlle. They eventually went for the larger-than-life Tommy Docherty, whose relationship with Dougan was hardly a marriage made in heaven.

"Derek Dougan is to football what King Herod is to babysitting," was the Doc's opening wisecrack soon after his appointment. The Doog was not amused. However, the controversial and jovial Scot was appointed to bring some light relief. It was thought his indestructible enthusiasm would bring a positive response from the club's rapidly declining support. Woodward, who had worked with Docherty at Villa, Hope and Hipkiss voted in favour. Dougan was firmly against, but had to submit to the majority vote.

Hope recalls, "Derek was becoming more marginalised at that time. We felt that Tommy was a big name and would give everyone a lift and maybe help us sell a few more season tickets even at that stage of the season. There was a clash of personalities between the Doc and the Doog, but they agreed to bury the hatchet, get on with it and work together for the sake of the club."

Docherty looks back at his spell in charge with a mixture of sadness and bemusement. He developed a love for Wolves, but could not believe the state of affairs that had dragged such a great club into such a wretched position. His sense of humour helped him through most of the hard times, but it was no laughing matter for Wolves fans as the slide towards the Fourth Division began to accelerate.

"To be honest, I never had any real problem with Derek when I was there," Docherty remembers. "He was always pleasant to me, at least he was to my face, and I don't think we had a single cross word. I managed to break the ice at the Press conference announcing my appointment when Derek said, 'Tommy Docherty can do for this football club what John F Kennedy did for the United States of America.' My response to that was, 'Yes, Mr Chairman, but he ended up getting shot!' I also made my King Herod crack, but I think Derek took that as a joke and wasn't upset by it. I didn't realise what a mess Wolves were in until I got there. The ground was collapsing around our ears and there was no more money for anything. I managed to get a striker called Jim Melrose on loan from Leicester and he helped us to improve things on the pitch, but we couldn't raise the £40,000 it would have taken to buy him permanently, He might just have made a difference if we could have kept him.

"I also brought through the ranks a young keeper called Timmy Flowers who went on to play for England (and win the Premiership with Blackburn Rovers). Wolves ended up selling him to Southampton for £80,000 which was a real giveaway, but they needed the money so desperately. I never got any of it to spend on the team. I guess it just went to pay off the debts. It was very sad for me to see such a massive club in such decline. There were some very good people there, men like Roger Hipkiss, working like mad to turn it around, but it was impossible. Eventually we were forced to see the funny side of things or we would have been driven crazy. My assistant Greg

Fellows and chief scout Sammy Chapman had to sleep in the boardroom some nights because the club could not afford to put us up in a hotel. At around 7.30 in the morning the cleaning lady, Mrs Clamp, used to come in and yell at us, 'Come on, you lot. Get up. I've got work to do.'

"Once, one of our players, Neville Hamilton, collapsed on the training ground with a suspected heart attack. They were just carrying him into the ambulance when Greg Fellows ran towards him and started taking the lad's boots off. It was a very grave situation for the boy so I said to Greg, 'What the hell do you think you are doing?' He replied, 'Gaffer, we have only got 14 pairs of boots in the whole club and we can't afford to lose these.'"

Docherty was sacked during the summer of 1985 after a run of 21 games without a win had sealed the inevitability of relegation to Division Three for only the second occasion in the club's history. He was wise-cracking until the bitter end and held a brief Press conference at a local tennis club to 'celebrate' his departure with champagne all round. Meanwhile, Derek Dougan was becoming increasingly morose. His dreams of guiding Wolves back to the top were slipping through his fingers. His Midas touch had deserted him and he was losing control of his power base. His days as the master of Molineux were numbered.

Chapter Thirteen

THE TAINTED HERO

THE QUESTION REMAINS UNANSWERED: Did Derek Dougan jump or was he pushed when he left his position as Wolves chairman in January 1986? The Doog always insisted that he walked away from an untenable situation, unable any longer to stand by and watch the club he loved disintegrating before his eyes. There is evidence, however, that his departure was forced upon him by the Bhattis and other directors.

His business acumen and even his integrity were being repeatedly called into question. What is indisputable is that in the eyes of a growing number of fans, his image as the saviour of the club was becoming tarnished. Not that Dougan would ever admit that. He left Molineux in those dark days of the winter of '86 convinced that he was the only person who had done right by the club and was battling against gross mismanagement and under-investment.

Up to a point, he was right. He was the only man in the boardroom with a football background and could recognise that the team, the facilities and the whole mood around the club were sinking into the abyss. Another miracle was needed, but his messianic qualities had run out. In typical Doog fashion he never could admit that he played any part in Wolves' downfall. In his interview with Peter Lansley he laid the blame for the club's decline at everyone's door but his own.

'This feeling of uncertainty grew when we fell out with Lloyds and I went to my own bank, NatWest, for an overdraft of £100,000 to cover a shortfall in staff salaries,' said Dougan. 'In all, over two and a half years I must have lent them between £150,000 and £200,000. If I had resigned that summer it might have all turned out better. I was chairman and chief executive, working for nothing, but the promise of a five-year contract that never materialised. You can't have any greater devotion to a club than that. Of course, people say, "But what did you get out of it?" At the end of the day it was bloody hard work. My role was to get resources for Graham Hawkins, but that experience taught me that you can have all the enthusiasm and energy in he world, but, if you don't have the resources to do the job it's like swimming against the tide.

'It was unfair of Allied Properties to say that I had £1 million to spend on players when I didn't. I financed that promotion season through my own sheer endeavour and ability, getting money to buy those three players (Burridge, Dodd and Kellock). I ran the club without losing money in that first year and I am proud of that. But the more I was into it, day in day out, the more I realised that, however hard I dug, I wasn't in an Aladdin's Cave. The council didn't give us the support needed to develop the ground. The supermarket was the big earner to help us redevelop, but we were turned down. The plan was to get about £8 million in grants and then another £8 million from the supermarket. The whole development would have cost £22 million. The worst thing that happened was getting promotion and then having to finance the jump up. Frankly it would have been in our interests to finish third.'

As the debts mounted and the spirits sank, Wolves were becoming a laughing stock inside football with tales emerging of how the lights would go off inside Molineux because of unpaid electricity bills and there had to be a weekly whip-round among office staff to pay the milkman. Prize asset Andy Gray's sale to Everton had brought in £180,000 to ease the chronic cash-flow crisis and still the Doog thought there might be a way through the crisis.

"You can't convince yourself this is real," he said. "You keep on believing, wanting to believe, when the Bhatti brothers tell you another bank is coming in. It all came to a head when, fobbed off for months and with debts of about £100,000, we realised it had all gone pear-shaped. The Bhattis were always out of the office, out of the country, out of earshot. So unbeknown to the the other board members, Eric Woodward, Starkey and I entered into negotiations with a Swedish bank to buy the club for £2 million. Typical of Bhatti, he asked for £8 million."

Roger Hipkiss, for one, knew well in advance that time had run out for Dougan. He had to stand by and watch his pal, affected by a growing drink problem, lose his grasp on reality. It pains him now to admit that he voted against him during a boardroom debate on the Doog's future.

"Eric Woodward did a lot to try to save Derek, but it did seem to be getting away from him," recalls Hipkiss. "He didn't get my support when it came to a boardroom vote. People might have thought that was disloyal of me, but my first duty was to the football club. In the end he did resign, but it was under pressure. Eventually there was a unanimous boardroom vote inviting him to step down. It affected him when he left. He was disappointed and for a long time didn't want anything to do with us. We did what we thought was right for the club, but he resented the fact that, effectively, he had been removed. There were lots of reasons why he had to go, but they are probably best left alone.

"The problem was that he did not really have a good business brain. At first the Bhattis revered him, but they came to realise that he had great ideas, but couldn't see them through. Derek had become very volatile towards the end. He blew hot and cold. I hate to admit it, but he did have a problem with drink and it led to some embarrassing moments. On one occasion when we played at Aston Villa, he had enjoyed a very liquid lunch in their McGregor Suite and when he went across to the boardroom before the game he was quite inebriated. He had a right go at Doug Ellis and it all became very unpleasant. In the end the police were called and Derek had to be taken back to Wolverhampton."

Ellis, who had returned to Villa as chairman after his involvement with Wolves, remembers the incident quite vividly. "Derek was going on about how the Wolves fans had been locked out of the ground for too long. It all became very heated," he says. "He did take a swing at me, but I don't think he realised I had been a very accomplished boxer during my days in the Navy. Needless to say he didn't make contact. It ended with Derek trying to kick my boardroom door down. At that point I had to summon the deputy chief constable and had him removed. It was a very sad moment. I had plenty of time for Derek, but there were times when his temperament got the better of him."

Hipkiss remembers another occasion when the Doog caused a scene in an opposition boardroom. It was at Luton Town, where one of the directors at the time was the much-loved comedian Eric Morecambe. "Derek said something to Eric which upset him and words were exchanged," said Hipkiss. "In the end Eric just turned his back on him and ignored him. Anyone who could upset Eric Morecambe – well he must have had a serious problem of some sort.

"Don't get me wrong. He wasn't always like that. He could be charm itself and generally he was well received by the other clubs. On one occasion the Duke of Gloucester asked to use Molineux to land his helicopter on a visit to Wolverhampton. Derek was the perfect host to him in the boardroom.

"He had lots of fantastic virtues and good ideas. For instance, he had this scheme at one time to move the ground from Molineux to an out-of-town site near Featherstone. We would have had a better stadium near the motorway with plenty of room for expansion and parking. It was a great scheme, but that's all it was – an idea.

"Derek was very generous with his time when it came to needy causes. He was also visiting sick children in their homes and in hospital. He loved going to working men's clubs and spending time with the people there. He had a human touch. The fans loved him and he loved them. But he was very much a law unto himself at times, especially at the football club. The only person who could really control him was the cleaner, Mrs Clamp. She knocked on the boardroom door one day in the middle of a meeting and said, 'Derek, if you don't stop these silly buggers using the front entrance after I have cleaned the floor, I'll smack you round the head.' Mrs Clamp's word was law. Derek stopped everyone going through the front door once she had finished her cleaning."

Doug Hope saw at close hand the effect Dougan's departure from Wolves had on him. He took it badly, but felt that he had not been given the backing he deserved. "It hurt him very deeply," says Hope. "He wanted to take the club back to its glory days. He had the opportunity and the vision to do that. But Derek wasn't a man for detail. He was a man for the big picture. Usually someone had to follow behind him to sweep up and tidy around after him. By the time Derek left, the rot had set in. It seemed as if the world was conspiring against us. They hit us with everything. Two sides of the ground were condemned as unsafe and closed down. The Molineux Hotel was falling into decay and the council spent thousands on repair work before sending us the bill. It felt as if they tried to drive us out of business so someone else could get their hands on the club. We tried to hold on, Roger, myself and Akbar Bhatti, but eventually a receiver was appointed again in 1986."

Hope remained friends with Dougan until he died. They worked on various business projects including an unsuccessful attempt to take over Stoke City. "We ended up swapping houses," Hope recalls. "I took his home in Codsall which he had lived in for over 30 years. He moved into my bungalow in Stockwell End. His partner at the time, Virginia Taylor-Potts, had elderly parents who did not enjoy the best of health. Derek helped to take care of them. My bungalow was next door to an old people's home and that gave them some respite from time to time. For the last couple of years, Derek and I spent a lot of time together socially. I know that to the average man in the street, he was still the great Wolves hero. When you went into a pub he was instantly recognised. He had this way with him which would make people feel special. He would never refuse an autograph and would willingly support any good cause, even when everything was going pear-shaped for him at Wolves. He got a phone call at Molineux one day from a player at Ayr United asking if he would make a contribution for a fund-raising event. Derek jumped in his car, drove up to Scotland and made a speech. He was back at his office desk next day.

"When he heard one of the former Wolves players, Ian Cartwright, needed help with some life-saving treatment, he personally went to the Primary Care Trust in Dudley to plead his case. He attended many of his fund-raisers and organised a dinner for him.

"Derek worked very hard to set up Xpro, an organisation to help former football professionals who had fallen on hard times. Twice I went with him to the Houses of Parliament for meetings with the chairman of the all-parties football committee, Alan King, to try to get some legislation through in support of retired players. But despite all his good work, there was a lot of animosity towards him from some quarters. He could fly off the handle for no reason and was a difficult man to live with, but much of that was down to his poor health. A lot of the new people at Molineux didn't like him and he was excluded from events organised by the Wolves old players' association. He was invited back towards the end, but Derek, being Derek, chose not to go."

No-one is better placed to illustrate the extreme limits of the Doog's personality than Roger Hipkiss, who knew him from the day he first joined Wolves and enjoyed a relationship with him which fluctuated from being the best of friends to sworn enemies. They fell out many times, kissed and made up and, sadly, at the time of Dougan's death were not on speaking terms. Hipkiss can look back through a lifetime of experiences with Dougan which brought him pleasure, frustration and resentment. "I first met Derek shortly after he was signed for Wolves by Ronnie Allen. I was a Wolves fan since I was a boy and often I was invited into the directors' box by the chairman John Ireland. One of the first things Derek said when he arrived was that he could have got Gordon Banks to join him from Leicester for £50,000, but the board thought that was too much for a goal-keeper.

"My first impression of the Doog was that he was flamboyant and full of his own self-importance, but I liked him very much. I got to know him even better when he rented an office from me in Lower Green, Tettenhall, for a short time. He ran some kind of promotional business and I would see him every day. When Ronnie Allen left and Bill McGarry took over I was amazed by Derek's relationship with the new manager. They didn't like each other at all, but I think Bill got the best out of him. He made him into a better player and I believe that was the outstanding period of Doog's career. Underneath the mutual feeling of hatred, I think Derek did respect him. He used to call McGarry 'that cunt' – behind his back, of course, but when the manager was around he was disciplined and did what he was told. He always said McGarry knew his football.

"Derek was a fearless player. He never took any nonsense from the so-called hard men of that time, Norman Hunter, Tommy Smith and 'Chopper' Harris. If it all kicked off on the field the Doog would be there in the thick of it, protecting and standing up for his team-mates. Derek opened a lot of doors for me into the football world and I would regularly attend the annual PFA dinners with him. I remember meeting Bill Shankly once. Derek went up to him and said, 'Shanks, why did you sign that big so-and-so Tony Hateley when you could have had me?' Shankly replied, 'Aye son, that's correct, you were a better player than Hateley, but I always knew where he would be on a Friday night. I could never be sure where you would be.'

"Derek was a bit of a lady's man. Long after he had split from his wife, Jutta, there was always plenty of female company. When I became a director of Wolves he often used to ask me to open his post in the Molineux boardroom. One day I opened an envelope and a toothbrush dropped out with a hand-written note. It said, 'I am returning this and never want to see you again.'

"Derek was great fun, but while he did open a lot of doors he ended up closing a few of them as well. I lost touch with him for a while when he resigned from the Wolves board and he obviously felt I had let him down. Eventually I gave him a call and he came to my office and we made it up. He always had something big going on in his mind. There was always some great scheme he was working on and he would run things past me. But we parted company again after we had another disagreement. He came and asked if he could see the books of the 1982 Wolves company that I had obtained from the receiver. I said he could borrow them. He had a claim against the club and wanted to study the accounts, so he took them away. I was pleased to help him. We fell out when he refused to bring them back. The books should have gone back to the Bhattis. We were never friends again after that.

"Of course, I was very very upset when he died. It was very sad. We'd known each other for a long time and shared some wonderful experiences together."

For years Dougan was vilified, certainly by the Wolverhampton establishment and by some sections of supporters, for aiding and abetting the collapse of the club in the Bhatti years. Towards the end of his life he confessed his regret at becoming involved.

"Looking back, I didn't need all the hassle, especially not getting paid," he admitted. "But the adrenaline was flying at 100 miles per hour and here were a club who meant so much to me. I'm still Wolves' highest goalscorer for a season in Europe, a record I am sure will never be passed and my goals helped keep the club in the First Division for eight years."

That's the Doog as Wolves fans will prefer to remember – lean, long-legged, flamboyantly blowing kisses to the North Bank after scoring another match-winning goal.

The man who hitched up with two brothers who appeared to be trying to make a property killing off the back of a world-famous football club? No, that must have been some other fella.

Chapter Fourteen

TWO OF US

JOHN RICHARDS WAS STILL STUDYING for his A levels at Warrington Grammar School in March 1967 when Derek Dougan signed for Wolves. The career paths of these two strikers from widely differing backgrounds and age groups, would eventually meet, They would merge, interlink, and eventually collide quite painfully over the next decade and a half.

Some partnerships are born, others manufactured and occasionally they happen by chance if the force of destiny thrusts two characters together to create a unique bond. It happened when two young Liverpool lads met at a church fete in Woolton in the late 1950s to forge the greatest songwriting partnership of the 20th Century. It happened too when a much-travelled Ulsterman and a fresh-faced Lancashire teenager stumbled into each other at Molineux to form the most productive goal-scoring double act in Wolves history.

The Doog and JR did not need to work on their partnership. There were no lengthy tactical discussions or blackboard debates. This was a duo which thrived on pure instinct. They happened to be at the right place at the right time – and that is the hallmark of great strikers, whether they are working in tandem or solo. If Dougan was the Clown Prince to Wolves fans, Richards, though the junior partner, became King John. One was the craggy, experienced leader of the line and the mentor. His sidekick was the young buck keen to learn at his elder's feet. It was a classic striker combo. One was the rangy, target man, good in the air, great positional awareness. The other was quick, sure-footed, a deadly finisher.

Of course, any star duo needed a support act and that Wolves team of the late '60s and early '70s had a chorus line to call upon with the robust energy of skipper Mike Bailey and his midfield partner Jim McCalliog, the defensive strength of Frank Munro, the irrepressible wing play of David Wagstaffe and, in later years, the astute delivery of Kenny Hibbitt.

'Wagstaffe to Dougan to Richards – goal.' It rolled off the tongues of commentators so frequently and effortlessly down the years and became music to the ears of Wolves fans. In little over two and a half seasons as regular partners they plundered well over 100 goals.

However, just like Lennon and McCartney, Dougan and Richards split up, acrimoniously and irreparably. It was long after the Doog's playing days were over when he was occupying the chief executive and chairman's desk at Molineux in 1983. Their fall-out occurred when Richards was still a Wolves player, albeit by then in an occasional walk-on role.

Richards can still talk of their playing days with fondness and reverence of his one-time partner, but refuses to allow the bitterness of their bust-up to fade into the dimness of his memory. Typical of the relationship with some of the central characters in his life, Dougan could make friends and enemies of the same person in the blink of an eye.

"I remember Derek Dougan before I joined Wolves," recalls Richards. "I was watching on television when he scored that hat-trick on his home debut against Hull City. That stuck in my mind. Two years later when I signed for Wolves he was still the main man at Molineux. I was 18 when I arrived. I had stayed on at grammar school to do my A levels. I signed a temporary contract, so I could play in a reserve game against Derby County. We won 4–1 and the chairman, John Ireland, came to the dressing room afterwards and said, 'Well done, son. Would you like to come and play for Wolves?' I was offered a one-year contract. I had played for the England schoolboys team so it was not as if they were plucking me from nowhere. To start off with I was in the away team dressing room at Molineux with the apprentices and young professionals. It was everyone's aim to get in the first team dressing room.

"I enjoyed a good spell in the reserves and after scoring five goals in one game against Blackburn, I gained a bit more prominence and started training with the first team. There would be a group of about 20 training together. I was well down the pecking order when it came to strikers, behind Bobby Gould, Hughie Curran, Paul Walker, Derek Clarke, Jimmy Seal and, of course, Derek Dougan. I would see Derek around the club all of the time. Everyone treated him with a great deal of respect. He was regarded as THE Wolves player of the time, along with Peter Knowles. They were the ones with the high profile.

"In those days you treated all your seniors respectfully. Derek was always very friendly towards the younger lads. He was Wolves' union rep and was our figurehead. If there were any problems he was the man you could go to. He was approachable, but at the same time you could not help being a bit in awe of him.

"I made my debut against West Bromwich Albion in February 1970 because of an injury to Dougan. I was substitute for most of the next season, but by then I had moved up to the first team dressing room. At that stage you were looking to get one of the pegs numbered 1 to 11. I was about number-25 to start with and Derek had number-10, so I still had a fair way to go. It was by now that I started to see more of the first team, but as a young player I still knew I had to keep my distance. You were their underlings and you knew your place. Youngsters like me, Kenny Hibbitt and John McAlle never joined in any of the team discussions. It all came from Mike Bailey and Dougan. You did not feel you could offer an opinion in front of a dressing room full of internationals.

"Derek was the voice of the dressing room. There was friction between him and Bailey, who was very much seen as the manager Bill McGarry's man. Mike was the team captain, so he had to be close to the manager. Derek didn't like McGarry and because of that he didn't seem to like Mike. You never heard Mike say anything bad about Derek, whereas Derek would have a go at Mike and McGarry when they were not in the room. Usually that was just within Derek's own little clique of players, which included John Holsgrove and Les Wilson. We were never part of those groups. We never associated with them socially. There was a massive age gap. We were different generation. Derek never mixed with us. He would kid everyone he was 29, but everyone knew he was well into his 30s.

"We were young lads who would be out on the town in Wolverhampton at a place called the Club Lafayette. We had a totally different lifestyle. He was married with a stunning wife and children. The only real contact I had with Derek away from the club was when I became Wolves' PFA rep and he was the union chairman. We would travel up to meetings in Manchester together. It was fascinating to watch him in action. He was a real players' champion and a natural orator. I just used to sit there listening and learning because I was only 22."

Dougan and Richards began to combine more regularly and effectively from the 1971/72 season and McGarry eventually made a double positional switch, which made the partnership more complete. Soon the goals began to flow as Richards began to appreciate Doog's skill and fitness levels. Richards explains, "I was naturally right-footed and Derek favoured his left. But McGarry moved me to play down the left and Derek down the right. It suited our runs because I was cutting inside on to my stronger side towards goal and so was Derek from the right. We worked on that in training and it started to gel. Waggy would get the ball and I would know exactly where he was going to put it. It would be he same from Kenny (Hibbitt) on the other side.

"Derek was one of the fittest players I ever saw. He was always at the front when it came to running, over long distances and sprints. On a Tuesday we would do these staggered runs around the pitch and he would be right out in front. Only John McAlle and Derek Parkin would beat him regularly. We never sat down and talked about our partnership. It just seemed to come instinctively and from the bits of work we did on the training pitch. We didn't need to have big discussions about it. It was just something natural that worked. When he went up for the ball I knew whether he was going to flick it on or knock it down from his body shape. It was my job to anticipate this and hopefully get on the end of it and go past him. It was simple stuff really. Mike Bailey or Jim McCalliog would get it in midfield and give it Waggy or Kenny and they would try to pick out me or Derek. It was not complicated, but very effective.

"Derek never seemed to get injured, although I do remember him once getting a fractured cheekbone and concussion which kept him out for a while courtesy of Stoke City's hardman Denis Smith. Generally people didn't mess with the Doog and you knew he was always looking after you. In many ways Doog took me under his wing. It was a great comfort to know that you had someone like that alongside you who was willing to put himself about. In those days defenders would tackle you from behind and come right through you, but you rarely saw him retaliate."

The team of the Dougan-Richards era hit their peak by winning the League Cup with a 2–1 defeat of Manchester City at Wembley in 1974. Richards scored the winning goal despite carrying an injury that had stopped him training in the build-up to the game. Ironically, Dougan was perceived to have one of his quieter games, but his partner reckons his contribution was immense and went unrecognised. Richards remembers, "During the final I wasn't able to give Derek much support. I was doubtful right up to the kick-off with a pelvic injury. I had to have treatment rather than train. I was not firing on all cylinders so Dougan was the lone man up front. He had to do most of the running for me.

"I was due to come off in the second half, but Waggy got injured, I stayed on and scored the winner. I was more pleased for Derek and Mike Bailey than for myself after we won that Wembley game. They were not just the two most senior and respected players in the team, but they had been in the sides which lost the UEFA Cup final against Spurs and in the previous season's semi-finals of the FA and League Cups. They were desolate after those defeats. Each time I am sure they were thinking that it was their last chance to win something. They didn't say it, but the rest of us knew what they were feeling. We had plenty of time in front of us because we were still young. It was a fitting tribute to Mike and Doog when we won at Wembley in '74. They were two people who didn't always see eye to eye, but it was just great to see them celebrating that win together."

A little over a year later Dougan had retired. Richards went on to even greater success scoring even more goals with various partners although he did not add to the lone England cap he had won in 1973. He reckons the debt he owed to the Doog as far as his playing career was concerned was incalculable.

"The time we had playing together regularly was just a little over two seasons in total," says Richards. "According to records we scored 125 goals between us in that time. Any partnership that is going to get you 50 goals in a season isn't doing too badly, is it?' It was very condensed spell of our careers. But it was a golden period. I don't think I would have been the same player without the influence of Derek Dougan – certainly not so effective."

If only they could have wrapped up their partnership in a gold and black shirt and preserved it for all time. It would have remained untouchable and unblemished. Unfortunately, it was fractured seven years later when Dougan took over as chairman and chief executive following the 1982 takeover. Richards was then the club captain and desperate to help Wolves through their troubled times. He was relieved that a consortium had come to the rescue and happy that Dougan was part of it because he had so many good memories of their playing days. However, a chance conversation with the then Wolves manager Ian Greaves made him question what lay ahead.

"If you ask people like Kenny Hibbitt, they will tell you Ian Greaves was a cracking bloke and a very good manager," Richards said. "During pre-season training I was talking to Ian and it was coming towards the deadline for the takeover bids. Ian said to me, 'If Dougan comes here, that's me finished.' That surprised me because I liked Ian and thought he was doing a fine job for Wolves. Then I found out there was some history between him and Dougan. They had clashed when Derek was on one of those television panels and clearly it hadn't been laid to rest.

"Within a few days of Derek taking over, Ian Greaves was gone. That made me think straight away that if you upset Dougan, he won't forget it. You were either for him or against him. He held grudges. But there was a new regime in charge and we had to get on with it. As club captain I had to sort out the players' bonuses with Derek as he had taken up his role as chairman and chief executive. We got Gordon Taylor, the players' union boss, down and Derek was doing the negotiations for the club.

"It was clear to me from the start that Derek was playing a game. He was trying to renege on the bonuses we had fixed the previous season, even though he had said before he would honour everything in our contracts. Gordon and I spent a couple of hours going backwards and forwards from the boardroom to the dressing room to talk to the players. Derek was the man who was supposed to be a players' champion and who had fought so hard for players' rights. You might have thought he would have been more sympathetic to our position. This was the Derek Dougan I had played alongside and the man who had warned us not to trust directors. Suddenly he was on the other side. In the end, after hours of talks, he agreed to our demands, but he had been playing a game. He wanted to make a point that he was now in charge. It taught me a lot about how he had changed – the bonuses and the Ian Greaves episode. It was an indication of how he was going to run the club. The players were to be subservient. I was looking at a different bloke across that boardroom table from the one I had known before."

Worse, much worse, was to follow for Richards. He knew he was approaching the twilight days of his career, but still felt he had something to offer a team, managed by Graham Hawkins, who were relying to a large extent on youngsters to win promotion to the First Division. The striker did not figure in the side which got off to a flying start to the 1982/83 season and was relieved eventually to get a loan move to Derby where the chance of playing regular first-team football in the Second Division gave him some respite from his frustrations, even if it meant turning his back temporarily on his beloved Wolves.

"I was getting on by then," recalls Richards. "I was 31. I was playing all right, but I couldn't get a look in. It was very frustrating, so I jumped at the chance to join Derby. They were struggling and Brian Clough's old partner Peter Taylor was the manager. We eventually went on a bit of a run in the FA Cup. Although I did not play, we beat Nottingham Forest in the third round and Chelsea in the fourth. Wolves went out in that round, while we were due to face Manchester United at home in the fifth. I was looking forward to that when I got a call saying Wolves wanted me back. There was nothing I could do about it. They had a few injuries and wanted me back for the next league match. It meant I couldn't rejoin Derby and had to spend the rest of the season at Wolves, but that was OK if I was going to get some games."

Richards was not selected immediately after his surprise recall on 4 February, even though he was named in Wolves' squad for the following day's visit to Barnsley. It was six weeks after returning to Molineux that he finally made an appearance and a very brief one at that – at Grimsby. "When we got to the stadium nothing had been said to me until Graham Hawkins announced the team and I was the substitute!" recalls Richards. "There I was sitting on the bench on a freezing day at Grimsby which, to be fair, isn't one of the most appealing of places. It was 0–0 and with a couple of minutes to go I was thinking how glad I would be to get out of there. Then Graham asked me to warm up and I went on for a minute, touched the ball once and then the referee blew the final whistle.

"The following week I was training with the reserves. I kept my thoughts to myself, but obviously wasn't very happy. I was doing a bit of writing for the local Saturday paper, the *Sporting Star*, and eventually that was where I let my frustration come out. I wrote in my column, 'Rarer than a penny black, more elusive than the abominable snowman. What is it? A picture of me in a Wolves shirt this season. The Christians had a better chance in the Colosseum than I've had at Molineux this year.'

I had played in the reserves the day the article came out and had gone straight home, rather than back to Molineux. Dot Wooldridge, one of the secretaries, rang me at home at around 7.15pm and said, 'Derek Dougan wants you at the club, now.'

"I drove down to Molineux, thinking it was something important and that maybe another club had come in for me. Virtually everyone had left the club by then and I knocked on the boardroom door. Roger Hipkiss opened it and as he walked past me he said under his breath, 'I don't blame you for what you've done. I understand it.'

"I saw the newspaper with my article in it on Derek's desk. Then he launched this attack on me about how disloyal I had been after all he and the club had done for me. All I said in response was that I was just expressing the way I felt and I was not happy with my situation.

"But I realised there was not much point arguing with him. He had obviously been doing some entertaining in the board room after the first-team game and there were still drinks over the table. This was the same Derek Dougan who had campaigned all his life for freedom of speech for players and had always been outspoken with his own views. At that moment all my respect for Derek had gone. There he was slagging me off, effing and blinding. After about ten minutes I just walked out without saying any more. I was club captain, I had been at the club for 14 years and all I was trying to do was explain my frustration at being badly treated. I think the least I deserved was an explanation as to why I was not playing.

"I knew when I left that boardroom, it was the end at Wolves for me as a player. For the rest of the season I played only two games and came off the bench in another. Whether that was Dougan's influence or not, I don't know. I had to get away, but I still had two years left on my contract which would take me up to 1985. I wasn't going to give that up even if it meant just sitting around picking up my money and doing nothing. I was on good money by then, but still had a mortgage and bills to pay."

An escape came Richards's way from an unlikely source. Maritimo, a team in the Portuguese Second Division, had been recommended to sign Richards by former Wolves manager Ronnie Allen. At first, the move did not appeal to the striker. They only wanted to offer him a one-year deal and the wages were not great. However, Wolves finally went out of their way to ease his departure and promised him a payment to make up for the missing year of his contract. The promise was broken and that led to another, crushing, final, fatal blow in the declining relationship of Dougan and Richards.

"I didn't even know where Maritimo was," said Richards. "I found out it was in Madeira and even had to look that up in the atlas. I didn't want to play Second Division football in Portugal, but they kept trying to persuade me and after Wolves agreed to make me a payment to compensate me, I agreed to give it a try. I was over in Madeira and my wife Pam was back home sorting things out before joining me. The payment was due by the end of July, but they reneged on it. Communication between Madeira and home wasn't easy in those days, so Pam was ringing Wolves on my behalf. She was leaving messages with the club secretary Keith Pearson to pass on to Dougan. She was getting no calls back. It was September by now and she was due to come out in time for the kids to start school.

"I had to tell her to leave a message with the club and say if the money wasn't paid, we would get in touch with the PFA and ask them to pass it on to their solicitors, George Davies and Co. Within half an hour Derek was on the phone to Pam. He was swearing, using the most abusive language and asking who the hell did we think we were. He was taking it out on my wife and that was uncalled for. I was brought up to believe you don't talk like that to women. If he'd got an issue he should have sorted it out with me, not my wife. The way he behaved was cowardly and unforgivable.

"In the end we did put it in the hands of the PFA and I got my money a couple of months later. I never spoke to Derek again after that. I bumped into him a couple of years ago at a party for Frank Munro. I had Pam with me. We just about acknowledged each other. I saw him at other functions subsequently and it was the same – just a nod of acknowledgment. We deliberately avoided conversation. He was invited to join the activities of Wolves Former Players' Association, but he didn't respond. I know some of the senior members of that group were not too disappointed that he chose not to join because he had said some critical things about Billy Wright, who was possibly the greatest Wolves player of all time."

There was one more indirect clash between the two former playing partners. When Richards helped to organise a reunion dinner to celebrate the 30th anniversary of the 1974 League Cup final win, Dougan decided to boycott it and persuaded former team-mates John McAlle and Derek Parkin to do the same.

"Basically, two local lads I knew, both Wolves supporters, wanted to put on a dinner and it was a great opportunity to get all the team together," Richards says. "It was a non-profit making event and it was even agreed to cover the costs of the players' travel and accommodation. Derek took exception and said he was organising something similar himself. He claimed the old players were being exploited. They weren't. They were all delighted that someone had made an effort to organise the event and they had a cracking night out. Alan Sunderland came over from Malta and he insisted on paying all his own costs. He just wanted to be there with the other lads. But there was a lot of bad publicity in the local paper about Derek's so-called boycott and that left a bit of a sour taste."

When Dougan died in the summer of 2007, a notable absentee from his funeral was John Richards. It raised a few eyebrows among Wolves fans, but Richards chose not to attend for his own very personal reasons. "I was just sad to hear about Derek's death, just as all his old team-mates were," he says. "But I never gave a second thought to going to the funeral. He lost any respect I had for him when he treated my wife in the way that he did. I have my own memories of Derek Dougan and they are of the times we had when we were playing together in the same team and scoring goals. They are good memories and I treasure them."

Chapter Fifteen

UNWANTED HEADLINES

AFTER HIS DEPARTURE FROM MOLINEUX, Dougan could have kept a low profile, but it was not long before he re-emerged to spearhead a project which began with the best of intentions, but eventually failed to materialise – the Duncan Edwards Sports Medicine Centre Appeal. The plan was to build a unit which would specialise in treating sports injuries and, as it was to be based at Russells Hall Hospital in Dudley, there could be no-one better after whom to name it than the town's most famous son. Duncan Edwards had died on 21 February 1958, 15 days after being injured in a plane crash at Munich Airport, which claimed the lives of seven of his Manchester United colleagues as they returned from a European Cup tie against Red Star Belgrade in Yugoslavia.

The call which led to Dougan's new venture came barely a month after he had quit Wolves. Irshad Ahmad, a consultant surgeon at Russells Hall wanted him to speak at a gathering of top medical men. Dougan was a late replacement for the Bishop of Birmingham and felt that deputising for a top clergyman may have been divine intervention – for his attendance at the meeting led to him learning about the work of Mr Ahmad and his colleague Dr Terry Pinfold. They shared Dougan's view that a unit specialising in treating sporting injuries was long overdue. The doctors had pioneered the idea for several years by holding weekly clinics to look at sports-related injuries. To mark the launch of the charity, a book, Duncan Edwards, was published in 1988. In the foreword to it, Dougan recounted how the plans took shape.

'I had never realised that just 12 miles from my home in Wolverhampton was the finest limited treatment in the Midlands. When Dr Pinfold and Mr Ahmad told me it was not possible to have a clinic seven days a week 52 weeks of the year, because of lack of resources, I replied, "Put the cash element to one side and let's start talking about the concept of a complete sports medicine centre." Over six months of increasingly exciting talk, involving the consultants, Alan Horwell the hospital administrator at that time, Isobelle Rees district head of physiotherapy and architect Gerry Perrin, the project came alive.

'Imagine the concept – to provide the finest comprehensive diagnosis involving rehabilitation and prevention of injuries. A community project with treatment free of charge to anyone in the United Kingdom with sports-related setbacks. We decided to form ourselves into a charity, which took almost a year to achieve, even with the superb administrative help of John Brocklebank, a senior partner in George Davies Law Practice in Manchester. For the record, they have looked after the Professional Footballers' Association for over 30 years. The Charity Commissioners and the Inland Revenue were left complimenting us on "the finest charity of its kind in history" being registered.

'In the middle of 1986, I knew the charity was finally going to be registered and felt confident that we were going to launch the project in the form of an appeal. I arranged a meeting with the three trustees, Dr Pinfold, Mr Ahmad and Ken Parton, and asked if they would call the centre the Duncan Edwards Sports Medicine Centre, in memory of Dudley's most famous son. They unanimously agreed.'

The Duncan Edwards book, as well as Dougan's explanation of how the charity came into being, also included a tribute from journalist Hugh Jamieson to the former England star who was only 21 when he died. Jamieson was a United fan and, as a youngster, had watched Edwards in action. There was also an excerpt from The Day A Team Died, a book about the Munich disaster written by Frank Taylor, the only journalist to survive the crash. The rest of the contents were a reproduction of *Tackle Soccer This Way*, a book Edwards had just completed at the time of his death. Dougan's acknowledgements at the beginning of the book said that Edwards's mother, Sarah, had given her support to the appeal.

On the back cover of the charity's book, which sold at £9.95, was an artist's impression of how the sports medicine centre would look. It said all proceeds from the sale of the book would go towards building the centre and added, 'Our slogan at appeal headquarters is "We've done our bit! Have you?" This is an opportunity for you to do your bit.' The charity was registered with the Charity Commission on 25 July 1986 as 'The Sports

Medicine Centre Russells Hall Hospital'. Its registration number was 327199.

In the months that followed many events were held to raise money for the charity, such as sports forums, dinners and sponsored events at local pubs, schools and clubs. Kingswinford resident Cedric Grove, who had devoted many years to staging charity events, managed to raise £5,000 for the cause. He approached Billy Wright and asked if Billy's wife Joy could arrange for her and her singing twin sisters – the trio were known as the Beverley Sisters and had been world famous in the 1950s – to perform at one of the charity evenings. It could not be arranged, but because the cause bore the name of Duncan Edwards, the Wolves legend donated one of his England caps which was duly raffled to raise the £5,000 sum.

Dougan tried to cover every angle and recruited a local journalist to help publicise the charity – John Field. He was, like Dougan, a larger-than-life character. Field, who would die at a comparatively early age, had been a reporter at the *Express & Star's* Dudley office before starting his own free- lance agency.

For a while the charity maintained a high profile, but when it finally ground to a halt there was found to be very little money left in the kitty. A lot of people were unhappy about the situation and not merely because it seemed the medicine centre was not going to happen, but also because the revered name of Duncan Edwards had, they claimed, been tainted by the episode. There were certainly many only too eager to criticise Dougan.

As of March 2008 the charity is still registered with the Charity Commission and Dudley solicitor Graham Dean is listed as its contact. He told us there was very little cash left in it. He had become involved when things ground to a halt. Mr Ahmad had died some years ago and Dean said the dream of the clinic had been Mr Ahmad's and Dr Pinfold's even before Dougan came along, but it was Dougan who took up the challenge and tried to make it happen.

Someone once said that never put down to malice what can be put down to stupidity. In other words, the failure of the Duncan Edwards appeal was in all probability not down to any wrong-doing by Dougan, but was merely due to his inability to organise the venture sensibly. He may well have been over-ambitious and unwise in some of his actions – like committing the charity to the long-term hire of a large Portakabin as their head-quarters in the grounds of Russells Hall Hospital. It may have been that the Duncan Edwards book did not make the sort of profit to justify the cost of it. The trustees of the charity were all reputable people and as one of them,

Ken Parton, told us, if there had been anything untoward happening, they would surely have spotted it. Perhaps the simple truth in this ultimately sad chapter in Dougan's life is that he went into it full of enthusiasm and with the best intentions, but had not got the ability to see it through.

That broad summing-up is confirmed by highly respected broadcaster Nigel Pearson. A regular on sports chat radio station talkSPORT and much in demand as a speedway and darts commentator on TV, Pearson was a teenager with ambitions to be a journalist when he joined the charity head-quarters for work experience and remembers the Portakabin at Russells Hall. "It was not just a little wooden hut, it was a huge, luxurious Portakabin. Derek had a massive office. It would befit a Premier League manager. There were toilets and a kitchen where Derek would make a coffee now and then. He had a PA and a lottery manager, who was on commission only. Derek did not have a salary, just expenses. When it came to an end, independent auditors were brought in and everything was subject to close scrutiny." The lottery manager was former Albion striker Keith Smith, a playing colleague of Dougan's at Peterborough.

One of the big fund-raising ventures was a walk from Old Trafford to Dudley that would end on 21 February 1988, the 30th anniversary of Duncan Edwards's death. The same afternoon Dougan arranged a match between a Manchester United XI and an England XI at Albion. Before these events Dougan was forecasting in the Express & Star that the fund would pass £100,000 by the end of the month. The walk duly took place and the last leg was completed by over 60 Dudley youngsters. Dougan told the newspaper, 'So much character has emerged in these children this week and I would be proud to be the father of any of them. They are true ambassadors of Dudley.'

However, there were still those around happy to undermine Dougan at every chance. "There was a local reporter who had it in for Derek and absolutely crucified him," says Pearson.

The match at the Hawthorns was an anti-climax, however, as Pearson confirms. "I ended up playing the second half in an England shirt with number-seven on my back. Tony Morley of Villa played, so did Martin Hodge the Sheffield Wednesday goalkeeper and Dave Bennett of Coventry. Certain football managers promised players, but let Derek down at the last minute. That summed it all up – he was let down by others.

"The overheads really killed us, but don't anyone ever try to tell me there was any fiddling going on. It was given the blessing of Duncan's mother Sarah Anne Edwards and was backed by reputable people. If you are questioning the integrity of Derek Dougan you are questioning the integrity of absolutely everybody else involved, including two eminent surgeons."

Pearson recalls the trek from Manchester to Dudley, "I did the whole walk and it included stops at places like Altrincham and Stoke. When we got to the hotel in Stoke they had not heard of us. We blagged our way in and got free accommodation and free meals so it turned out all right, but Doog assured us he had booked us in. I think there must have been about £10,000 raised by the walk and we also had a sort of reunion when about 30 of us climbed Ben Nevis with Bert Bissell (a legendary Dudley walker) and then had a relay run of 400 miles back to Dudley."

The story of how Pearson teamed up with the charity reflects well on Dougan as he obviously recognised enterprise and a youngster of talent. Pearson explains, "I organised a charity basketball match in my last year at Kingswinford School in 1986, when I was 16, all for the SMC appeal. I publicised it and even wrote to Birmingham Bullets and asked for a player and they sent one of their American stars, Tyrone Shoulders. It was a massive success and Derek was so impressed he invited me to the office and asked if I'd like to be involved on a regular basis through the summer. The rest is history."

It must have been a helter-skelter time working with Dougan, but Pearson would not have missed it for the world. "He was not perfect. He could be the kindest man on earth one day and a real bastard the next. He made my life difficult at times, but overall it was an absolute pleasure to work under him. It was a fantastic experience for me to be involved with Derek – the stories he told me about his career and football people and introducing me to proper adult drinking. It was an experience which no-one aged 18 could ever buy. I learned more about life in six months than I would have done in three years at university. Derek was great with the youngsters as well when they came in with their ten pounds or 50 pounds, he would take down their names and addresses and a letter was sent to their parents thanking them. But it was never going to add up to a million quid. It needed corporate backing. John Field became a close friend of Doog's and promised him the earth, saying he would get him publicity in national newspapers and take it to a new level but it did not happen. Derek tried his butt off, he did everything he could to make it work. Towards the end he even left the Portakabin and hired an office on Pensnett trading estate out of his own pocket."

Pearson also backs up the theory that the Duncan Edwards book was not a money-spinner. It was far more likely a money-loser. Pearson says,

"There were boxes of the book left and the print bill must have outweighed sales. Derek was giving copies away just to empty the boxes. Very sad but true. He never had the support of book shops and, actually, Manchester United who were so generous as to allocate a couple of paragraphs in their match programme. A classic case again of no suspicion over Derek's deals. It was just that the book flopped – fact, simple. I suspect many boxes were thrown in the skip, tragically. Yet the bill still had to be paid by the charity."

In the summer of 1989 the *Express & Star* reported on June 29 that Dudley Health Authority had finally lost confidence in Dougan's ability to reach his target. The paper ran a story, headlined 'Backing on sport clinic appeal is withdrawn', and reported, 'A statement issued today said members and officers of the authority have felt considerable concern about the progress of the major fund-raising exercise. And they have failed to establish the current financial position of the trust despite repeated attempts to obtain up-to-date certified accounts. "Regrettably, these acounts have still not been produced. Members of the health authority agreed it must publicly dissociate itself from the charity until such time as the current position has been satisfactorily clarified." A mobile office at Russells Hall Hospital has been closed and calls transferred to Mr Dougan's office on Pensnett Trading Estate. Appeal organisers have so far refused to reveal the present fund total – but it is believed to have raised only £30,000 so far.'

A day later the paper reported that Dougan had described the health authority's decision as a 'bombshell' and had vowed to carry on his quest to have the sports injuries clinic built. The paper confirmed, 'Today a furious Mr Dougan said the Dudley Health Authority had not provided so much as a second class stamp to help the appeal. It had earmarked a site for the centre and provided a portable office building. But Mr Dougan said he had even paid some of the rent for that out of his own pocket. "This has been a dream of mine for 23 years and I am not giving up now. I am 200 per cent committed to this dream despite this insult from the DHA to me, the memory of Duncan Edwards and to the thousands of people who have raised money so far. But I am going to stay involved with this although the centre may not now be built in Dudley."'

It was clear matters were coming to a head and just a few days later the trustees of the charity met and announced afterwards that Dougan had given up his role as project co-ordinator. A statement issued after the meeting by solicitor Graham Dean said the trustees were still fully committed to the scheme for a centre, which would be built at Russells Hall, and a firm of accountants had been appointed as auditors to produce accounts for the health authority and the Charity Commissioners. Dean said the trustees hoped to persuade the health authority of the viability of the project and added, "Whilst the commitment and enthusiasm of Mr Dougan has led to the raising of moneys to establish the fund, the trust is now moving into a new era. Some time ago Mr Dougan relinquished his role as project co-ordinator."

Dougan denied he had quit and stormed, "It was agreed we should meet and either myself or both of us should make a statement afterwards. I was not even given the chance to put my views and it was the height of discourtesy. As for leaving the project, I have never ever said I was giving up and indeed without my help now the accountants could not produce any figures. As of this afternoon I am still project co-ordinator."

Despite the bold words, it was clearly the end of the road. The dream was over.

It emerged later in the year that Dougan had tried other avenues to raise the cash for the medicine centre. He was questioned by a courtroom investigation looking into a crashed company linked with the fallen Eagle Trust empire. The *Express & Star* reported on 20 September 1989, 'Dougan was questioned by Northampton County Court after the collapse with £1m plus debts of Hydrodam (Corby), a former subsidiary of Eagle Trust. Dougan had previously been linked with missing Eagle Trust chief executive John Ferriday when he claimed the businessman would underwrite his £1m Duncan Edwards sports medicine centre appeal. The claim was later soured by a public dispute between Mr Dougan and the trustees of the charity. Dougan gave evidence after it emerged he was chairman of Landsaver, a company apparently linked to Hydrodam. Landsaver operates from the same business premises in Corby which housed Hydrodam. Mr Peter Sargent, handling Hydrodam's liquidation for Huddersfield accountants Revell, Ward and Hexton, said, "Mr Dougan was questioned and he was most helpful." He added it was unlikely he would be questioned further.'

However, nine days later Landsaver also collapsed. The *Express & Star* reported that shareholding in the firm which had offices in Corby, Northants, was split evenly between Dougan, the chairman, and Alan Lambert, the chief executive, with two per cent owned by registration agents. It was announced in October that a winding-up petition was being issued against Landsaver, creditors claiming they were owed thousands of pounds. Liquidators were appointed after complaints from the insolvent associated company Hydrodam that Landsaver owed £9,000 to them. The newspaper added that Dougan was in Northern Ireland and unavailable for comment. To put it mildly, 1989 had not been a good year for Alexander Derek Dougan, who a year earlier had experienced more financial strife when his Wolverhampton-based promotions company had to be wound up

The charity story dragged on and police were eventually asked by the Health Authority to look into the matter because of concern over the failure to produce any accounts. Detectives made inquiries but no charges were brought, which tends to confirm the theory that it was all down to bad management.

It eventually emerged that of £90,000 raised some £70,000 had gone on expenses. Duncan Edwards's mother Sarah said she was deeply hurt that so much had been spent on running the charity, the auditors rapped those involved for not keeping proper accounts and when activities finally ceased there was just a few thousand pounds left in the kitty.

In 1996 Dougan completed work on a revamp of his book *The Sash He Never Wore* which would be published as *The Sash He Never Wore . . . Twenty Five Years On*. He hoped to throw himself into promoting the book and also announced his intention to run for Parliament. However, fate, yet again, was about to deal him a blow. In mid-January 1997 he suffered a massive heart attack and it took all his fighting qualities to survive it. Under a banner heading 'Doog saved from death by doctors' this is how the *Express & Star's* front lead story of 14 January covered the incident:

'Wolves' former hero Derek Dougan was brought back from the brink of death by doctors after he collapsed and his heart stopped beating. The 58-year-old striker – nicknamed The Doog – was taken to hospital in Belfast on Sunday night with a heart attack. Mr Dougan, who until recently lived in Keepers Lane, Codsall, was described this afternoon as "comfortable" in the city's Royal Victoria Hospital. A spokeswoman said "There has been a slight improvement in his condition but he is still pretty poorly." At one point the Northern Ireland player's heart stopped beating, but doctors were able to resuscitate him, according to a close friend. Mr Dougan was Wolves chairman and chief executive during the club's darkest days when it was owned by the Bhatti Brothers. He recently became involved in a legal battle with Wolverhampton Council. He claims the council owes him up to £25,000 which he said he pumped into the club. It stemmed from the turbulent times which followed the authority's 1986 takeover of the Molineux stadium under a rescue package to save Wolves from extinction.'

Incredibly not even this setback could dampen Dougan's fire. Two months after his heart attack Dougan confirmed he would fight DUP deputy leader Peter Robinson's East Belfast seat in the 1997 General Election. At his campaign launch he reckoned he would give Robinson "a fair run for his money". He said his policies were for a referendum in Northern Ireland on its political future, integrated education and peace through appreciation of human differences. He added, "When I drove myself to hospital in January I knew somehow I would come through and that I would offer myself to serve the people of East Belfast. I am one of them. I have been away. I am back among them. My politics are the politics of trust, tenderness and togetherness – the three Ts. When you have come back from the door of death you see life and the future in a very different light."

They were fine words, but the sincerity of them has to come into question when one listens to Dougan's son Nick. He told us of a slightly more practical reason for his father's apparently serious political aspirations. "I was working with my dad in Belfast on a few projects, including the launch of his book. I read a draft copy and he asked me what I thought and I said, 'It's a good read, not the best, but a good read.' He asked how many should we print and I said 5,000. He said, 'No, let's go for 10,000.' I was the cautious one. He would just want to go for it. Just before Christmas, he was doing some signing sessions in the bargain book stores around Belfast. Suddenly he said to me, 'Do you know what I am going to do? I am going to stand for Parliament as an independent candidate.' Really all he wanted to do was use the campaign to promote the book. It was a clever move. He didn't get many votes and he lost his deposit – but we sold a fair few books."

All his campaigning did not help Dougan make an impact in the election. Robinson polled 16,640 votes and held onto his seat with a majority of 6,754. Dougan's 541 votes represented 1.4 per cent of the poll and placed him seventh.

Dougan's views did not meet with everyone's approval, particularly his vision of an all-Ireland football team. He had no time for sectarianism and it may have been these beliefs that saw a mural of him in Woodstock Road, Belfast, defaced in 2005. His portrait, which adorned the wall along with other Northern Ireland footballing greats Danny Blanchflower, Sammy McIlroy and George Best was daubed with black paint.

Dougan said people misunderstood him. He was expressing personal views not political ones. 'I'm proud that I was born off the Newtonards Road and lived in Dee Street,' he told the *Belfast Telegraph*. 'I genuinely believe that, like rugby, there should be a team from the 32 counties. If morons, and I'm not saying football morons, get some sort of pleasure out of defacing the mural, then good luck to them. They want to segregate me into a category and I'm not allowed to have an opinion. Every now and then the minority seems to shame the majority. But I do believe the majority in the 32 counties are decent people.'

East Belfast Ulster Unionist Jim Rodgers came to his defence – "Derek is a guy who says what he thinks. Some people may not agree with his views but this is totally uncalled for."

The defacing of the mural does indeed seem to tell us more about the state of Belfast politics and the turmoil which had divided the community for so long than Dougan's unpopularity, although lack of votes hints that he was not connecting with the same divided populace either. Perhaps, once again, Dougan was a man ahead of his time.

In April 2000, Dougan was making headlines yet again after an incident which may have provided the newspapers with a story to titillate their readers but which did little for the reputations of Dougan and the others involved. Dougan appeared in court on charges of assault and aggravated burglary. The charges were thrown out by the jury at Wolverhampton Crown Court, but the allegations and counter-allegations were the sequel to a rather tacky episode. It was the sort of story tabloid newspapers love – an alleged attack by a football legend with a pool cue on a man known as 'Rambo' at the home of an ex-lover with some threatening letters part of the saga, too. Dougan was alleged to have visited the home of his ex-lover Patricia Thompson and assaulted ex-US marine Eylande Mason, a kitchen-fitter.

Obviously something had occurred and it was all a question of which version the jury accepted. The prosecution claimed three letters sent to Mason's girlfriend in Telford could be traced back to Dougan as his left-hand palm print was found on the back of one of them. The first included lines like 'Would you please inform your partner Rambo, the ex-Vietnam soldier and helicopter pilot, the war is only just beginning' and 'he will in time receive a personal digging from the boss.' Another letter claimed Mason had gambling debts and would be visited by people to collect while the third stated 'This is all about adultery committed by the scumbag.' They were signed by 'a well-wisher'. Dougan said his print may have been on the letters as he had taken stationery to Mrs Thompson.

It was claimed that Dougan had used the butt of a pool cue in the alleged assault, Mrs Thompson saying she had seen it at Dougan's home and recognised it as it had a stars and stripes motif on it. Her relationship with Dougan had lasted 18 years, but broke down in 1998. She said Dougan had arrived at her home in Graiseley, Wolverhampton, on the day of the alleged offence in July 1999 and began hammering on the door and window. She said he burst past her and searched her home before attacking Mason. She threatened to telephone the police, but that Dougan pulled the telephone plug out of the wall before going upstairs to attack 57-year-old Mason. She agreed she had made several attempts on her own life between 1977 and 1998 and was receiving treatment for serious clinical depression. She denied she had pestered Dougan to the extent that he had to change his mobile phone and land line numbers.

Mason, who said he had become friends with Mrs Thompson after fitting a kitchen in her house, was getting ready to go out with her and was wearing her bathrobe when Dougan entered the bathroom with a pool cue. Mason maintained he was struck on his head and charged at Dougan as a way of stopping him.

Dougan's version of events was that he had been invited round by Mrs Thompson to speak to Mason about work he had left unfinished. He had been invited into the house but before he had a chance to talk to Mason he was punched by Mason and was knocked backwards into the porch. He followed Mason upstairs but he shut himself in the bathroom. Dougan said he kicked the door open and it hit Mason and the force sent him into the opposite wall. Mason regained composure and then came at him again and threw two punches, Dougan went on.

As part of his defence Dougan was supported by PFA colleague Gordon Taylor and former Northern Ireland team-mate Pat Jennings. Taylor said he succeeded Dougan as PFA chairman in 1979 and added, "I've known Derek over the past three decades as a very proud and fearless leader of players and also a very caring person." In a statement, Jennings said, "Derek Dougan has always acted during his time as a football player with the greatest professionalism. I have never known him to show violence or aggression to anybody."

The jury of six men and six women deliberated 90 minutes before rejecting the aggravated burglary charge and a further 45 minutes on the assault allegation. When the 'not guilty' verdict was announced on the latter charge, Dougan mouthed 'Thank you'. After the verdict was announced, Judge Frank Chapman told Dougan, "Your ordeal is over but perhaps it is wise to keep away from Mrs Thompson in future."

The *Express & Star* reported that Dougan had shown little emotion during the trial and one of the freelance reporters who covered it said his eloquence impressed the court. As he put it, "He had the jury eating out of his hand." Typical of Dougan was the way he dealt with photographers detailed to take a snatch picture of him arriving at court. Usually taking this sort of photo can be a hazardous business as people hide their faces or run quickly into the court building. Dougan was exactly the opposite and an *Express & Star* photographer said Dougan stopped and posed for him and his colleagues.

Despite his failure in the 1997 General Election Dougan was still attracted to politics and joined the United Kingdom Independence Party – UKIP. His first public speech for them was during the 2005 election when he lent support to the campaign of Malcolm Hurst for the South Staffordshire seat. Although Hurst finished fourth in the poll he had over 10 per cent of the votes and Dougan was confident that the foundations were being laid for UKIP to make an impact. Dougan cut a confident figure when he appeared on BBC TV's long-running *Question Time* programme in June 2006. Broadcast from Sheffield, the programme also included Lord Falconer, the Lord Chancellor, leading Conservative Theresa May and Liberal Democrat Mark Oaten.

UKIP's West Midlands MEP Mike Nattrass recalled Dougan's speech to the meeting in Codsall. "This quietly spoken and naturally good speaker told us that he had been one of those recruited to advocate a 'Yes' vote to the Common Market referendum. He came to regret this action and considered that he had been used and that joining UKIP rectified the situation." Paying tribute to Dougan after his death, Nattrass recalled that he had watched him during his Leicester City days. "He filled us with emotion and our respect for his football talent was beyond doubt. The crowd recognised him as the star that he was and the chant 'Dougan, Dougan' would be almost deafening. My delight found overdrive when our Doug Hope introduced him into UKIP. I found out that the man with the soft Irish accent and broad smile was a modest man who quietly helped former footballers who had fallen on hard times." Party leader Nigel Farage said, "For many in the West Midlands he was the face of the party. He was always enthusiastic in helping the party and his death is a great loss."

Mention of his helping former players was reference to Xpro or to give it the full title – the International Association of Ex-Professional Footballers. Among its stated objectives were: to improve the quality of life for ex-professional footballers and their families, to represent and serve the interests, rights and entitlements, benefits and welfare of ex-professional footballers and to promote and further the good name and tradition of professional football and foster a spirit of fellowship, sportsmanship and goodwill among former professional players and others.

Dougan felt many former players did not know their rights and entitlements. Many, he said, would have strong grounds for industrial injury claims on the pitch and during training. They did not know there was a huge amount of funds available for the treatment of injuries, operations and benevolent support. One of the areas Dougan thought Xpro should look at was players getting image rights from their playing days. In other words, if a picture of them was used they should get payment. He was also concerned about the growing memorabilia industry and claimed there were a few 'parasites' trying to steal players' footballing memories from them and their families.

While Dougan was chairman of Xpro its chief executive was Neil Rioch, brother of Bruce, the former Scottish international. Rioch had been on the books of Luton, Aston Villa, York, Northampton and Plymouth and helped found the Aston Villa Former Players' Association in 1996. When Xpro was launched in June 2005, Rioch told the Birmingham Evening Mail, "Although there are a number of former players' associations around the country, all doing a sterling job, there are thousands and thousands of former players out there who are just not covered. Some former players have terrific lives and have been very successful away from football, but there are many others who haven't. We're looking to support former players, looking at their welfare and entitlements, which they are largely unaware of. Many don't know the funds that are out there for operations needed as a result of football injuries and things like that. There are also benevolent funds in cases of hardship.

"We're talking about former players who were earning about £20 or £30 a week, not the £20,000 or £30,000 a week that players are earning today. So they need help. With the Aston Villa FPA for example, we've helped over 40 players in that way, for operations and other things. I've been getting calls for years now from former players at other clubs saying: 'I understand this is what you do for former Villa players, can you help me?' So I certainly found there was a real need out there for a national organisation."

So how did Dougan and Rioch join forces? Rioch explained, "I was speaking about it to a former player at a function a few years ago and, unknown to me, Derek Dougan was listening to what I was saying. He phoned me the next day and revealed he had been working on it for a number of years too. When we met up our aims were almost identical, so we joined forces. Since then it's taken a lot of time to set the thing up, getting the structure right and getting enough people involved." He felt a national organisation was needed as the individual ex-players groups were all well and good, but they were run by volunteers and it was difficult to get people who had the time and commitment.

Possible sources for its funding were listed on the Xpro website as the PFA, the FA, Premier League, Football League, the clubs and the organisers of the annual Community Shield game. They could also approach organisations indirectly involved in the game – like the Sports Council, Sport, England and the National Lottery – and others associated with the game, like Sky TV and sporting goods manufacturers. There could also be cash via dinners, members' personal appearances, memorabilia sales as well as various publications.

Before the end of 2005 Dougan had a prominent role in a sad event that captured world attention – the funeral of football genius George Best at Stormont Castle in Belfast. Dougan carried Best's coffin on part of its journey, helped by fellow former Northern Ireland stars Billy Bingham, Peter McParland, Harry Gregg and Gerry Armstrong as well as former Scotland hero Denis Law. Doog caught the moment perfectly when he said, "He carried us for so many years, it was an honour to carry him." Under two years later Northern Ireland was in mourning again, this time for Dougan himself.

The death of Dougan robbed the Xpro organisation of its driving force but Rioch is determined to see Xpro fully functional. He said, "Derek had a real passion for footballers and the welfare of footballers. With the loss of Derek there are things we have to discuss, but people are looking to make this a reality. We have already done things under the Xpro banner, but there are still things to be done before it is up and running on a day-to-day basis. It does need funding because it is not something that can be done in your spare time. We need to get members and people on board who share our objectives and once we have some substance then we can look to funding."

Rioch hopes to talk to the various former players' associations around the country and feels they will join forces with Xpro once they realise the benefits of such an organisation. Shortly before his death, Dougan had arranged to see his old Portsmouth and Northern Ireland team-mate Norman Uprichard to see how he could help him and was clearly full of enthusiasm for this new project. Sadly he will not be around to see the dream fulfilled, but Rioch and many others are working to make it happen. As Rioch says, "It would be a good legacy for Derek and one that everyone should be proud of."

Chapter Sixteen

AND IN THE END

FOR SOMEONE WHO LIVED HIS LIFE in the eye of a storm to the echo of raging cheers and laughter, Derek Dougan died a lonely, peaceful death. He was sitting in an armchair in the lounge at his bungalow in Wolverhampton's Stockwell End. His last desperate plea for help as he suffered a heart attack was too late. For once he was in the wrong place at the wrong time. Hours earlier, he had been in his element, surrounded by pals holding court at a nearby pub. And though his passing was a quiet one, it was followed by a period of mourning which brought glowing tributes from friends and followers in massive numbers.

Dougan's health had been a constant concern for his friends and family. He had suffered a heart attack, and was having treatment for other ailments. He underwent surgery for arthritis in his toes and was taking various medications. However, that did not drain his energy or commitment to the causes he believed passionately in. Nor did it curtail too much his zest for life.

The Doog spent the final day of his life with Doug Hope and other friends. He returned home alone and his family believe he stayed up all night to watch the middle-of-the-night television coverage of boxer Ricky Hatton winning his world light welterweight title fight against Jose Luis Castillo in Las Vegas. A phone call to Merlyn Humphreys, his partner for three years, who lived a few minutes from his home, was his dramatic last act.

"I always went round to Derek's house on a Saturday," Hope revealed. "We would have a bite to eat and watch the live lunchtime football match on television. That day we decided to go the Bentlands pub in Codsall. One or two other pals joined us and Derek was in good form.

"I dropped him off at the end of his lane at about 2.30pm. I didn't go into his bungalow. Normally I would have gone in for a cup of tea, but I think he felt a wee bit tired. He had a meeting in Eastbourne next day where he was due to speak on behalf of the former Portsmouth goalkeeper

Norman Upritchard as part of his Xpro work. I had loaned him a 4x4 vehicle to give him a bit more comfort on the long journey.

"On reflection I was probably the last person to see him alive. I got a phone call the next morning to say he was dead. I was absolutely stunned. My belief was that he had not gone to bed, had fallen asleep in the armchair and made a distress phone call for help to Merlyn."

Ms Humphreys, who declined to be interviewed for this book, told the *Express & Star* the day after Dougan's death, 'He called me at my home yesterday at 10.10am and all he could say was "Merlyn". I raced round and found him dead in the chair with the phone still in his hand. I called the ambulance and they told me to resuscitate him which I tried, but it was too late.'

Apart from family, Hope was the person closest to him for over 40 years and is best qualified to comment on the Doog's final days. "He liked to give the impression he was healthy and he was looking forward to his 70th birthday," he said. "But I don't think anyone really knew what a sick man he was. He had far too much stress in his life, but he did always live off his nervous energy. On the outside he looked in great nick for a 69-year-old, but he was under the doctor for various complaints. He had a couple of arthritic toes, a legacy of his playing days, and had been in hospital to have them straightened. That put him on his back for six weeks. He had various tests on his heart, but no-one knew with any certainty what toll the heart attack had taken on him nine years earlier. I learned later that apparently his heart was only 35 per cent as effective as it should have been. He had a few problems which would have caused him stress. He was on various medications, including Warfarin to keep his blood thin. But he wouldn't slow down and take things easy. Usually he was at war with someone over something.

"I felt privileged to know Derek Dougan. He certainly enriched my life. He still comes into my thoughts every day. And I don't think his name should be forgotten. I would like to see one of the stands at Molineux named after him, There is a precedent when they took the name of John Ireland off one of the stands and replaced it with Steve Bull's. Derek is just as much a legend as Bully. They were both great goalscorers who did such a lot for the club but, don't forget, when Derek played for Wolves he scored most of his goals at the very highest level."

Hundreds of fans lined the streets of Wolverhampton on the day of the funeral which took place at a packed St. Peter's Church in the city centre. It was filled with ex-colleagues from his Wolves and Northern Ireland teams and among those who addressed the congregation were former Molineux skipper Mike Bailey, ex-Stoke City star Terry Conroy, Aston Villa manager Martin O'Neill, sons Nicholas and Alexander, his niece Josephine Long, ex-partner Ms Humphreys and BBC presenter Nick Owen. The service was relayed to a larger congregation outside.

There were long queues forming too for the many people wanting to pay their own personal tributes. One of the most moving was from his former team-mate John McAlle, who enjoyed a regular ritual with him during rounds of golf at the South Staffs course which was overlooked by the Doog's bungalow.

McAlle said: "Like many thousands of Wolves fans, I'll never forget Derek Dougan. For all the headlines about him, the lessons we learned from Derek as a professional footballer stood the likes of myself, Derek Parkin and Frank Munro in good stead throughout our careers. If you speak to any of the fans they will put Doog right up there with the best payers to have worn the shirt. Yes, he had those difficulties during the Bhatti era, but let's not forget some of his other achievements off the pitch. There are an awful lot of footballers who are earning huge amounts of money because of the role Derek played fighting for freedom of contract when he led the PFA.

"I play golf regularly at South Staffs and Derek's house overlooks the ninth tee. Whenever I played through that hole, I would see Derek at his kitchen window and we would wave and smile. Sometimes we were able to stop for a chat. When I spoke to him a few weeks before he died he looked very well. He had just had an operation on his feet which was giving him some discomfort, but he was more upset about the death of Alan Ball (the England World Cup winner). He was anxious to get to his service and pay his respects and was worried because, following his operation, he wasn't finding it easy to get about. I was back on the golf course the morning he was found dead. I reached the ninth, looked up at the kitchen, but there was no Derek at the window. The house looked empty and I reasoned he must have popped out and I had missed him. It was only when I got home and took a call from Phil Parkes (former Wolves goalkeeper) that I found the real reason he was not there."

The Rev David Frith highlighted Dougan's work outside football and described him as "an unsung hero of peace and reconciliation." He went on, "Not only did Derek have ideas about people from different backgrounds living in harmony, he also took action to bring it about. The story of his off-the-field work to put together an all-Ireland football team ought not to be lost among the tales of his on-the-field prowess.'"

His son Nick said, "The day of the funeral and the service itself was a fitting memorial to dad. You know what. He would have loved to have been there. But I am sure he was looking down on it, smiling and itching to stand up and say a few words himself. There were times soon after he died that I was half expecting him to pop his head round the corner and say: 'Fooled you. I'm still here.' That was my dad."

An on-line book of condolences was filled with the memories of legions of Wolves fans from across the globe and included one from a supporter who called himself Hong Kong Wolfie. 'Doog was quite simply one of the all-time great Wolves players. For me he was the greatest. I actually saw him in the Gold 'n Black and his partnership with King John and Waggy was as good as any forward trio of the time. I met the Doog a few times and he was always a real gentleman with lots of time for the fans. We all loved the big man. There will mostly never be another one like him. May he rest in peace in the Molineux in the sky.'

The Doog would have loved that tribute most of all.

STATISTICAL RECORD

Full name   **Alexander Derek Dougan**
Date of birth   **20 January 1938**
Place of birth   **Belfast**
Playing position   **Centre-forward**

Domestic Playing Career - Appearances

Season	Club	Lge	FAC	LC	Oth	Tot
1957–1958	Portsmouth	26	2	-	3	31
1958–1959	Portsmouth	7	1	-	-	8
	Total	33	3	-	3	39
1958–1959	Blackburn Rovers	4	-	-	-	4
1959–1960	Blackburn Rovers	33	9	-	-	42
1960–1961	Blackburn Rovers	22	5	3	-	30
	Total	59	14	3	-	76
1961–1962	Aston Villa	23	4	-	-	27
1962–1963	Aston Villa	28	1	4	-	33
	Total	51	5	4	-	60
1963–1964	Peterborough Utd	38	2	1	-	41
1964–1965	Peterborough Utd	39	8	2	-	49
	Total	77	10	3	-	90
1965–1966	Leicester City	37	4	-	-	41
1966–1967	Leicester City	31	1	3	-	35
	Total	68	5	3	-	76
1966–1967	Wolves	11	-	-	-	11
1967–1968	Wolves	38	1	1	-	40
1968–1969	Wolves	38	2	3	-	44
1969–1970	Wolves	26	1	2	4	33

1970–1971	Wolves	23(2)	2	1	5(1)	31(3)
1971–1972	Wolves	38	-	1	12	51
1972–1973	Wolves	36(1)	5	5	2(1)	48(2)
1973–1974	Wolves	30(8)	1	8	4	43(8)
1974–1975	Wolves	3(3)	-	1	2	6(3)
	Total	264(14)	12	22	29(2)	307(16)

	League	**FAC**	**LC**	**Oth**	**Total**
Career Total	**552(14)**	**49**	**35**	**32(2)**	**648(16)**

Domestic Playing Career – Goals

Season	Club	Lge	FAC	LC	Oth	Total
1957–1958	Portsmouth	8	-	-	1	9
1958–1959	Portsmouth	1	-	-	-	1
	Total	9	-	-	1	10
1958–1959	Blackburn Rovers	1	-	-	-	1
1959–1960	Blackburn Rovers	14	3	-	-	17
1960–1961	Blackburn Rovers	11	1	4	-	16
	Total	26	4	4	-	34
1961–1962	Aston Villa	10	2	-	-	12
1962–1963	Aston Villa	9	-	5	-	14
	Total	19	2	5	-	26
1963–1964	Peterborough Utd	20	-	1	-	21
1964–1965	Peterborough Utd	18	7	-	-	25
	Total	38	7	1	-	46
1965–1966	Leicester City	19	1	-	-	20
1966–1967	Leicester City	16	-	5	-	21
	Total	35	1	5	-	41
1966–1967	Wolves	9	-	-	-	9
1967–1968	Wolves	17	-	-	-	17
1968–1969	Wolves	11	2	1	-	14
1969–1970	Wolves	8	-	-	2	10

1970–1971	Wolves	12	-	-	1	13
1971–1972	Wolves	15	-	-	9	24
1972–1973	Wolves	12	-	3	2	17
1973–1974	Wolves	10	2	3	2	17
1974–1975	Wolves	1	-	-	1	2
	Total	95	4	7	17	123
Career Total		**222**	**18**	**22**	**18**	**280**

International Playing Career
NORTHERN IRELAND CAPS

Fixture	Opponents	Result	Gls
8 June 1958 (Halmstad, Sweden, WCF)	Czechoslovakia	W 1–0	
3 Oct 1959 (Belfast, HIC)	Scotland	L 0–4	
8 Oct 1960 (Belfast, HIC)	England	L 2–5	
12 April 1961 (Belfast, HIC)	Wales	L 1–5	1
25 April 1961 (Bologna, Friendly)	Italy	L 2–3	1
3 May 1961 (Athens, WCQ)	Greece	L 1–2	
10 Oct 1962 (Katowice, ENC)	Poland	W 2–0	1
7 Nov 1962 (Glasgow, HIC)	Scotland	L 1–5	

Fixture	Opponents	Result	Gls
28 Nov 1962 (Belfast, ENC)	Poland	W 2–0	
2 Oct 1965 (Belfast, HIC)	Scotland	W 3–2	1
10 Nov 1965 (Wembley, HIC)	England	L 1–2	
24 Nov 1965 (Tirana, WCQ)	Albania	D 1–1	
30 March 1966 (Cardiff, HIC)	Wales	W 4–1	
7 May 1966 (Belfast, Friendly)	West Germany	L 0–2	
22 June 1966 (Belfast, Friendly)	Mexico	W 4–1	
22 Oct 1966 (Belfast, ECQ)	England	L 0–2	
16 Nov 1966 (Glasgow, ECQ)	Scotland	L 1–2	
12 Apr 1967 (Belfast, ECQ)	Wales	D 0–0	
21 Oct 1967 (Belfast, ECQ)	Scotland	W 1–0	
28 Feb 1968 (Wrexham, ECQ)	Wales	L 0–2	

Fixture	Opponents	Result	Gls
10 Sep 1968 (Jaffa, Friendly)	Israel	W 3–2	1
23 Oct 1968 (Belfast, WCQ)	Turkey	W 4–1	1
11 Dec 1968 (Istanbul, WCQ)	Turkey	W 3–0	
3 May 1969 (Belfast, HIC)	England	L 1–3	
6 May 1969 (Glasgow, HIC)	Scotland	D 1–1	
10 May 1969 (Belfast, HIC)	Wales	D 0–0	
10 Sep 1969 (Belfast, WCQ)	USSR	D 0–0	
22 Oct 1969 (Moscow, WCQ)	USSR	L 0–2	
18 Apr 1970 (Belfast, HIC)	Scotland	L 0–1	
21 Apr 1970 (Wembley, HIC)	England	L 1–3	
11 Nov 1970 (Seville, ECQ)	Spain	L 0–3	
3 Feb 1971 (Nicosia, ECQ)	Cyprus	W 3–0	1

Fixture	Opponents	Result	Gls
21 Apr 1971 (Belfast, ECQ)	Cyprus	W 5-0	1
15 May 1971 (Belfast, HIC)	England	L 0–1	
18 May 1971 (Glasgow, HIC)	Scotland	W 1–0	
22 May 1971 (Belfast, HIC)	Wales	W 1–0	
22 Sep 1971 (Moscow, ECQ)	USSR	L 0–1	
13 Oct 1971 (Belfast, ECQ)	USSR	D 1–1	
20 May 1972 (Belfast, HIC)	Scotland	L 0–2	
23 May 1972 (Wembley, HIC)	England	W 1–0	
27 May 1972 (Wrexham, HIC)	Wales	D 0–0	
18 Oct 1972 (Sofia, WCQ)	Bulgaria	L 0–3	
14 Feb 1973 (Nicosia, WCQ)	Cyprus	L 0–1	

Career Total   43 caps   8 goals

Key
WCF = World Cup Finals, HIC = Home International Championship, WCQ = World
Cup Qualifier, ECQ = European Championship Qualifier

BIBLIOGRAPHY

Aston Villa: A Complete Record 1874-1988
(Breedon Books)
David Goodyear and Tony Matthews

Attack!
(Pelham Books)
Derek Dougan

Banksy, My Autobiography
(Michael Joseph, Penguin Books)
Gordon Banks

British and Irish Special and Intermediate Internationals
(SoccerData)
Edited by Keith Warsop

Doog
(All Seasons Publishing)
Derek Dougan

Duncan Edwards
(The Duncan Edwards Sports Medicine Centre Appeal)
Derek Dougan, Hugh Jamieson, Frank Taylor

Football League Players Records 1946–1992
(Tony Williams Publications)
Barry J Hugman

Gray Matters: Andy Gray, the Autobiography
(Pan)
Andy Gray

League Football And The Men Who Made It
(Collins Willow)
Simon Inglis

Revelations of a Football Manager
(Sidgwick & Jackson)
Terry Neill

Running With Wolves
(Thomas Publications)
Peter Lansley

Scoring At Half-time
(Ebury Press)
George Best, with Martin Knight

The Essential History of Blackburn Rovers
(Headline for W H Smith)
Mike Jackman

The Essential History of Leicester City
(Headline for W H Smith)
Tony Matthews

The Park Drive Book of Football
(Pelham Books for Gallaher)
edited by William Luscombe

The Sash He Never Wore
(Mayflower)
Derek Dougan

The Sash He Never Wore . . . Twenty Five Years On
(Lagan Books & All Seasons Publishing)
Derek Dougan

The Wolves: An Encylopaedia of Wolverhampton Wanderers
(Breedon Books)
Tony Matthews with Les Smith

Those Were The Days
(Geoffrey Publications)
Clive Corbett

World Cup 1958
(Ruper Hart-Davis)
John Camkin